Handbook
of
SCHOOL
IMPROVEMENT

For Sammy, and in memory of Sam.

—Jo

In memory of Nan.

—Joseph

In memory of Dad and Kit.

—Dana

Handbook
of
SCHOOL
IMPROVEMENT

How High-Performing Principals
Create High-Performing Schools

FOREWORDS BY
William D. Greenfield, Jr.,
Joseph Hunter,
and Susan M. Usry

Jo Blase
Joseph Blase
Dana Yon Phillips

CORWIN
A SAGE Company

For information:

Corwin
A SAGE Company
2455 Teller Road
Thousand Oaks, California 91320
(800) 233-9936
Fax: (800) 417-2466
www.corwin.com

SAGE Ltd.
1 Oliver's Yard
55 City Road
London EC1Y 1SP
United Kingdom

SAGE India Pvt. Ltd.
B 1/I 1 Mohan Cooperative
  Industrial Area
Mathura Road, New Delhi 110 044
India

SAGE Asia-Pacific Pte. Ltd.
33 Pekin Street #02-01
Far East Square
Singapore 048763

Printed in the United States of America.

Library of Congress Cataloging-in-Publication Data

Blase, Jo Roberts.
Handbook of school improvement : How high-performing principals create high-performing schools/Jo Blase, Joseph J. Blase, Dana Yon Phillips; forewords by William D. Greenfield, Jr., Joseph Hunter, and Susan M. Usry.
    p. cm.
Includes bibliographical references and index.
ISBN 978-1-4129-7997-9 (pbk.)

    1. School improvement programs—United States—Handbooks, manuals, etc. 2. School principals—United States—Handbooks, manuals, etc. 3. School management and organization—United States—Handbooks, manuals, etc. 4. School supervision—United States—Handbooks, manuals, etc. I. Blase, Joseph. II. Phillips, Dana Yon. III. Title.
LB2822.82.B54 2010
371.2′07—dc22   2009051372

This book is printed on acid-free paper.

10   11   12   13   14   10   9   8   7   6   5   4   3   2   1

Acquisitions Editor:	Arnis Burvikovs
Associate Editor:	Desirée Bartlett
Editorial Assistant:	Joanna Coelho
Production Editor:	Eric Garner
Copy Editor:	Adam Dunham
Typesetter:	C&M Digitals (P) Ltd.
Proofreader:	Susan Schon
Indexer:	Judy Hunt
Cover Designer:	Michael Dubowe

Contents

List of Figures   x

The Book in Brief   xii

Foreword by William D. Greenfield, Jr.   xiii

Foreword by Joseph Hunter   xvii

Foreword by Susan M. Usry   xix

Preface   xxii
    Outline of the *Handbook of School Improvement*   xxiv
    The Double Helix Model of Leadership:
        A Systems-Development Approach   xxv
    The Resources   xxv
    The Study   xxvi
    Overview of High-Performing Principals' Administrative
        and Instructional Leadership Approach   xxvii
    Some Findings About Principals Who
        Create High-Performing Schools   xxviii
    How to Use This Book   xxix

Acknowledgments   xxx

About the Authors   xxxi

Part I. Administrative Leadership for School
Improvement: Action Foci of High-Performing Principals   1
    Introduction to Part I of the *Handbook*   1
    What Is a High-Performing School?   2
    What Is a High-Performing Principal?   3
    The New Challenge of Administrative
        Leadership for School Improvement   4

1. Learning   6
    Principals of high-performing schools are models of learning.   6
    How Did They Learn?   6
    What Did They Learn?   8
    Summary   20
    Tips and Suggestions   21

2. Modeling   **23**

*Principals of high-performing schools are exemplars of
the field's standards of leadership.*   23
     Activities for Becoming an Exemplar of Leadership Standards   25
     Summary   27
     Tips and Suggestions   27

3. Focusing   **28**

*Principals of high-performing schools focus on school
and teacher practices associated with increased student achievement.*   28
     Jigsaw Activity for School- and Teacher-Level
       Practices Influencing Student Achievement   30
     Summary   30
     Tips and Suggestions   31

4. Leading for Achievement   **32**

*Principals of high-performing schools lead in
ways that have maximum impact on student achievement.*   32
     Summary   36
     Tips and Suggestions   36

5. Improving Instruction   **37**

*Principals of high-performing schools work with teachers on the
school mission: They engage in ongoing, collaborative study
of schoolwide instructional improvement efforts.*   37
     Summary   41
     Tips and Suggestions   41

6. Developing Systems   **42**

*Principals of high-performing schools use a systems-development
approach to dispatch with administrative/managerial responsibilities
and to support instructional aspects of work.*   42
     Use a Systems-Development Approach to Create
       Efficient and Effective Self-Sustaining Structures   43
     Use Time Wisely   45
     Plan Well   50
     Manage the Budget Efficiently and Effectively   51
     Manage the Physical Plant Efficiently and Effectively   56
     Prevent Problems From Begetting Problems   61
     Summary   62
     Tips and Suggestions   63

7. Empowering   **65**

*Principals of high-performing schools take an
empowering (team) approach to almost everything and create
learning communities in their schools.*   65
     The Leadership Team   69
     Summary   74
     Tips and Suggestions   74

8. Hiring   **75**

Principals of high-performing schools hire strong
people for administrative, faculty, and staff positions.   75

     Know Who You Need   76
     Involve Everyone in Hiring   78
     Establish Hiring Protocols   80
     Correct Hiring Mistakes   83
     Summary   86
     Tips and Suggestions   86

9. Using Data   **87**

Principals of high-performing schools insist on using
data to inform instructional decisions.   87

     Questions About Data Use in Your School   92
     Additional Helpful Materials About Data Use   93
     Summary   97
     Tips and Suggestions   97

Part I. Suggested Reading for Further Learning:
Administrative Leadership   **98**

     A Research Base on Leadership for School Improvement   98
     Leadership for Effective Change   99
     Assistant Principals   99
     Hiring   99
     Teacher Leadership   99
     Mentoring   100
     Peer Coaching   100
     Observing and Teacher Talk   100
     Beginning Teacher Assistance   100
     Teachers' Work   101
     Data Use and Action Research   101
     Technology   101
     Instructional Leadership   102
     Teacher Empowerment   102
     Effective Communication   102
     Group Development   102
     Developing Trust   102
     Caring in Schools   102
     Working With Parents and Other Stakeholders   102

Part II. Instructional Leadership for School
Improvement: Goals of High-Performing Principals   **103**

     Introduction to Part II of the *Handbook*   103

10. Teaching and Learning   **105**

Principals of high-performing schools maintain a
focus on teaching and learning.   105

     Summary   109
     Tips and Suggestions   109

11. Culture   **111**

Principals of high-performing schools develop a schoolwide
culture that supports and sustains instruction.   111
    Summary   113
    Tips and Suggestions   113

12. Dialogue   **115**

Principals of high-performing schools establish a context (i.e., a
specific set of practices and routines) for dialogue about instruction.   115
    Faculty Meetings: A Sea Change   117
    Encouraging Frequent Teacher Dialogue and Collaboration   118
    A Note About the Need for Common Planning
        Time Among Teachers   121
    Summary   123
    Tips and Suggestions   123

13. Research   **124**

Principals of high-performing schools reference
research-based instructional elements when observing
instruction and when talking with teachers.   124
    Element 1: Factors Influencing Achievement   124
    Element 2: Planning for Instruction   127
    Element 3: Standards-Based Instructional Units   128
    Element 4: Components of Instruction   131
    Element 5: Student Abilities That Teaching
        Strategies Should Enhance   132
    Element 6: Effective Teaching Practices Across Content Areas   133
    Element 7: Ordering and Pacing of Content and
        Instructional Strategies   137
    Element 8: Addressing Diverse Students' Needs   138
    Element 9: Use of Technology in Instruction   139
    Element 10: Models of Teaching   140
    Element 11: Classroom Management (Discipline)   141
    Considering the Value of Walk-Throughs   149
    Considering Formal Evaluations   153
    Summary   154
    Tips and Suggestions   155

14. Development   **157**

Principals of high-performing schools provide effective,
ongoing professional learning (staff development).   157
    A Professional Learning Community   159
    The Right Approach   161
    Going Further   163
    A Multitude of Personalized Learning Opportunities   163
    A Good Use of Money   164
    The National Staff Development Council Standards   165
    The Special Case of Empowering Special Education Teachers   166

Professional Learning for Administrative Teams   169
Summary   170
Tips and Suggestions   170

**Part II. Suggested Reading for Further Learning:
Instructional Leadership**   **171**

Leadership for Learning   171
Walk-Throughs and Observing in Classrooms   171
Planning and Organizing for Teaching   172
Maintaining High Expectations and Developing
    Critical-Thinking Skills   172
School Effects Research   173
Integrating Curriculum   173
Cooperative Learning   173
Addressing Every Child's Needs   174
Challenged and Culturally Different Students   174
Technology in Learning   175
Discipline and Classroom Management   175
Developing Professional Learning Communities   176

**Part III. Conclusion: Systems Thinking
and the Systems-Development
Approach in Educational Leadership**   **177**

Introduction to Part III of the *Handbook*   177

**15. The Importance of Systems Thinking and the Systems-
Development Approach for School Improvement**   **178**

Using the 4 Cs Model as a Diagnostic and Prescriptive Tool   180
Summary   183

**16. Afterword: A Summary and A Note About
Preparation for Educational Leadership**   **184**

High-Performing Principals   185

Research Method and Procedures   **187**

References   **190**

Index   **197**

List of Figures

Figure 0.1   The Double Helix Model of Leadership: A Systems-Development Approach to Administrative and Instructional Leadership for Creating High-Performing Schools   xxvi

Figure 2.1   Educational Leadership Policy Standards of the Interstate School Leaders Licensure Consortium (ISLLC) 2008   24

Figure 3.1   School- and Teacher-Level Practices and Student Factors Influencing Student Achievement   30

Figure 4.1   21 Research-Based Leadership Responsibilities and the Average Effect Size of Their Impact on Student Achievement   34

Figure 5.1   Study Group Resources and Activities for Schoolwide Instructional Improvement   38

Figure 6.1   Time-Usage Activities   48

Figure 6.2   What We Talk About During Meetings and Its Influence on Learning   49

Figure 8.1   Six Qualities of Effective Teachers   77

Figure 9.1   A Framework for Data-Driven Instructional-Improvement Systems   88

Figure 9.2   Links to Support the Use of Data in Schools   93

Figure 12.1   Establishing a Context for Principal-Teacher Dialogue About Instruction   116

Figure 12.2   Teachers' Perspectives on Teacher-To-Teacher Assistance (e.g., Peer Consultation, Teacher Conversations)   119

Figure 12.3   Instructional Improvement Activities for Teachers, Principals, and Parents   120

Figure 13.1   School- and Teacher-Level Practices and Student Factors Influencing Student Achievement   125

Figure 13.2 Factors Emphasized in 90/90/90 (Milwaukee)
and Brazosport (Texas) Schools   126

Figure 13.3 Research-Based Models Cited by Principals
Who Created High-Performing Schools   127

Figure 13.4 Eight-Step Process for Planning for Learning in
Brazosport Schools   128

Figure 13.5 Different Types of Standards   128

Figure 13.6 Questions for Teachers Developing
Standards-Based Instructional Units   129

Figure 13.7 The Framework for Teaching: Components of
Professional Practice   132

Figure 13.8 Student Abilities That Teaching Strategies
Should Enhance   133

Figure 13.9 Enhancing Student Learning Through
Research-Driven Practices Across Content Areas 134

Figure 13.10 Planning Guide for Use of Instructional Strategies 137

Figure 13.11 Families of Teaching Models   141

Figure 13.12 Teachers' Research-Based
Classroom-Management Actions   142

Figure 13.13 Activities for Developing Research-Based
Schoolwide and Classroom-Management Systems   143

Figure 13.14 Lessons From Peer Consultants   148

Figure 14.1 The Value of Teachers Teaching Teachers:
Excerpts From Research   160

Figure 14.2 Action Planning for Professional Development 162

Figure 14.3 Variations on Staff Development Activities and
Strategies: Beyond Lecture-Style Workshops   164

Figure 14.4 Standards for Staff Development   165

Figure 15.1 The 4 Cs Model for School Improvement:
Diagnosing and Overcoming Educational Problems 182

The Book in Brief

The *Handbook of School Improvement: How High-Performing Principals Create High-Performing Schools,* in contrast to other published books, is a complete guide to *administrative and instructional leadership for school improvement.* The book highlights (1) findings from a ground-breaking study of high-performing principals who create high-performing schools; (2) the double helix model of leadership, a systems-development approach; and (3) the best resources (i.e., books, articles, Web sites, standards, videos, kits, tools, workbooks, career planning materials, interviews with experts, as well as individual and group activities that can be used by district- and school-level administrators, staff developers, teachers, and parents working together for school improvement). The *Handbook* can also be used as the core textbook in university- and district-based leadership preparatory programs and coursework focused on school improvement.

Foreword

William D. Greenfield, Jr.

This is a genuinely superb book! The authors bring together, in a highly readable and engaging format, the professional wisdom of high-performing principals and the guidance offered by the research on effective leadership for school improvement. A key feature of the book is that these high-performing principals' observations about their administrative and leadership practices solidly confirm what research studies have reported as effective school-leadership and instructional improvement practices.

School principals and superintendents in large as well as small districts will find very clear and helpful insights and guidance regarding concrete steps they can take to provide more effective leadership. Administrators working in urban as well as rural communities will find applicable high-quality examples of how effective leaders develop higher-performing schools and systems. Students in educational-administration–preparation programs and their university professors will appreciate and learn much from the very real accounts by these high-performing principals of the challenges and strategies associated with leading and improving schools. Researchers interested in studying effective school leadership will gain a more complete and robust appreciation of the complexity of leading schools and improving instruction, and they will be drawn to further clarify and confirm known as well as emergent variables and relationships informing the field's understandings of school leadership and school improvement.

This book represents a major departure from most of the professional literature in educational administration. Concrete examples of the day-to-day practices of high-performing principals are described by each principal in his or her own words. The authors very clearly illustrate how those practices are reflected and validated in the research that has been done on effective leadership to improve teaching and learning. Practically every observation offered by these high-performing principals contains a valuable insight or a useful guide to action. The authentic voices of successful leaders highlight key ideas and critical issues that will stimulate readers to reflect and consider the implications for their leadership and their schools.

Readers also will be pleased to find that this book departs in important ways from the typical handbook narrative. It is not the usual laundry list of prescriptions for being an effective school leader, nor is it composed of the dense and voluminous reviews of theory and research that characterize many such efforts. In contrast to those more typical formats, the authors have successfully woven together a rich tapestry that includes, first and foremost, concrete descriptions by principals of exactly what it is they do on a day-to-day basis to be effective in leading and managing their schools and in developing them into high-performing communities of teaching and learning.

The book has three main strengths:

1. It offers beginners as well as more experienced school administrators a well-informed and succinct guide to what research tells us about what works and what makes a difference for improving instruction.

2. It provides, in the words of principals themselves, a clear set of actions that reflect what effective leadership in a school entails. Specifically, it offers the reader concrete examples of specific actions school leaders can adopt to enhance their effectiveness as leaders. It is this latter "leadership map" that has for so long been missing in books and research and policy recommendations about school leadership.

3. It vividly captures the ways in which these various teacher, principal, and school conditions interact as a socio-cultural-political system.

The descriptions of these high-performing principals' daily activities are complemented by illustrations and exercises to assist the reader in adapting and applying the key ideas to their particular school and community contexts. Each chapter also includes a very rich and focused set of references—the most important resources available for informing and guiding school improvement. These include not only the usual list of key articles, research papers, and books, but also links to a wide variety of sources available electronically.

Running throughout the narrative and pulling together these observations of high-performing principals and the research on effective leadership focused on school improvement into an easily understood and coherent whole, is a comprehensive and well-integrated *theoretical framework* that reflects a socio-technical–systems conception of schools as highly complex organizations situated in socio-culturally diverse and often politically unpredictable community environments.

A significant feature of this book is that it illustrates the importance of applying a *systems-development approach* (i.e., the double helix model of Leadership) as a guide to one's work on school improvement. As the authors so vividly illustrate in drawing on the observations of the principals they studied, school improvement that is effective often requires changes in multiple subsystems within the school.

For their efforts to succeed, these high-performing principals frequently found it necessary to reorganize and to reculture the school's administrative, management, and instructional leadership functions into an integrated whole. That is, one cannot successfully change and improve instruction in a school on a piecemeal or ad hoc basis.

The authors' detailed and theoretically informed analysis of the data provided by high-performing principals enabled them to paint a very vivid and highly realistic picture of what is involved in improving a school. It is one thing to *understand the idea* of teachers working collaboratively to improve a school's instructional effectiveness, and it is quite another thing to *understand what a principal needs to do* to actually develop and sustain such practices in one's school.

Leading a school successfully requires very complicated and sophisticated work on the part of a principal. He or she must first have a well-informed sense of the problem to be addressed; the principal needs a certain level of relevant knowledge in order to competently communicate and interact with teachers about the instructional matter of concern. She or he must have or develop the interpersonal skills, relevant technical knowledge, and professional sensitivity to be able to work effectively with teachers and other staff to develop and implement the organizational systems, routines, and supports needed for goal-directed and instructionally focused teacher collaboration.

Additionally, if a desired change is really to occur and be self-sustaining over the long haul, the principal must cultivate an awareness of and support for the key beliefs and assumptions underlying instructionally focused collaboration among teachers. One must put the needed supports in place for teachers, and, if necessary, change or reculture the school to some degree. For this to happen, teachers and staff must genuinely believe that what they are attempting to improve by their change and implementation efforts is important and should be accomplished.

Schools are very complicated sociocultural systems, and changing virtually any aspect of what occurs instructionally in a school is not easily accomplished. The myriad examples of attempted and failed efforts to reform and improve schools over many decades stand as mute testimony to the difficulty of this challenge. Exhorting principals or teachers to change their practices, or inviting or requiring them to participate in specific training programs to learn the knowledge or skill associated with a desired change in practice, simply are not powerful enough to induce the desired change. For authentic and self-sustaining change to occur not only must administrative routines and support systems be in place but also antecedent and concurrent cultural change must occur. That is, for real change to occur, teachers and others need to change not only what they do: They must also change their beliefs about what is important and needs to be done. This is change of the second order, and it is not easily achieved in any type of organization. The nature of the school as a highly normative and loosely organized group of largely autonomous professionals makes such change especially challenging.

Most efforts to reform and improve schools, to improve teaching and learning, ignore all of the above. *The principals whose actions and beliefs are described in this book are high performing largely because they understand these things.* They know that change is difficult; and if real change is to occur, both the managerial and instructional aspects of the school must be working in a well-integrated and complementary fashion; and instructional support systems and administrative routines as well as the school's culture (underlying assumptions, core beliefs, and attitudes) must be oriented so as to support the desired practices.

While mapping and understanding the terrain of successful school leadership has eluded educational administrators and researchers for many decades, The *Handbook of School Improvement* brings us much closer to realizing this goal, and for this reason the book will serve its readers well. I am confident that readers will find these pages very engaging, readable, useful, and mentally stimulating as well!

—William D. Greenfield, Jr.
Professor Emeritus
Portland State University
Portland, Oregon

Foreword

Joseph Hunter

Many years ago, as a teacher-leader working with staff development and then as an administrator for curriculum, instruction, and school improvement, I learned that one of the most difficult challenges principals face is developing teacher commitment to improvement activities that require significant change. Indeed, I have observed this truly daunting challenge of inspiring continuous improvement from a number of vantage points over the years—as a teacher-leader, as an administrator of both secondary and elementary schools, and as a principal of both small rural schools and in large suburban districts—and I have successfully led small-scale first-order change as well as complex, organization-wide second-order change initiatives which resulted in significant student achievement gains. Currently, I am superintendent of a small, fast-growing school district, which I am leading through significant improvement activities; this I do in a community and environment long committed to local traditions and provincial viewpoints that have been embedded and permeated the schools and community for generations. Based on my experience in diverse settings, I believe The *Handbook of School Improvement* will be invaluable to practitioners across a wide range of contexts.

I wish a handbook such as this had been available when I stepped into school leadership 20 years ago because what I had to learn through trial and error, long hours of research and study at university libraries, and countless hours poring over books written by nationally recognized experts has been distilled and organized into this inspiring volume. As a superintendent striving to develop the leadership and performance capacities of the schools and principals in my district, I will use this book with teacher-leaders, aspiring and beginning administrators, veteran administrators, and even our school's board of directors. I believe the information in this book is presented in a usable format that will allow me to simplify and contextualize sophisticated concepts for neophyte leaders and noneducators and to provide reinforcement and extension for leaders who are already well grounded in school improvement. Honestly, I have never seen a more successful attempt at making complex processes straightforward and easily understood. This book is a welcome addition to the field: Educators who need a quick introduction to theory and practice will be able to wrap their minds around the authentic words and examples of the exemplary leaders presented in this book; novice and beginning administrators will be able to better inform their action planning and daily behavior; and competent and veteran administrators who need to look deeper into theory and empirical evidence to develop their own commitment to more-effective practice have, in this book, easy access to the information they need.

Most importantly, the concepts presented in this book will help novices and veterans develop and sustain first- and second-order change. For instance, Chapter 3 provides a clear, coherent description of research-based concepts which undergird and sustain a focus on variables that significantly impact student achievement; after noting the work of Robert Marzano, the importance of teacher collaboration, principal modeling, and instructional leadership, the authors quickly move to practical suggestions about how to encourage staff discussions and commitment to best practice.

In comparison with leadership books I have used in the past, school administrators will find this book refreshingly easy to use despite it being filled with a wide variety of resources. The wealth of practical tips, group discussion ideas, citations, and references to free online resources makes this a must read. The suggested activities and study-group resources give administrators concrete examples that demonstrate how exemplary administrators guide schools through consideration of proven ideas and practices which result in organizational reculturing that sustains a focus on best practice and continuous improvement on teaching and learning. Detailed examples and suggestions about time management, systems thinking, and use of support staff and volunteers to free principals from the tyranny of the urgent in order to focus on long-term, deep school improvement activities will be extremely valuable to system leaders. The authors give simple, practical, usable ideas in a clear and concise manner; school leaders will find this approach exciting, enlightening, and reinforcing.

One of the most powerful aspects of this book is that it goes beyond presenting research-based practice: It provides a forum for private and individual or public and group analysis of theory in practice. Unfortunately, educators are so accustomed to talking "about the research" that we often fail to engage in personal and group reflection about our actual practice—followed by action. In contrast, this book encourages—even inspires—reflection and self-assessment leading to action; it thereby functions as a handbook for novices and veterans alike. Furthermore, this book not only fosters self-reflection but also invites and frames reflection in the educational organization, where collectively thinking about our work and having frank and open discussions about what is working and what can be improved is vital. In sum, this book is well conceived and will serve an important role in revealing and reducing existing gaps between espoused theory and educational practice, which is the place where real change starts.

—*Joseph Hunter, EdD*
Superintendent of Schools
Central School District
Independence, Oregon

Foreword

Susan M. Usry

School leaders cannot ignore the current emphasis on creating high-performing schools: Local, state, and federal school leaders, the media, the general population, and other public and private organizations demand school improvement. This means that school leaders and teachers face ever-increasing time constraints and are expected to work miracles in managing schools while increasing student achievement. Unfortunately, while they may be aware of their respective school's rankings, school leaders and teachers often stop short of thorough analysis of factors that inhibit school improvement.

Heretofore, what has been missing from school leaders' repertoire is clear direction on exactly how to foster school improvement. In The *Handbook of School Improvement,* Blase, Blase, and Phillips provide the answer to the question, "How do I move my school to higher levels of performance?" Finally, school leaders have an outstanding, research-based book that can be used as a comprehensive guide to creating high-performing schools.

Unquestionably, creating a high-performing school is a monumental challenge, so the authors went straight to the heart of the issue with their latest research: They collected data from a wide array of high-performing principals and schools and critically analyzed common threads in the data. Indeed, they produced a research base focused directly on leadership for school improvement. Then, the authors blended existing and emerging research, observations, and theory into a highly readable and beneficial handbook. This book is comprehensive in nature; it clearly merges elements into a powerful publication that will prove incredibly helpful to practicing and aspiring school leaders.

Three crucial aspects make this a significant book. First, because the *Handbook* is replete with excerpts from numerous interviews with principals from elementary, middle, and high schools, it speaks to all of us; hearing other principals plainly confirm our daily experiences rings of truth, and detailed descriptions of their approach to leadership will help us all improve. Over and over again in the *Handbook,* high-performing principals describe myriad, complex, administrative and managerial aspects of their work and emphasize the need to organize, take control of, and balance such tasks in support of instruction.

Second, from my perspective as a practicing principal, one of the most salient lessons of this book is this: The authors' identification of *a systems-development approach* for merging the two most demanding and important aspects of leadership, administrative and managerial tasks, and instructional improvement. Essentially, the principals the authors studied demonstrated the crucial importance of systems that enabled them to get everything done while focusing on instruction in order to improve academic performance. Virtually all school principals encounter conflict emanating from administrative or managerial tasks that shift one's focus away from school improvement. And yes, administrative and managerial tasks are extremely vital; indeed, they form the needed framework upon which schools operate. However, failure to understand the link between administrative and managerial tasks and supervision of good instruction undermines overall school performance. The authors' *systems-development approach* streamlines and integrates all leadership tasks and in so doing eliminates any weakening of school improvement efforts.

Third, the *Handbook* reveals that principals who use a *systems-development approach* achieve a unique organizational structure comprising subsystems that reflect individual school culture. In the *Handbook,* we learn that high-performing principals approached restructuring in a similar manner despite working in different types of schools and in different contexts: Each shared a focus on instruction, developed trust, created a sense of ownership, and fostered real collaboration. This yielded a host of school-based subsystems that proactively interacted to facilitate a smoothly running organization; this, in turn, freed principals to focus on school improvement efforts.

The authors also found that the development of a school's system and its supporting subsystems was a bottom-up rather than top-down process; principals and administrative groups provided leadership and guidance, but success derived from teachers, who were always a significant part of the process. Most principals, me included, have experienced top-down administration in which planning is done at higher levels and presented to school administrators and faculty for implementation. In such cases, trust is abridged, and ownership of improvement efforts is reduced. In effect, teachers revert to *private practice,* in which they take refuge. In my opinion, when principals encounter such situations, it is imperative that they use a systems-development approach as presented in the *Handbook* to create the needed subsystems required for a healthier, more-productive organizational structure. For example, one subsystem might be a school-level design team focused primarily on instructional issues rather than on administrative and managerial aspects of the issues. Naturally, personnel must collaborate as this subsystem is merged with other parts of the system and as all subsystems are continuously evaluated. This results in increased school achievement and improvement efforts.

The authors have produced a comprehensive book that is unique in content and structure. Educators now have a go-to guide that combines salient research and findings from the authors' study. It is also filled with annotated bibliographies, reference lists, and Web sites, all of which have been reviewed by the authors and recommended as the best available school improvement resources. This book is also original in its use of professional exercises, tips, and suggestions designed to stimulate the kind of thoughtful discussion among school leaders and faculty members required for serious school improvement.

Without question, this excellent book has much to offer leaders regardless of experience level. For beginning leaders who want to avoid typical mistakes to veteran leaders focused on achieving higher-performance levels, the *Handbook* details a systems-development approach to creating and managing all of the moving parts of a school as a well-coordinated whole. Personally, it truly is a joy to see a school in which everyone is a meaningful participant and in which trust, ownership, and collaboration yield a high level of performance, all driven by a well-planned *systems-development approach.*

Being part of a high-performing school is a privilege and a challenge. The *Handbook* is the key to meeting that challenge and enjoying that privilege. The *Handbook* offers substantially more than any traditional here-is-another-study-and-here-are-the-results book. I, for one, am excited to have all the essential information for building a high-performing school in one easy-to-access-and-use location. The *Handbook* will help me continue to grow as a principal while I develop sustainable leadership within our school and as I prepare others to move into leadership positions. I strongly recommend that aspiring and practicing leaders add the *Handbook* to their professional libraries.

—Susan M. Usry, EdD
Principal
Putnam County Primary School
Eatonton, Georgia

Preface

*To be a great principal you have to be a great manager and a great leader.
. . . Don't do either well and the school fails.*

—Middle School Principal

True leaders are not born but made and not made as much by others as by themselves.

—Bennis (1989, p. 37)

There is nothing more satisfying than seeing hordes of people engaged to do good together because of the leadership you helped to produce.

—Fullan (2005, p. 104)

Throughout the past century, the work of school administrators has emphasized "management" functions rather than leadership and, in particular, instructional leadership. Since World War II, factors such as the increasing size of schools and school districts, increasing numbers of students, expanding school bureaucracies, community expectations, pressure from unions, and expectations of state governments have reinforced a principal-as-manager model (Drake & Roe, 2003; Kowalski, 2003).

During the past two decades, demands that principals focus on instructional leadership have been made by the National Policy Board for Educational Administration (NPBEA) and the Council of Chief State School Officers (CCSSO) (Gronn, 2002). This led to the work of the Interstate School Leaders Licensure Consortium (ISLLC) and the creation of "standards" for school leaders (McCarthy, 1998) that emphasize "leadership" rather than old-style school management/administration[1] (Thompson, 1998). The new standards derived from research that demonstrated a strong link between school leadership and student learning (Gronn, 2002).

Clearly, the role of school leaders has dramatically expanded and intensified in recent years and now includes a host of new expectations for both management and instructional leadership. Cusick (2003), for instance, found that principals work 10-to-12-hour days, the number and types of responsibilities in which they engage have increased, and many of their duties and responsibilities are overlapping and conflicting. Other studies have demonstrated that principals work, on average, between 60 and 70 hours per week (Buckley, 2004; McPeake, 2007). Moreover, despite a string of strong new demands by educational scholars and policy makers, the actual work of school principals today comprises *more school management than school leadership;* for example, in a major study of principals' time-on-task from 1960 to the twenty-first century, McPeake (2007) found that principals have devoted the greatest amount of time to school management as compared to all other task areas. Several studies have reported that although principals valued instructional leadership and school improvement, routine management and administration and the demands of "putting out fires" have increased and consume most of principals' work days (Buckley, 2004; Chan & Pool, 2002; Gould, 1998). Similarly, Kellogg (2005) reported that regardless of their career stage, principals devoted more time than they preferred to managerial responsibilities. McPeake (2007) concluded that, in part, requirements of the No Child Left Behind (NCLB) legislation have been largely responsible for the recent proliferation of management responsibilities.

Indeed, new responsibilities and activities have been added to the principal's role, but the old responsibilities and activities have remained. The role is now considered overloaded, highly complex, and composed of a multitude of conflicting demands (Cunningham & Cordiero, 2006; Cusick, 2003; Fullan, 2007; Kowalski, 2003; Murphy, 1994). The National Association of Secondary School Principals (NASSP) has attributed the shortage of qualified leaders for the school principalship to the problematic nature of the principal's role (Quinn, 2002), which includes

> increased job stress, inadequate school funding, balancing school management with instructional leadership, new curriculum standards, educating an increasingly diverse school population, shouldering responsibility that once belonged at home or in the community, and then facing possible termination if their schools don't show instant results. (p. 1)

Upon reviewing the voluminous additions to the principal's role, Fullan (2007) remarked,

> The net effect is that the principalship is being placed in an impossible position. In short, the changes required to transform cultures are far deeper than we understood; principals do not have the capacity to carry out the new roles; and principals are burdened by too many role responsibilities that inhibit developing and practicing the new competencies—add-ons without anything being taken away. Hard change, low capacity, plenty of distractions—a recipe for frustration. In sum, the principal is key, but we haven't yet figured out how to position the role to fulfill the promise. (p. 165)

Similarly, Elmore (quoted in Farrace, 2002) noted,

> Although instructional leadership is a central article in the belief system about principals, the empirical evidence has always indicated that a relatively small proportion of principals are actually able to practice instructional leadership. (pp. 39–40)

It appears that federal and state policies designed to promote a principal-as-instructional-leader model have largely failed and, in fact, may have inadvertently reinforced a principal-as-manager model in practice. *This is particularly discouraging in light of strong evidence that effective instructional leadership by the school principal is a key within-school factor in promoting school improvement and is second only to teaching in contributing to student learning.* This point is supported by numerous studies and discussed in subsequent sections in this book.

In the end, most scholars agree that principals must be knowledgeable and competent in management and administration without undermining leadership and instructional leadership. School principals must create both well-managed and well-led schools; they must be able to balance the overwhelming number of competing and often conflicting demands of the role (Achilles, Keedy, & High, 1999; Boris-Schacter & Langer, 2006; Kowalski, 2003; Owens & Valesky, 2007; Pounder & Merrill, 2001; Sharp & Walter, 2003). Unfortunately, this is easier said than done. To state the problem differently, *school principals must now be able to do what most have failed to do in the past—provide instructional leadership—but in the context of more management responsibilities, responsibilities which have consistently negated that possibility*, at least for most principals. Our study goes a long way in cracking open what has historically been considered a "black box" in educational research; in this book we provide a research-based answer to the question, *How do principals create instructionally-effective schools?*

OUTLINE OF THE *HANDBOOK OF SCHOOL IMPROVEMENT*

Part I of the *Handbook*—Administrative Leadership for School Improvement—begins with a brief discussion of two key questions: What is a high-performing school? And, What does a principal do to create a high-performing school? The chapters in this part of the book describe defining *action foci* of principals who create high-performing schools derived from our study of 20 such principals. In the perspectives of these principals, their work on nine action foci promoted the development of school-based *learning subsystems* that support school improvement. Thus, the term *administrative leadership* includes managerial and organizational leadership functions, responsibilities, and behaviors that provide the foundation (i.e., support structure) for school improvement and, thereby, impact teaching and learning.

Part II of the *Handbook*–Instructional Leadership for School Improvement—focuses more directly on high-performing principals' approaches to instructional leadership for school improvement. Drawn from our study, the chapters in this part of the book describe *five primary goals* of high-performing principals that directly impact teaching and student learning, including (1) maintaining a focus on teaching and learning, (2) developing a culture that supports and sustains instructional improvement, (3) establishing a context for dialogue about instruction, (4) referencing research-based elements when observing and talking with teachers, and (5) providing effective, ongoing professional learning. Gleaned directly from our study data, the *systems-development approach* (i.e., the systematic development of coordinated subsystems in the school to address all administrative and instructional leadership functions) is discussed throughout this book.

Part III of the *Handbook*—Conclusion: Systems Thinking and the Systems-Development Approach in Educational Leadership—includes a discussion of Wagner et al.'s (2006) "systems framework," a powerful and practical diagnostic approach to school improvement; and a discussion of the importance of a systems perspective and the systems-development approach for school improvement and for preparation programs in educational leadership.

THE DOUBLE HELIX MODEL OF LEADERSHIP: A SYSTEMS-DEVELOPMENT APPROACH

According to our study data, high-performing principals create high-performing schools through both (1) administrative leadership for school improvement (Part I of the *Handbook*) and (2) instructional leadership for school improvement (Part II of the *Handbook*). We found that these two dimensions of high-performing, school-based leadership were, in practice, highly connected and interrelated (as well as supported by a systems-development approach, as discussed in Part III of the *Handbook*); thus, we refer to the double helix model of leadership, which is graphically illustrated in Figure 0.1. In geometry and molecular biology (the latter represents the structure of DNA), a double helix consists of two helices with the same axis and grooves connecting the two. In high-performing schools, principals enact the nine *action foci* discussed in Part I (Chapters 2–9) of this book while maintaining their focus on the 5 *goals* discussed in Part II (Chapters 10–14). Each of these action foci and goals, in turn, revolves around the *axis of student achievement/school improvement* and is pursued by way of carefully developed *subsystems* (i.e., the workhorses of school improvement) at the school level. In sum, all of what is done by high-performing principals is more or less *administrative* or more or less directly *instructional*; but all major leadership actions are structured in subsystems (as discussed in Part III, Chapters 15–16), appropriately interrelated, and serve the metagoal of student achievement and school improvement.

THE RESOURCES

In addition to presenting our findings about how high-performing principals create high-performing schools, throughout the *Handbook* we refer the reader

Figure 0.1 The Double Helix Model of Leadership: A Systems-Development Approach to Administrative and Instructional Leadership for Creating High-Performing Schools

ADMINISTRATIVE LEADERSHIP
Action Foci

Be a **model** of learning.

Be an exemplar of leadership **standards**

Focus on practices associated with increased student achievement

Lead for maximum **impact on achievement**

Work with teachers on the mission: ongoing, collaborative study of schoolwide **instructional improvement.**

Use a **systems-development** approach.

Take an **empowering** approach to create a learning community.

Hire strong people.

Use **data** to inform instructional decisions.

INSTRUCTIONAL LEADERSHIP
Goals

Maintain a focus on **teaching** and learning

Develop a **culture** that supports and sustains instruction.

Establish a context for **dialogue** about instruction

Reference **research-based instructional elements**

Provide ongoing, effective **professional development.**

AXIS: student achievement/school improvement

to the *best* resources available for professional learning and school improvement, including books, annotated bibliographies, articles, Web sites, standards, videos, kits, tools, workbooks, career plans, and interviews. We also describe individual and group activities that can be used by administrators and teachers working together for school improvement; thus, the *Handbook* is a complete guide to leadership for school improvement.

THE STUDY

The study that serves as the basis for this book investigated the question, How do high-performing school principals create high-performing schools, establish and manage effective administrative routines, and how do they manage inevitable daily crises and ongoing administrative challenges? This incredibly important question has dogged the field of educational leadership for decades. Our goal was to describe principals' perspectives on this critical issue. Therefore, we conducted a series of in-depth interviews with 20 principals in one southeastern state, *each of whom had been designated by the state department of education and/or recognized by other education-based organizations, agencies, and entities as a high-performing principal of a high-performing school or a significantly improving school.* Given space limitations, we present excerpts from our database to illustrate select ideas. (For a detailed description of the study, see the Research Method and Procedures section at the end of this book.)

OVERVIEW OF HIGH-PERFORMING PRINCIPALS' ADMINISTRATIVE AND INSTRUCTIONAL LEADERSHIP APPROACH

We found that all high-performing principals use a bottom-up *systems-development approach* (a concept we derived from our study data) to create high-performing schools. That is, they systematically create or build, in collaboration with others, a deeply embedded network of mutually-reinforcing *organizational* and *cultural* subsystems, large and small, to effectively cope with both managerial and administrative, and instructional leadership responsibilities while *persistently and single-mindedly focusing on school improvement.* They create a school-based system to maximize each subsystem's ability to contribute directly and/or indirectly to school improvement. In essence, all principals use a systems-development approach to *reorganize* and *reculture* their schools to focus on school improvement, as both reorganization and reculturing are required to create a high-performing school.

Reorganizing a school requires that a principal create and sustain, in collaboration with all relevant others (as in distributed or shared leadership), a school-level system (and subsystems) that include, among other things, teams, policies, procedures, plans, schedules, and routines to address all major management and administrative responsibilities (e.g., technology, hiring, physical plant) and leadership and instructional leadership responsibilities (e.g., professional development, instructional observations, and conversations) to maximize school-improvement efforts; usually the creation of these subsystems derived from the principals' realization that their schools were, in varying degrees, instructionally problematic (i.e., stagnant, underachieving, or inefficient). The reorganization of each school is a bottom-up process, and its particular development is dependent upon its context (i.e., a school's specific human and physical needs and available resources). *The system developed at each high-performing school we studied was unique, but all were predicated on school improvement.*

Reculturing a school requires that each principal's approach to leadership and instructional leadership promote values, beliefs, ways of thinking, and behaviors of individuals and teams based on trust, ownership, commitment, collaboration, responsibility, accountability, risk taking, mutual respect, reflection, and problem solving to focus on school improvement. *The cultures of the high-performing schools were similar: They consisted of the same configuration of values, beliefs, ways of thinking, and behaviors that emphasized school improvement.*

SOME FINDINGS ABOUT PRINCIPALS WHO CREATE HIGH-PERFORMING SCHOOLS

1. Becoming a high-performing principal is an evolutionary, ongoing, incremental process of recurring efforts to improve things coupled with reflection that, for most, began when the principals were teachers and assistant principals and has continued to the present. Principals also learn that, in practice, administration and instructional leadership are highly interrelated and intertwined. However, high-performing principals derive most of their knowledge about effective instructional leadership and effective teaching and learning from published research and other empirically based professional resources.

2. At the start of their administrative careers, most high-performing principals tend to be control-oriented rather than empowering and inclusive; as a result, they are neither effective administrative leaders nor instructional leaders. Over time, they learn that both efficient and effective administrative and instructional leadership require the best from all stakeholders and that an empowering approach (i.e., distributed or shared leadership) is essential to achieving deep levels of "ownership" in pursuit of school improvement.

3. High-performing principals learn that hiring strong educators who are team players is essential to addressing the overwhelming array of administrative and instructional leadership responsibilities. Further, such principals employ a professional development approach that is extensive and compelling, and it includes the principal (who models lifelong learning), assistant principals, teachers, and staff in a range of ongoing informal and formal professional-development experiences.

4. High-performing principals, assistant principals, grade and department chairs, and lead teachers work collaboratively to create and maintain a school's focus on school improvement via, for example, frequent classroom walk-throughs, professional dialogue, instructional planning, emphasis on standards-based instruction and effective teaching practices, and professional learning.

5. Once viable school-improvement-oriented organizational and cultural subsystems have been created, high-performing principals require ongoing vigilance (monitoring) by all stakeholders. The organization and culture of each school is always, to some extent, a work in progress that requires occasional tweaking.

6. High-performing principals are excellent administrative and instructional leaders. All believe that effective administrative leadership provides a stable, predictable, and supportive foundation for a high-performing school. All insist that effective administrative and instructional leadership are inextricably intertwined and interdependent processes and that leadership in schools frequently requires being engaged in both types of processes simultaneously. In other words, effective school-level leadership is an integrated, holistic, complex, dynamic process—one that cannot be understood by simply identifying behaviors associated with either administrative leadership or instructional leadership

alone. Therefore, principals use a bottom-up, systems-development approach to understand and to create an effective, integrated system (i.e., configuration) of both organizational subsystems and cultural components that *focus* the school on instructional improvement. As noted above, excellent performance in administrative and instructional school leadership is double helical in nature; this reflects the interactions among the principals' action foci and goals and a systems-development approach to student achievement and school improvement. In his classic book, *Why Leaders Can't Lead*, Warren Bennis (1989) noted,

> Leaders are people who do the right thing; managers are people who do things right. Both roles are crucial but they differ profoundly. I often observe people in top positions doing the wrong things well. (p. 18)

HOW TO USE THIS BOOK

The *Handbook of School Improvement* will demonstrate that the double helix model of leadership, a systems-development approach to school improvement, should be seriously considered by all prospective and practicing school leaders. Because every school is different, we strongly recommend that school leaders and their colleagues study the *Handbook* in its entirety before developing a school improvement plan; it will become apparent that a leader's readiness to take a systems-development approach to school improvement requires not only having the action foci and goals of high-performing principals (e.g., being a learner, understanding teaching and learning, empowering others, effectively hiring and using data, and developing subsystems) but also the ability to *reorganize* and *reculture* the school. This book was designed especially to help school leaders develop and refine all of the knowledge, attitudes, and skills represented on the double helix model of leadership.

NOTE

1. Throughout this book, we use the terms "administration" and "management" synonymously.

Acknowledgments

We wish to express our gratitude to the extraordinary school principals who participated in the study that serves as the basis for this book. We also want to thank Professor Emeritus William D. Greenfield, Jr. for his valuable feedback on early manuscripts of this book and especially for his contribution to the conceptualization of the systems-development approach and the double helix model of leadership.

Additionally, Corwin gratefully acknowledges the following peer reviewers for their editorial insight and guidance:

Sean Beggin
Assistant Principal
Andover High School
Andover, MN

Roxanne Cardona
Principal
PS 48
Bronx, NY

Suzanne L. Gilmour, PhD
Chair, Educational Administration Department
Executive Director, New York State Association for Women in Administration
Oswego, NY

About the Authors

 **Jo Blase,** PhD, is a professor of educational administration at the University of Georgia, a former public school teacher, high school and middle school principal, and director of staff development. She received a PhD in educational administration, curriculum, and supervision in 1983 from the University of Colorado at Boulder, and her research has focused on instructional and transformational leadership, school reform, staff development, and principal-teacher relationships. Through work with the Beginning Principal Study National Research Team, the Georgia League of Professional Schools, and public and private school educators with whom she consults throughout the United States and abroad, she has pursued her interest in preparation for and entry to educational and instructional leadership as it relates to supervisory discourse. Winner of the W. G. Walker 2000 Award for Excellence for her coauthored article published in the Journal of Educational Administration, the University of Georgia College of Education Teacher Educator Award, the University of Colorado School of Education Researcher/ Teacher of the Year, and the American Association of School Administrators Outstanding Research Award, Blase has published in international handbooks and journals such as *The Journal of Staff Development, The Journal of Curriculum and Supervision, Educational Administration Quarterly,* and *The Alberta Journal of Educational Research;* her eight book editions include *Empowering Teachers* (1994, 2000), *Democratic Principals in Action* (1995), *The Fire Is Back* (1997), *Handbook of Instructional Leadership* (1998, 2004), *Breaking the Silence* (2003), and *Teachers Bringing Out the Best in Teachers* (2006). She has authored chapters on becoming a principal, school renewal, supervision, and organizational development; her recent research examines the problem of teacher mistreatment. Professor Blase has published over 90 academic articles, chapters, and books, and she also conducts research on supervisory discourse among physicians as medical educators and consults with physicians in U.S. hospitals and medical centers.

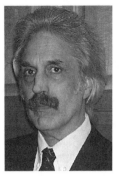

Joseph Blase, PhD, is a professor of educational administration at the University of Georgia. Since receiving his PhD in 1980 from Syracuse University, his research has focused on school reform, transformational leadership, the micropolitics of education, principal-teacher relationships, and the work lives of teachers. His work concentrating on school-level micropolitics received the 1988 Davis Memorial Award given by the University Council for Educational Administration, and his coauthored article published in the Journal of Educational Administration won the W. G. Walker 2000 Award for Excellence.

In 1999, he was recognized as an elite scholar, one of the 50 Most Productive and Influential Scholars of Educational Administration in the world.

Blase's books include *The Politics of Life in Schools: Power, Conflict, and Cooperation* (winner of the 1994 Critic's Choice Award sponsored by the American Education Studies Association), *Bringing Out the Best in Teachers* (1994, 2000, 2008); *The Micropolitics of Educational Leadership* (1995), *Empowering Teachers* (1994, 2000), *Democratic Principals in Action* (1995), *The Fire Is Back* (1997), *Handbook of Instructional Leadership* (1998, 2004), *Breaking the Silence* (2003), and *Teachers Bringing Out the Best in Teachers* (2006). His recent research (coauthored with Jo Blase and Du Fengning, 2008), a national study of principal mistreatment of teachers, appeared in *The Journal of Educational Administration.* Professor Blase has published over 120 academic articles, chapters, and books.

Dana Phillips, EdD, is a middle school administrator and former elementary school administrator in Georgia, part-time Assistant Professor at the University of Georgia, and part-time Instructor for Piedmont College. She completed her EdD in educational leadership at the University of Georgia in 2004, where she focused on shared governance, instructional leadership, and teacher leadership. At the University of Georgia, she now teaches organizational leadership, change for school improvement, and ethics.

During 1999 and 2000, Phillips produced and was host of *School Talk,* a weekly cable television program exploring educational trends and issues with school leaders. In 2003, she delivered a paper on the topic of parental involvement at the National School Reform Conference.

Prior to her return to the field of education in 2000, Dr. Phillips owned and operated a nursing home management company for 26 years. Recognized as a service-oriented organizational leader, Dr. Phillips also provided management consulting services and conducted numerous seminars and workshops on topics such as staff development and training, operational policies and procedures, and federal and state long-term health care requirements for trade associations and nursing home and assisted living facilities. She is author of *Policies and Procedures for Long-term Health Care Facilities* (1993) and *Manual of Staff Orientation and Training for Long-Term Health Care Facilities* (1994).

Part I

Administrative Leadership for School Improvement

Action Foci of High-Performing Principals

INTRODUCTION TO PART I OF THE *HANDBOOK*

Today's emphasis on accountability for achievement in schools has made educational leaders eager for answers to the overriding question, How do we develop instructionally effective schools? Specifically,

- How do we develop a school organization and culture that promotes and sustains learning?
- How do we lead for continuous school improvement?
- How do we encourage and enable teachers to engage in the kinds of behaviors that are linked to increased student achievement?
- What leader behaviors are linked to increased student achievement?

The *Handbook* is written to provide answers to these and other crucial leadership questions. By studying principals who create high-performing schools, we can now describe the attitudes, beliefs, values, and actions of extraordinarily successful educational leaders. These findings, coupled with the best existing knowledge base in education, provide powerful guidance to achieve instructional and school improvement.

WHAT IS A HIGH-PERFORMING SCHOOL?

A solid body of highly respected research demonstrates that in high-performing schools the components that matter most for school improvement include the following 10 school conditions and five teaching strategies (Cotton, 2003):

10 School Conditions

1. Safe and orderly school environment
2. Strong administrative leadership
3. Primary focus on learning
4. Maximizing learning time
5. Monitoring student progress
6. Academically heterogeneous class assignments
7. Flexible in-class groups
8. Small class size
9. Supportive classroom climate
10. Parent and community involvement

5 Teaching Strategies

1. Careful orientation to lessons
2. Clear and focused instruction
3. Effective questioning techniques
4. Feedback and reinforcement
5. Review and reteaching as needed

In short, in high-performing schools, the *focus* of administrators and teachers is instruction; that is, both sets of educators engage in day-to-day efforts to assess and enhance student learning. This body of research also reveals that the components of school improvement—or successful school reform—include the following factors, all of which support effective classroom instruction:

1. Effective, research-based methods and strategies
2. Comprehensive planning and instructional design with aligned components

3. Professional development

4. Measurable goals and benchmarks

5. Support within the school

6. Parental and community development

7. External technical support and assistance

8. Evaluation strategies

9. Coordination of resources

Throughout the *Handbook,* we demonstrate that organizational conditions and teaching strategies as well as instructional leadership in the high-performing schools we studied are generally consistent with those found in related studies of high-performing schools (Cotton, 2003; Elmore, 2000).

WHAT IS A HIGH-PERFORMING PRINCIPAL?

Again, we turn to the existing research base to define a high-performing principal. In fact, this research base centers on the leader behaviors that have strong *effects* on student achievement. An effect is a statistically derived, predictable result; thus, a high-performing principal exhibits behaviors (also called "best practices") that yield statistically greater student learning than if the leader did not engage in those behaviors. This is a bottom-line definition of a high-performing principal. In brief, the six largest student achievement effect sizes derive from the following (Waters, Marzano, & McNulty, 2003), which will be discussed in depth later in this book:

1. *Situational Awareness:* The principal is aware of details and occurrences in the school and uses the information to address current and potential problems.

2. *Intellectual Stimulation:* The principal ensures that faculty and staff know current theories and practices and make related discussions a regular part of the school culture.

3. *Change Agent:* The principal is willing to and actively does challenge the status quo.

4. *Input:* The principal involves teachers in the design and implementation of important decisions and policies.

5. *Culture:* The principal fosters shared beliefs, a sense of community, and cooperation.

6. *Monitors/Evaluates:* The principal monitors the effectiveness of school practices and their impact on student learning.

More specifically, Blase and Blase (2006) found that principals and teachers of high-performing schools routinely ask questions such as,

- How do we enhance our commitment to improving student learning?
- Are we engaged in ongoing study of the teaching and learning process?
- How effective are our assessment procedures and our use of data for school improvement?
- What decision-making structures enable teachers, parents, and others to be meaningfully involved in decision making?
- Is teacher leadership emerging?
- What opportunities exist for collaboration and professional growth?
- Do teachers engage in creative problem solving?

THE NEW CHALLENGE OF ADMINISTRATIVE LEADERSHIP FOR SCHOOL IMPROVEMENT

The field of education is rife with debates about approaches to effective school leadership, including managerial, instructional, transformational, distributed, and balanced leadership. Such debates notwithstanding, *effective approaches invariably include leader and teacher behaviors that link to student achievement.* Thus, some educational scholars argue that an excellent analytical tool for explaining "best leadership practices" in complex organizations such as schools is *distributed leadership* (Spillane, Halverson, & Diamond, 2004). To improve teaching and learning, educational leaders engage in the social distribution of tasks (e.g., delegating and sharing) and the situational distribution of support (e.g., coaching and providing instructional materials) to enhance instructional practice; *in other words, principals structure the entire school context to facilitate instruction).* It is argued that distributed leadership increases the number of people concerned with improvement and involves a broader range of participants in collaboration to achieve school improvement goals; it also blends traditional practices (i.e., program evaluation, teacher evaluation, curriculum design, and professional development) with external accountability expectations (i.e., coupling of teaching and leadership, teacher collaboration, professional learning aligned with instructional goals, and monitored instructional outcomes) (Halverson, Grigg, Prichett, & Thomas, 2007).

Similarly, other scholars argue that a traditional instructional leadership approach should be conceptualized broadly as "instructional improvement." This suggests a combination of (1) *leadership for instructional matters* (e.g., development of strong staff development programs, ongoing curriculum review, instructional supervision, and oversight of evaluation and assessment) and (2) *creation of school-level conditions* that enable teachers to collaborate, to do the complex and often-messy work of finding more effective ways to teach (e.g., providing opportunities for teachers to collectively create, adapt, and refine instructional lessons that are framed by "best practices"; developing communities of teachers who are committed to continuous inquiry and the teaching of one another; and engaging in incremental, schoolwide improvement informed by data and aimed at increasing achievement for all students) (Elmore, 2000; Fullan, 2001; Joyce & Showers, 2002).

Moreover, according to our study, high-performing school principals improve teaching and student learning by creating accountable *learning subsystems,* and these subsystems derive from the principal's nine action foci. Principals who create high-performing schools:

1. Are *models* of learning;

2. Are exemplars of the field's *standards* of leadership;

3. *Focus* on school and teacher practices associated with increased student achievement;

4. Lead in ways that have *maximum impact on student achievement;*

5. Work with teachers on the *school mission:* They engage in ongoing, collaborative study of schoolwide instructional improvement efforts;

6. Use a *systems* approach to dispatch with managerial responsibilities and to organize instructional aspects of work;

7. Take an *empowering (team) approach* to almost everything, and create learning communities in their schools;

8. Hire *strong people* for administrative, faculty, and staff positions; and

9. Insist on using *data* to inform instructional decisions.

In Chapters 1 through 9, we will explore each of these nine action foci.

The school is a learning community!

1 Learning

> Principals of high-performing schools are models of learning.

During our research, we examined each high-performing principal's background with respect to his or her approach to leadership. Without exception, principals asserted that they were lifelong learners and models of learning. We asked how they learned what they know and use in day-to-day school leadership; we also asked them *what* they had learned that they believed was most crucial to the successful practice of school leadership.

HOW DID THEY LEARN?

How did high-performing principals learn what they know? Principals told us they learned a great deal from experience, especially from positive and negative role models they had encountered, and through trial and error.

Learning From Positive and Negative Role Models

According to our findings, high-performing principals attributed much of their effectiveness to *disciplined reflection* throughout their careers as teachers, assistant principals, and principals on experiences with both positive (i.e., effective) and negative (i.e., ineffective) principals:

> *I have been very blessed to have worked with excellent principals, assistant principals, and teachers—people who have accomplished a great deal; I have been able to ask all of them questions and figure out what makes them tick. I worked with a National Middle School Association principal-of-the-year; I really enjoyed working with her and getting her feelings about how to be an effective administrator. Prior to that, I worked with the faculty and staff in another school, which became a national School of Excellence. Those experiences were extremely helpful to me.*
>
> —Middle School Principal

I have been exposed to great leaders in my life, from a very young age until now. I was a teacher in a school where the principal empowered us. Then I was an assistant principal; and for seven years, I had conversations with many great principals. I have worked with principals who were both great leaders and great managers.

—Elementary School Principal

I took everything I could from the principals I knew—what to do and what not to do. The first principal we had, all he did was worry about how he looked. The second principal, all he did was worry about discipline; if you moved out of place, he got all over you. He jumped on me one time because I moved the seats in my classroom! Then there was the principal who was lazy; he did the announcements and then let the kids run the school. The next principal loved the kids, but he was disorganized, and the one after that was very organized but not very friendly. I got my organization skills from the last one.

—Elementary School Principal

I was an assistant principal, and I worked in the county office, and I worked with very effective and very ineffective principals. From them, I learned a lot about what to do and what not to do. I just absorbed it... and I find myself always thinking back to those experiences.

—Elementary School Principal

Learning Through Trial and Error

The principals we studied also learned to be exemplary leaders through trial and error:

I think 99% of the job is learned through trial and error; that's just gut honest. My education classes were wonderful, and I had some great classes, but until you sit in that big chair behind that desk...

—Middle School Principal

I have changed... I have grown. We get older, learn from our mistakes, learn from our teachers, and try to get better.

—Middle School Principal

You realize very early on how all encompassing the role of principal is. It has changed and evolved to such a degree and so fast that the majority of things that I am doing now I learned by doing and reflecting on mistakes. I had good preparation, but there's no way you could be fully prepared to do this job. I didn't become a principal to be a project director for major construction at our school, but that's part of it.

—High School Principal

WHAT DID THEY LEARN?

What did high-performing principals learn from role models and through trial and error? We identified nine valuable lessons related to balance, hiring, life-long learning, communication, motivation, empowerment, recognition, visibility, and public relations.

1. High-Performing Principals Learned to Balance Their Personal and Professional Lives

Principals reported that after several years on the job and with "constant thinking and planning ahead" they learned to better balance their professional and personal lives. Fundamentally, this required a high degree of organization and reorganization of most aspects of the school (as discussed throughout this book) and their personal lives.

> *Because of the hours, the stresses, the demands, you have to be very organized at school, have systems in place, and you have to organize your personal life as well.*
>
> —Elementary School Principal

> *I try not to make work my whole life, but I have to be careful. I have a husband who can certainly take care of himself, but I maintain my distance from work and my personal dignity by setting a time by which I am going to leave school; otherwise, I can be at work as late as 11:00 P.M. because I am new here, and I am still adjusting.*
>
> —High School Principal

> *There's a family factor, and you have to learn to balance work and home. I'm eleven years into it, and I'm better now than when I began; then, I was taking stuff home every night. But it can depend on what is going on; for example, at budget time, the budget's going home with me, and I am playing with it, manipulating things. And when I am doing annual summaries, I'm typing them out at home, but fast. I also do most of the accreditation report online at home.*
>
> —Middle School Principal

2. High-Performing Principals Learned to Fill a School With Strong People

All principals who participated in our study discussed the importance of having strong people to create a high-performing school (see the discussion about hiring later in this book):

> *Bottom line, you have to find good people and you have to make sure that everybody is basically on the same page. You have to let other people do things, and you have to let other people be leaders without losing touch with the direction things are going. In other words, you don't give it away, you entrust it.*
>
> —Middle School Principal

> *You've got to have people who have the strength of their convictions, who get the facts out, take decisive action at the right time, and who do what's right. There are very few things you can stew on.*
>
> —High School Principal

> *You've got to have the right people on the right bus in the right seats . . . committed to excellence.*
>
> —Middle School Principal

High-performing principals suggested using the following general rule of thumb for balancing the work of administrative leadership and instructional leadership: Time should be devoted to teachers, students, and instructional leadership matters when teachers and students are in the building; time should be devoted to reports and other administrative leadership tasks that require concentrated effort when they can be completed more efficiently and effectively (i.e., before and after school, when teachers and students are not in the building).

3. High-Performing Principals Learned That Everyone (Starting With Themselves) Must Demonstrate Lifelong Learning

Although the principals we studied excelled as educational leaders, they were not complacent; they modeled lifelong learning as they continued their journeys toward professional growth, and they included assistant principals and teachers in this journey:

> *I constantly take professional learning classes, usually things that I am interested in. I have learned so much about the ways children learn—it's fascinating to me!*
>
> —Elementary School Principal

> *I try to read everything I can, be involved with county-level committees, and go to workshops so that I will have an understanding of some of the horizon issues, instead of just living day to day.*
>
> —Elementary School Principal

> *I try to model. I have read several of Todd Whitaker's books, which are very short. One that I keep as a handbook is* Fourteen Things Effective Principals Do Differently, *and one I gave all my teachers is* What Great Teachers Do Differently. *They are short reads, not laborious, and several teachers said, "You know, this is a great book. I read this part and thought I did that very well, but I also do that and it's not very good."*
>
> —Elementary School Principal

> *I read the educational research, and I think it's important for teachers to keep their fingers on the pulse of the research. Every Monday, I send out an instructional*

> *bulletin covering priorities for the week; and in that, I encourage teachers by including something related to the research so they will have their curiosity piqued and pursue it.*
>
> —High School Principal

4. High-Performing Principals Learned to Develop and Sustain Good Communication and Constructive Relationships With Everyone

According to our findings, principals worked to build mutual trust, treat people with respect, and care about people; these were considered essential to open and honest communication and constructive relationships between and among individuals and groups.

> *When I first came in as principal, I set aside time to get to know people. I set up times for teachers to come in and just sit down and talk to me; it was rather scripted—kind of formal—but it gave me a good sense of who they were, and it broke the ice. Starting with relationships first has helped me tremendously, as not everyone will tell me when they like this initiative or that direction, but they know they can trust me, and they know that I'm not going to make a decision that is going to hurt the children or the school. I put them in front of those paper tasks, though I do have a reputation that things are in on time and done conscientiously.*
>
> —Elementary School Principal
>
> *Communication is one of those things I probably struggle with as much or more than anybody else, but I am learning to become a good communicator. One-on-one is where you start. You have to have respect for others and for their dignity or the work that they perform. It's important to build that mutual respect and trust when you speak with individuals or with small and large groups in meetings.*
>
> —High School Principal
>
> *Instructional leadership is about having frank conversations with people, but before you can do that you have to build up enough trust.*
>
> —Elementary School Principal
>
> *Anyone can be a good manager. During my first year as a principal, I managed people, and we didn't talk much. But I have evolved into an instructional leader with great communication and managerial skills.*
>
> —Elementary School Principal

Principals also used e-mails, bulletins, newsletters, team minutes, and conversations to communicate with others. Timely communication (i.e., quick responses) to queries is essential.

> *The grade-level teachers meet weekly and plan. If they need anything or have questions, they can note that at the end of their minutes, and I respond that evening before I go home or the next day so that there is a quick turnaround to concerns.*
>
> —Elementary School Principal

> *Every morning, I put out a bulletin to staff; it could be very lengthy if there is a current issue that affects everybody in the building, or it could be just kudos to an individual or grade level. There is usually some sort of inspirational quote that I put on there, too.*
>
> —Middle School Principal

Moreover, high-performing principals reported that responsiveness to personal teacher requests was a priority. For instance, when a teacher requested a principal's recommendation for entry to graduate school, the principal responded immediately; prompt action demonstrated support of ongoing professional growth and showed appreciation for the teacher's contribution to the school. Most high-performing principals used a 24-hour turnaround rule regarding teacher requests of this nature; they stated that such responsiveness enhanced teachers' feelings of being valued, their job satisfaction, and school morale.

Several high-performing principals reported that they created opportunities for children to communicate directly with them.

> *We are a school in which a child is listened to. Any child can come into the principal's office, take a Jolly Rancher (candy) from the bowl on my desk, and talk about problems. We may think something is great, but the kids think it stinks; even if the kid is off base, we need to know that.*
>
> —Elementary School Principal

> *I learn things that I didn't know about the teachers from the children, and it's really exciting and always very positive. But, there have been a few times in Principal's Lunch Bunch when I have heard something that makes me go back to ask the teacher to explain something, like "Johnny said you're not doing Digi-blocks though everybody else is doing Digi-blocks and he doesn't know what Digi-blocks are." Talking with kids is an effective tool.*
>
> —Elementary School Principal

Principals recognized parents as stakeholders, valued their input, and created opportunities to communicate with them:

> *My concept of shared decision making includes parents. You can have a school that falters if you don't keep abreast of parents' concerns. Shared decision making is listening to people's concerns and trying to strategize solutions that might be available.*
>
> —High School Principal

> *Whether I am communicating with parents or teachers, I think it all impacts student achievement. Having community support and parent support is especially important to effective instructional leadership. So, if you wait seven days before returning a parent's phone call about a concern, I think it can, in the long run, impact student achievement and instructional leadership by causing conversations to occur in the home about your failure to respond.*
>
> —High School Principal

> *You have to make sure parents don't feel like they are excluded. I have coffee with the parents four times a year; it is held in the morning, and they can bring their issues and concerns they want addressed.*
>
> —High School Principal

> *I communicate regularly with parents through a monthly newsletter, one of which I always dedicate to reading and what parents can do to help their child with it. Last year, I also dedicated one issue to math; in it, I explained details about the Everyday Math program.*
>
> —Elementary School Principal

5. High-Performing Principals Learned to Motivate and Energize People

Principals who participated in our study were very concerned with keeping teacher morale high; they believed that a "happy teacher is a better teacher" and routinely worked to inspire teachers:

> *It is my job to inspire teachers, help them discover the realities of best practice, and move them collectively toward that.*
>
> —Elementary School Principal

> *I have to be a quality-plus leader. I have to have energy and passion for the job that I do. I have to be able to energize people around me and execute my role in order to achieve student success.*
>
> —Elementary School Principal

Conversely, principals worked diligently to prevent teacher negativity, which they reported has an adverse effect on student achievement:

> *Teacher negativity is the worst. Our teachers realize that I care about them and that if there's a problem we are going to work it out. I keep the staff morale up because if teachers are happy the kids are happy and they are learning, and then parents are happy.*
>
> —Elementary School Principal

> *I can't remember ever making a decision in the past four or five years without talking with some of the staff because decisions affect everybody, and it trickles down to the students. If the teachers aren't happy, their negativity is going to come out, and it's going to affect student achievement.*
>
> —Elementary School Principal

> *I'll play music in faculty meetings, and faculty members come in upbeat. I've said, "Last week we didn't have music and you were not nearly as upbeat as now, guys. I wonder how our kids would react if you picked a song appropriate to whatever you are teaching…"*
>
> —Middle School Principal

6. High-Performing Principals Learned to Empower Others

All the principals we studied were, in varying but significant ways, strong advocates of empowerment (i.e., distributed and shared leadership). That is, they tended to include all relevant stakeholders in decision making, built trust with individuals and teams, shared power and responsibility/accountability, and encouraged ownership. *Ownership* refers to a deep, sustained commitment to school improvement goals based on stakeholders' internalization of core values, beliefs, ways of thinking, and behaviors reflected in school culture. This is discussed in more depth in Part II of this book.

> *I believe in shared decision making, input from a variety of perspectives—teachers, parents, students, and staff. Shared decision making is listening to people's concerns and strategizing together to get solutions.*
>
> —High School Principal

> *I think one of the secrets to success is that I don't do it all myself. Instead, I work hard to effectively enable others to lead, to surround myself with capable, trusted, qualified leaders; and I don't mean just my administrative team, but the teachers, clerical staff, the lady who welcomes people at the front door while monitoring for security purposes. I think people welcome this, and I think that the wisest leader is one who surrounds him- or herself with excellence and then backs away and allows people to unveil their excellence.*
>
> —Elementary School Principal

> *My leadership style is to give teachers as much power as they need. I guide them and help them, but I don't guard them, and I'm getting the school as I always dreamed it should be: a garden for children, a place they can be happy and comfortable.*
>
> —Elementary School Principal

> *The principal cannot be the only one who is responsible any more; we all have to be responsible. I learn from my teachers, and I want them to be better than me. Whether I stay in this job or not, school success is based on what the teachers do.*
>
> —Elementary School Principal

It is noteworthy that many of the individuals who participated in our study pointed out that during the initial phase of their careers as school principals they employed a strong, controlling "power over" approach to school leadership; however, over time, they evolved as "power with" leaders who trusted, respected, and supported others and worked collaboratively with others on *all* major aspects of school life.

> *As an assistant principal, I had to complete so many tasks that I assumed that when I moved into the principal's role I would still have to hold on to all those tasks, to certify, seal, and deliver everything with my name and my handprints all over it. But you cannot do that as a principal; you have to evolve as a sharing personality, trusting others around you to do tasks with great quality. If it's less than great quality, we work together until we get quality. For that to happen, teacher leadership must exist throughout the entire building.*
>
> —Elementary School Principal

> *I didn't start out as an effective principal; I used to think I had to be in control. I quickly learned that I could not be the know all, be all, see all, do all for everything! I was turning myself into a miserable, frustrated person because I couldn't keep up with everything. I learned you can't control people; you can't coerce them; you have to work with them.*
>
> —Elementary School Principal

> *As a leader, I have learned—and I'm glad I learned the lesson early—that sometimes you have to be a good follower; you have to let other people lead, let them shine, help them feel important, and just stand behind them.*
>
> —Middle School Principal

> *I have changed in that I have mellowed. When I first became a principal, I thought that I would have control, but I learned that when you give power away, you get more power; that has been a grand experience for me because I had been brought up to believe that it is more blessed to give than to receive.*
>
> —Elementary School Principal

This could be me if I'm not careful!

Principals discussed the importance of delegating toward people's strengths and providing opportunities for risk taking to promote professional development:

> *When you become a new principal, you tend to want to do it all, but it was learning to delegate that helped me balance instructional leadership with managerial tasks. (And, if you want to keep your family going, that has to be factored in.) I delegate to people's strengths but also give them jobs in which they can take risks so they can grow.*
>
> —Middle School Principal

> *We need to groom leaders, to even groom these young people—students—for leadership. We need teachers in the school who can lead others, pull people along; then, even if we are upset with each other, we work through it as professionals. I give people responsibilities, but then I start working and helping them to work on their weaknesses.*
>
> —Elementary School Principal

> *I have become more trusting of others' ability to do things, tasks of great quality. I had to release my mindset that I was the only one who could do something.*
>
> —Elementary School Principal

Several high-performing principals reported that they maintained a summary of teacher strengths for easy reference. Summaries included (1) each member of the leadership team's independent assessment of the strengths of each faculty member; (2) teachers' assessment of their own strengths; (3) a comparison of leaders' and teachers' assessments; and (4) a comprehensive reference list for use when matching teachers' needs with accomplished teachers' skills, sending school representatives to serve on district committees, and writing annual evaluations.

Empowering others meant delegating to their strengths; it also meant blending strengths and helping individuals and teams to move in the right direction together.

> *My role is to be the "better way" seeker at the school, the person who truly empowers people to be leaders, who moves us in the same direction. The system we build must be so strong that when I leave, our school will continue to move in the right direction, regardless of who sits in this office. To me, leadership is about empowering people around you to move in unison, almost like geese flying south with ease. That's really where the priority needs to be and that's what happens when you have all your systems in place.*
>
> —Elementary School Principal

> *I have to make sure that the whole operation of the school is sound. This requires good people who have strengths, and I need to make sure they have a lot of direction. They also have to have ownership in what they do, which means a great deal of input from them. You blend the different strengths and abilities people bring to the table.*
>
> —Middle School Principal

In addition to sharing power and delegating to strengths, in many cases high-performing principals encouraged everyone, especially teachers, to share their knowledge and skills with their colleagues. (Instructional modeling and peer consultation will be discussed further in Part II of this book.)

We have mentor teachers who show new teachers the ropes and add to their repertoire, like how to respond to certain circumstances like dealing with a smart-mouthed kid or a kid who just wants to sit and talk in class. I've also freed up time so teachers can plan and collaborate and come up with bright ideas. This brings people together so they can focus on certain goals.

—High School Principal

You don't want a faculty turning over every two or three years. So, we have teachers help one another by giving teachers who aspire to leadership positions some informal responsibilities in classroom observations. They observe and then suggest what they see as strengths and what might be improved on; this makes everyone a valuable member of the school who can also correct weaknesses, but it's nonthreatening and it doesn't produce any anxiety where a teacher freezes up.

—High School Principal

When I came to the school five years ago, there was no instructional leadership team, so I established a group of lead teachers, some of the best and the brightest, to build camaraderie within the teaching team.

—Elementary School Principal

Principals disclosed that sharing power with others occasionally resulted in mistakes; thus, they stressed the importance of using a constructive approach that helped others learn and grow from such mistakes.

To empower others you have to trust them and their abilities. When it doesn't work out, you put a bandage on the hurt feelings and move on, and you don't look at it as a disaster or make people feel bad because they perhaps misjudged something.

—Middle School Principal

I learned that I had to give other people the power and responsibility to do some things. I've known many principals who said, "Okay, you're in charge of—say—discipline," and then take it back by making some decision! I would never undermine anyone after I had given him or her the power, and if something didn't work we'd talk about it and maybe change what we do next time.

—Elementary School Principal

7. High-Performing Principals Learned to Recognize Others

Most of the principals we interviewed successfully created comprehensive and inclusive cultures of appreciation and recognition and motivational climates for all school-level personnel. For instance, principals encouraged all stakeholders to overtly recognize the range of contributions and achievements of others, as individuals and as groups (e.g., teachers, students, noncertified staff, parents, volunteers). In addition, principals initiated frequent daily verbal acknowledgements for achievements and written recognition via e-mails, letters of recognition, certificates of achievement, a Principal's List, and "freebies."

High-performing principals also reported that they began faculty meetings with kudos for teachers and staff members and with requests for thoughts and support of those going through difficult or special times.

> *You have to recognize people every time you have faculty meetings.*
>
> —High School Principal
>
> *I recognize students and teachers every morning, or a bookkeeper or our head custodian. I have these certificates of achievement that I give for whatever honor they have achieved.*
>
> —High School Principal

High-performing principals also used classroom walk-throughs to acknowledge teachers' everyday contributions in the classroom. (This leadership behavior will be described in detail in Part II of this book.)

> *Walk-throughs give us an opportunity to catch a teacher doing something good and to write something positive to them. That way, teachers know that you value and appreciate what is going on in the classroom.*
>
> —High School Principal

They also used walk-throughs to "inspect what they expect." For example, one principal in our study described "5 by 5s," a classroom monitoring strategy she learned at a Max Thompson Learning-Focused Schools conference. Each member of her administrative team visited five classrooms per day for 5 minutes each. The faculty created a list of best practices for all classrooms, and teachers in the school expected all teachers to use these best practices. The administrative team members use a form that they developed to document what they observed during walk-throughs; the form includes a checklist of the school's adopted and implemented best practices.

Awesome idea!

Principals encouraged others to recognize staff, volunteers, and students for their work as well:

> *I talk with students and parents about the importance of the noncertified staff, and I encourage them to do more to recognize them.*
>
> —High School Principal
>
> *When I see a volunteer in the building, I say, "Thank you for volunteering today," and I try to impress upon others to do the same. I can't force people to say thank you, but I try to model it in every way that I can.*
>
> —Middle School Principal

> *We recognize students individually and collectively and we let others be involved in it. As the school's instructional leader, I believe that the administrative team and I have to be at the forefront of putting students up front and making sure they are recognized for doing their best.*
>
> —High School Principal

> *I make sure that the faculty members I recommend for employment at this school understand that, as a team effort, we all have to be willing to support and recognize students outside of the classroom.*
>
> —High School Principal

Principals argued that for students, in particular, an inclusive approach to recognition produced positive effects in the classroom.

> *Students who participate in something more than lunch are more willing to do what you ask them to do—homework, being prepared for class, not being tardy, having their books and pencils, and being ready to learn.*
>
> —High School Principal

8. High-Performing Principals Learned to Be Visible and to Maintain an Open-Door Policy

A number of principals indicated that visibility at school-related events and recognition of students' accomplishments and parents' supportive roles were important symbolic responsibilities.

> *Unless I'm out of town, I go to every single banquet, whether it's for fine arts, national honor society, football, basketball, volleyball. Sometimes, I go to four banquets in one night. I thank the kids for being there and for all their effort, for their performance—whatever it is—and their achievements. I thank the parents for supporting them, and I make it clear to the kids that they would not be there if not for their parents. I thank the coaches, teachers, and sponsors, and community members. I ask the senior students to raise their hands and remind them that this is their last banquet and say that I hope they are taking very good memories with them. It's the little thing that I do that takes only about 90 to 120 seconds, and then I go to the next banquet.*
>
> —High School Principal

> *It's important to include every student group, to not overlook or sidestep any group. It's impossible to be at every event, but we try to get a good balance, and someone from the administrative team will always be there if at all possible.*
>
> —High School Principal

Principals also explained that having an open door policy—being accessible and approachable—was a form of visibility, and that it provided timely opportunities to respond to teachers' concerns.

> *If I am in my office and people need to talk with me about something, I encourage it. I am very approachable, I'm up front, and I'm a good listener. People need to feel they have a way to communicate with you, but with the former principal, the door was never open; the secretary guarded the gate and kept the staff at bay.*
>
> —Middle School Principal
>
> *I make myself available part of every class period, so that teachers or groups on their planning time who need me can access me and I can address their immediate needs. It doesn't require them to come in early or stay late.*
>
> —Middle School Principal
>
> *I tell the staff that they are more than welcome to knock on my door or open the door for me to respond to them, unless I am in a private conference with a parent or teacher. Once in a blue moon, I isolate myself. I close the door to work on something, but that takes second, third, or fourth place to the needs of the children and staff.*
>
> —Elementary School Principal

9. High-Performing Principals Learned to Establish and Maintain Good Public Relations

Principals learned that good public relations require communication and interaction with various community groups.

> *In public relations, I am talking about listening and then reacting. It's interfacing with a variety of groups to share important information about the school.*
>
> —High School Principal

Planning for good public relations is essential, according to our data. To illustrate, one principal discussed an "Annual Community Relations Plan," which included creating newsletters, maintaining a school marquee, and developing phone masters (directories). Newsletters, the school marquee, and Web sites were identified as major mechanisms used to communicate with parents. Principals also planned student recognition and parent appreciation events as part of their public relations programs. Planning to create good will and figuring out ways community groups could help improve the school were also discussed. Good will was seen as especially useful when mistakes were made.

> *You have to work hard, and you have to let people in the community know you are working hard. Then when you make a mistake, your community will be supportive; they remember you've had lots of successes in other areas.*
>
> —Middle School Principal

District- and school-level committees initiated climate surveys to formally elicit feedback about community satisfaction. In addition to expecting teachers and assistant principals to find ways to supplement what was being done in the classroom, high-performing principals encouraged parental involvement in decision-making processes to improve school climate and classroom instruction. These and a range of informal interactions with groups and individuals constituted the evaluation component of public relations.

At the same time, principals stressed that efficient execution of public relations plans was necessary for good public relations, asserting, for example, "You don't want to spend an inordinate amount of time on it." Consequently, principals created structures such as the School Governance Council or similar committees to organize and coordinate work with parents, students, and community groups. Furthermore, principals and assistant principals and technology leaders shared responsibility for attending important meetings (e.g., PTSA) and events (e.g., athletic games, Senior Night, Open House).

> *It takes all of us; we spread ourselves out, and we try to make sure that none of us works more than three nights a week.*
>
> —High School Principal

SUMMARY

Chapter 1 explored *learning*, the first of nine action foci of high-performing principals. The chapter dealt with how and what high-performing principals learned as they became high-performing school leaders. What they learned included a number of core leadership skills including balancing personal and professional spheres of life; hiring strong people; life-long learning; communicating and developing constructive relationships; motivating, empowering, and recognizing others; being visible; and maintaining good public relations. Readers should keep in mind that becoming a high-performing principal requires *critical reflection* on experience, not simply experience itself; such reflection is an essential component of lifelong learning.

TIPS AND SUGGESTIONS

Increasing Teacher Positivity and Decreasing Teacher Negativity

1. Ensure that work time and workloads are equitable among teachers. Make analysis of work time and duties a routine procedure when assigning duties and developing schedules. Publish teaching and duty assignments to demonstrate your concern for fairness and equity.

2. Adopt a policy requiring that a parent who has a concern about a teacher address that concern with the teacher before seeking an administrator's involvement. Communicate this policy to parents in writing and at meetings. Ask those who answer the school phone to remind parents of this policy.

3. Encourage a norm of public positivity and private negativity. Develop a system for private and/or anonymous reporting of concerns, issues, grievances, and complaints and for addressing the same.

4. Use uplifting notes and inspirational stories to express gratitude to individuals for what they do.

Empowering Teachers

1. Encourage innovation and risk taking.

2. Reward good work with detailed, specific praise and public recognition; if the budget permits, provide a gift card to the local school-resource store.

3. Involve teachers in all instructional decision making.

4. Involve teachers in reflective problem solving.

5. Defer to teachers as the experts when appropriate.

6. Build capacity to lead, then step back and follow the lead of those you have empowered.

Handing Over Responsibility for Critical Tasks

1. When assigning tasks, meet with the responsible faculty members to discuss your expectations for the process and work. Set guidelines for time frames and quality of the work.

2. Communicate your trust of and respect for the faculty as professionals capable of producing a quality product.

3. Hand over the reins of power and assume a "mentor and resource" role.

4. Drop in on faculty work sessions to lend support and monitor progress.

5. Provide positive feedback.

6. Give credit.

7. Celebrate efforts and showcase the products.

(Continued)

(Continued)

Tapping Teachers as Resources for Teacher Growth

1. Develop a directory of in-house talents and resources. Publish the directory for teachers and encourage teachers to tap the in-house talent.

Walk-Throughs

1. Walk-throughs should occur not only during teaching time but also during planning time to ensure effective, productive use of planning time and to ensure that planning time is not used as personal time.

2. Establish a quota of daily walk-throughs for administrators. Monitor compliance with the quota and identify obstacles to meeting walk-through quotas. Brainstorm ways, such as staggered walk-through times, to overcome obstacles.

Visibility (Walk-Abouts)

1. Maintain visibility through walk-abouts (i.e., walking through the school at various times of the day). Visit key spots, such as the cafeteria during breakfast and lunch times, buses when loading and unloading, before-school tutoring areas, bathrooms during transitions, and after-school extracurricular activities. Use checklists to ensure that administrators are regularly seen in all of these locations daily.

School Climate

1. Ask faculty and staff to design and to complete an anonymous climate survey. Analyze and present the data from the survey. Brainstorm an action plan with the faculty and staff to address areas of deficiency.

2. Create a list of offensive principal practices (i.e., The Do Nots of Effective School Leadership), and reflect on and self-evaluate against that list at the beginning, middle, and end of every year.

Modeling 2

Principals of high-performing schools are exemplars of the field's standards of leadership.

Holding administrators to the same high standards as teachers increases the likelihood that schools are led by people who can guide others in needed improvements and reforms. The Interstate School Leaders Licensure Consortium (ISLLC) standards, developed by the Council of Chief State School Officers (CCSSO) and member states, are now widely accepted as essential to best practice. Generally speaking, the standards address school vision, culture, operations, resources, constituencies, ethics, and context. However, the standards emphasize an administrator's abilities in the areas of instructional leadership and school improvement, use of data for decision making, and student achievement (Council of Chief State School Officers, 2008). We found that high-performing principals addressed almost every ISLLC standard (to varying degrees, of course); that is, they exhibited a whole-school (i.e., comprehensive), well-organized, and well-integrated systems-development approach to leadership at the school level. See Figure 2.1 for a brief overview of the ISLLC standards.

High-performing principals who participated in our study worked hard to become exemplars of educational leadership and in the process modeled the same level of excellence they expected from teachers. Indeed, they engaged in frequent, reflective self-assessment using ISLLC standards and also embraced stakeholders' assessments and surveys of their leadership for school improvement. One high-performing principal noted,

You read, you think, you try to measure yourself—where you are and where you want to be and how you get there. It's just a constant evaluation. You're never really satisfied to do what you're doing, and you're never convinced that you're where you need to be. I think good teachers do that as well.

—Middle School Principal

These principals are reflective thinkers who use results of assessments to compare their own performance to the standards and to inform their leadership practices.

Figure 2.1 Educational Leadership Policy Standards of the Interstate School Leaders Licensure Consortium (ISLLC) 2008

Standard 1: An education leader promotes the success of every student by facilitating the development, articulation, implementation, and stewardship of a vision of learning that is shared and supported by all stakeholders.

Functions

Collaboratively develop and implement a shared vision and mission

Collect and use data to identify goals, assess organizational effectiveness, and promote organizational learning

Create and implement plans to achieve goals

Promote continuous and sustainable improvement

Monitor and evaluate progress and revise plans

Standard 2: An education leader promotes the success of every student by advocating, nurturing, and sustaining a school culture and instructional program conducive to student learning and staff professional growth.

Functions

Nurture and sustain a culture of collaboration, trust, learning, and high expectations

Create a comprehensive, rigorous, and coherent curricular program

Create a personalized and motivating learning environment for students

Supervise instruction

Develop assessment and accountability systems to monitor student progress

Develop the instructional and leadership capacity of staff

Maximize time spent on quality instruction

Promote the use of the most effective and appropriate technologies to support teaching and learning

Monitor and evaluate the impact of the instructional program

Standard 3: An education leader promotes the success of every student by ensuring management of the organization, operation, and resources for a safe, efficient, and effective learning environment.

Functions

Monitor and evaluate the management and operational systems

Obtain, allocate, align, and efficiently utilize human, fiscal, and technological resources

Promote and protect the welfare and safety of students and staff

Develop the capacity for distributed leadership

Ensure teacher and organizational time is focused to support quality instruction and student learning

Standard 4: An education leader promotes the success of every student by collaborating with faculty and community members, responding to diverse community interests and needs, and mobilizing community resources.

Functions

Collect and analyze data and information pertinent to the educational environment

Promote understanding, appreciation, and use of the community's diverse cultural, social, and intellectual resources

Build and sustain positive relationships with families and caregivers

Build and sustain productive relationships with community partners

Standard 5: An education leader promotes the success of every student by acting with integrity, fairness, and in an ethical manner.

Functions

Ensure a system of accountability for every student's academic and social success

Model principles of self-awareness, reflective practice, transparency, and ethical behavior

Safeguard the values of democracy, equity, and diversity

Consider and evaluate the potential moral and legal consequences of decision making

Promote social justice and ensure that individual student needs inform all aspects of schooling

Standard 6: An education leader promotes the success of every student by understanding, responding to, and influencing the political, social, economic, legal, and cultural context.

Functions

Advocate for children, families, and caregivers

Act to influence local, district, state, and national decisions affecting student learning

Assess, analyze, and anticipate emerging trends and initiatives in order to adapt leadership strategies

SOURCE: Council of Chief State School Officers, 2008.

Activities for Becoming an Exemplar of Leadership Standards

Activity 1: Using the Leadership Reflection Guide

Rigorous reflection is essential to professional growth; it is a deliberative approach to professional self-improvement and development. Serious professional reflection about something (X)—an idea, model, program, strategy, process, theory, belief, experience, and so on—should address *some* of the following questions and will develop your ability to think like an effective leader.

Practice your reflection skills by using some of the questions listed below to consider a current issue; then, plan a course of action based on the conclusions you derive from your reflective experience.

(Continued)

(Continued)

1. What are my existing values, beliefs, and assumptions about X?

2. What are my feelings related to X, and how will these impede and/or facilitate my leadership?

3. What did I think before I was introduced to X, and why?

4. What are my strengths and weaknesses vis-à-vis X, and what will be my improvement plan, beginning tomorrow? What opportunities are available to me in my everyday personal and professional world to practice and refine X?

5. How would I explain X (i.e., what is the rationale) to others? Do I really have a solid rationale for my actions?

6. How should X be modified to be useful to me in my school situation?

7. What obstacles can I expect in implementing X?

8. What are the costs and benefits of X for me and my school situation?

9. What are the possible outcomes of implementing X for teachers, teaching, and learning?

10. What are the ethical considerations related to X?

11. How do issues of diversity (e.g., gender, race, ethnicity, sexual orientation) influence my thinking about X?

12. How will X affect how I want to spend my time?

13. What new issues/problems might result from X, and what will I do about these before and after they occur?

14. To whom or what can I turn for help or support regarding X?

15. In implementing X, how will I know if I have been effective?

16. What other social, economic, financial, cultural, political, and pedagogical (learning) factors should be considered with respect to X? What influences does each of these factors have on X and its implementation?

Activity 2: Defining a Positive School Culture (ISLLC Standard 2)

Step 1. As a faculty, create a Culture Committee composed of faculty volunteers interested in school culture.

Step 2. Ask the Culture Committee to spearhead research on school culture and share their findings at a faculty meeting.

Step 3. Divide the staff into smaller work groups, possibly utilizing already existing teams or departments. Ask each work group to engage in development of positive culture guidelines based on the presented research, on the school's existing culture, and on the staff's vision for the school's culture.

Step 4. Work groups will share their positive culture guidelines with the Culture Committee, which will compile the results into one document and distribute it back to work groups.

Step 5. Work groups will identify the culture guidelines they feel should be included in the final document and will submit their results to the Culture Committee, which will create a draft of the guidelines on which there is consensus.

Step 6. The Culture Committee will present the guidelines draft and will lead the faculty through discussion and decision making on remaining guidelines (those on which there was not consensus originally).

Activity 3: Assessing and Improving the School Culture (ISLLC Standard 2)

Step 1. Create a Likert scale culture survey based on your school's Positive Culture Guidelines.

Step 2. Have teachers complete the survey.

Step 3. Have the Culture Committee analyze and interpret the survey results and distribute them to the work groups established in Activity 1 above.

Step 4. Have the staff work groups brainstorm action steps for realization of a positive school culture and submit their results to the Culture Committee.

Step 5. Have the Culture Committee create an action plan for building the desired culture.

SUMMARY

Chapter 2 included a brief description of the ISLLC standards, which comprise a comprehensive framework of administrative/management and instructional leadership tasks and benchmarks for principals. High-performing principals used these standards to reflect on their leadership performance. Activities and resources for enhancing one's professional knowledge and skills as an educational leader were presented.

TIPS AND SUGGESTIONS

School Leadership Performance Standards

1. Using the ISLLC standards as a self-survey, evaluate your performance on each function. Identify your performance weaknesses, and create an action plan to improve your performance.

2. Ask teachers and parents to generate a list of specific expectations for school leadership for each of the ISLLC standards. Use this list to inform your leadership.

3. Create leadership performance surveys based on teachers' and parents' specific expectations for each ISLLC standard. Periodically, ask random samples of teachers and parents to complete surveys. Use the resulting leadership performance ratings to assess the degree to which you are meeting stakeholders' expectations.

4. Ask various constituency groups (particularly nonparent community members and business leaders, as well as civic organizations) to share their expectations for the principal. Also, ask them what they expect of your school's graduates.

3 Focusing

> Principals of high-performing schools focus on school and teacher practices associated with increased student achievement.

Richard Elmore (2003), the highly respected expert in school improvement from Harvard University, has concluded that the key to improving schools and student achievement is having the right focus, and this focus then drives all that is administrative as well as instructional. In *Knowing the Right Things to Do: School Improvement and Performance-Based Activity*, he said:

> Knowing the right thing to do is the central problem of school improvement. Holding schools accountable for their performance depends on having people in schools with the knowledge, skill, and judgment to make the improvements that will increase student performance. (p. 9)

The high-performing principals we studied exhibited leadership consistent with Elmore's conclusions. Two high-performing principals summarized the shared beliefs of all of the principals in our study:

> *Instruction and instructional leadership drive everything in the school—budget, discipline, everything. If instruction is the engine that drives a school, then it is going to be successful.*
>
> —Middle School Principal
>
> *Having the right people doing the right thing is one of the biggest issues.*
>
> —Elementary School Principal

Surely, increasing student performance is the right thing to do, but how can school leaders do this? Unfortunately, most attempts at school reform fail because school principals do *not* sustain a focus on what, according to the best research, has an impact on student achievement (Levin & Wiens, 2003). This was not the case for high-performing principals.

What did the high-performing principals in our study do differently? They hired the right people, put them in the right places, held them accountable for meeting high expectations and standards for research-based teaching, and ignited in them an ongoing passion for student achievement and school improvement. Principals in our study shared their thoughts:

> *I insist. . . . We are absolutely about increasing student achievement, especially in the areas of reading, writing, and math. We, as a school and as a community, set very specific action plans, maintain a clear direction, and monitor to ensure that we are moving in that direction, accomplishing our goals.*
>
> —Elementary School Principal
>
> *My personal mission is to be a distinguished, quality professional who is committed, passionate, and driven to move our school forward.*
>
> —Elementary School Principal
>
> *The people here have a very strong work ethic. From the custodian all the way to the assistant principal, they care about students, and they're passionate about what they do.*
>
> —Elementary School Principal

High-performing principals relied heavily on research to guide their instructional leadership and to inform the ongoing focus on student achievement and school improvement in their schools. Robert Marzano and others (Marzano, Pickering, & Pollock, 2001; Marzano, 2003) at the Mid-continent Research for Education and Learning (McREL) were among the scholars frequently mentioned by principals; they specifically referred to their meta-analyses of classroom and school practices to determine the correct focus of instructional improvement efforts in schools. Principals concluded that leaders and teachers should continuously focus on 11 practices and factors strongly associated with increased student achievement (See Figure 3.1).

The magnitude of change associated with using best practices can account for as much as 20% of the variance in student achievement; for example, engaging in the most effective practices can improve a school's passing rate on a standardized test from 50% to 72%. According to our data, principals who created high-performing schools emphasized all the practices identified with school- and teacher-level variables; one principal in our study stated that he had "taken the research by Marzano and created a kind of mantra" by which instructional leadership in his school and classrooms would "live or die." Other principals in the study reported that Marzano, Pickering, and Pollock's (2001) book, *Classroom Instruction That Works,* served particularly well as a template for their school's instructional improvement efforts. (The full details of the

Figure 3.1   School- and Teacher-Level Practices and Student Factors Influencing Student Achievement

School practices	1. Guaranteed and viable curriculum
	2. Challenging goals and effective feedback
	3. Parent and community involvement
	4. Safe and orderly environment
	5. Collegiality and professionalism
Teacher practices	6. Instructional strategies
	7. Classroom management
	8. Classroom curriculum design
Student factors	9. Home environment
	10. Learned intelligence/background knowledge
	11. Motivation

SOURCE: Marzano, Pickering, & Pollock, 2001; Marzano, 2003.

Jigsaw Activity for School- and Teacher-Level Practices Influencing Student Achievement

Step 1. Divide faculty members into 8 groups and assign each group one of the school or teacher practices listed in Figure 3.1.

Step 2. Ask each of the 8 groups to use the resources listed above to develop a PowerPoint presentation of the research on their respective practices influencing student achievement as well as to develop practical applications derived from the research.

Step 3. Ask each group to present its research, PowerPoint, and practical applications at faculty meetings.

research described in this book are available in the McREL report, "A Theory-Based Meta-Analysis of Research on Instruction" (1998; free download at www.mcrel.org/PDF/Instruction/5982RR_InstructionMeta_Analysis.pdf) in "A New Era of School Reform: Going Where the Research Takes Us" (available free at www.mcrel.org/PDF/SchoolImprovementReform/5002RR_NewEraSchoolReform.pdf#search=%22a%20new%20era%20of%20school%20reform%22), and in two books published by the Association for Supervision and Curriculum Development, (1) *Classroom Instruction That Works* (Marzano, Pickering, & Pollock, 2001) and (2) *What Works in Schools* (Marzano, 2003). This research is discussed further in Part II of this book.)

SUMMARY

Chapter 3 described high-performing principals' focus on school-teacher-student factors that contribute to school achievement. This chapter also included the best available resources for helping educators develop the requisite knowledge and skills to enhance student achievement. To be sure, "knowing the right things to do" (Elmore, 2003, p. 9) can improve a principal's instructional leadership.

TIPS AND SUGGESTIONS

Best School- and Teacher-Level Practices for Influencing Student Achievement

1. Ensure that teachers know the standards they should teach, and ensure that they reliably cover those standards in accordance with established pacing guides. To monitor curricula, carry standards and pacing maps on all walk-throughs. Further, conduct walk-throughs on the same day for the same content area, course, and grade level; for example, conduct walk-throughs of same-placement-level 5th-grade math classes back to back on the same day (teachers should be together or close to the same point on the pacing schedule). Investigate concerns.

2. Monitor teacher expectations of students, and ensure that expectations are posted for students. Ask students to tell you what their teachers expect of them and where they can find that information.

3. Encourage student-teacher conferencing for goal setting and goal monitoring.

4. During walk-throughs, look at feedback provided to students on their graded class work and homework. Does feedback consist of a grade only, or is there other meaningful feedback?

5. Require teachers to use department meeting time to work on inter-rater reliability of their feedback to students. Specifically, ask teachers to provide feedback on a common piece of student work and compare their feedback. When discrepancies are significant, ask teachers to work collaboratively to establish guidelines for meaningful feedback and to find ways to provide effective, specific feedback in a time-efficient manner.

6. Create a Safe and Orderly Environment Checklist. Ask various departments, grade levels, and/or teams to complete the Checklist during a designated month. Use the results to guide and inform additional measures to secure a safe and orderly environment.

7. Encourage the establishment and adoption of schoolwide professional norms by teachers. Serve as a resource when faculty members desire assistance and direction in creating norms.

8. Ask teachers to investigate best practices in general as well as best practices for their content areas. Encourage teachers to develop a best-practice checklist for their departments.

9. Ask teachers to create a monitoring document for administrative walk-throughs, including the checklist of general and content-specific best practices; use this when conducting walk-throughs.

10. Utilize a schoolwide discipline plan to achieve consistency in practice at the classroom level and at the school level. Ensure that teachers consistently follow the adopted plan. Ensure that administrators are consistent about what constitutes misbehavior and in their use of consequences (in other words, that inter-rater reliability exists).

11. Adopt a schoolwide design for effective lesson planning and delivery. Train faculty and build an in-house training team to ensure best practice and consistency throughout the school.

12. Create opportunities for parents to be involved, and encourage parent involvement.

4 Leading for Achievement

Principals of high-performing schools lead in ways that have maximum impact on student achievement.

We mentioned earlier that a solid body of research demonstrates that principal behaviors are second only to teacher behaviors in terms of effects on student learning (Leithwood, Seashore-Louis, Anderson, & Wahlstrom, 2004; Marzano, Waters, & McNulty, 2005). Principals in our study concurred—teachers are the critical factor in effecting increases in student learning:

Hiring well is what results in student achievement and school improvement; both rise and fall on the quality of the men and women who work with our children.

—Elementary School Principal

When you have highly qualified, well-trained, hard-working, dedicated teachers in classrooms, your chances for high student achievement are high. You need people who know their content, know how to adapt it, know how to deliver it, and who are willing to learn.

—Middle School Principal

At the same time, high-performing principals neither marginalized their own role nor abdicated their responsibility as instructional leaders:

What makes the difference is me generally keeping that pendulum swinging further away from managerial things and toward instructional things.

—Elementary School Principal

To determine the effects of school *leadership* on student achievement, scholars at McREL conducted a meta-analysis derived from three bodies of knowledge, including a quantitative analysis of 30 years of research, a review of theoretical literature on leadership, and the research team's collective years of experience (over 100 years) in school leadership. The research team determined that the 70 studies chosen for meta-analysis (from among over 5,000 studies) met rigid standards for design, controls, analysis, and rigor. The team described 21 specific leadership responsibilities that significantly correlated with student achievement (the full report of this work is available for download from McREL at http://www.mcrel.org/topics/productDetail.asp?topicsID=7&productID=144 and in a book published by the Association for Supervision and Curriculum Development, *School Leadership That Works: From Research to Results,* (Marzano, Waters, & McNulty, 2005). In essence, these researchers concluded that

- Leaders do make a significant difference in student achievement;
- Specific leadership responsibilities are correlated with higher student achievement;
- Effective school leaders know what to do, when, how, and why to do it; in particular, effective leaders understand faculty, parents', and community members' concerns and adjust their leadership approach for maximum results; and
- There is a strong empirical relationship between the 21 leadership responsibilities and change.

Figure 4.1 identifies leader responsibilities and *average effect size* (impact) of each on student achievement.

We found that the principals of high-performing schools engaged in "balanced leadership" (Waters, Marzano, McNulty, 2003); that is, their leadership reflected all 21 leader responsibilities that impact student achievement, with particular emphasis on situational awareness, intellectual stimulation, being a change agent, input, culture, and monitoring/evaluating, each of which has a particularly high impact on student achievement. Principals described how they maintain both balance and focus:

How do I find a balance between the pulls of managerial realities and my designated role as an instructional leader? To keep my focus, I frequently reflect on my purpose as an instructional leader. I know I must lead by example in order to gain a commitment from others to our vision and mission, so I remind myself every day that I need to pull myself together, center my mind, and be here for the children, staff, and community.

—Elementary School Principal

You can't be a great leader if you are not a great manager as well, but you have to understand what is important and take care of that business; our business is people and teaching and learning, not cranking widgets.

—Elementary School Principal

Figure 4.1 21 Research-Based Leadership Responsibilities and the Average Effect Size of Their Impact on Student Achievement

Leader responsibilities	The extent to which the principal . . .	Effect size (impact on student achievement)
1. Culture*	Fosters shared beliefs and a sense of community and cooperation	.29
2. Order	Establishes a set of standard operating procedures and routines	.26
3. Discipline	Protects teachers from issues and influences that would detract from their teaching time or focus	.24
4. Resources	Provides teachers with materials and professional development necessary for the successful execution of their jobs	.26
5. Curriculum, instruction, & assessment	Is directly involved in the design and implementation of curriculum, instruction, and assessment practices	.16
6. Focus	Establishes clear goals and keeps those goals in the forefront of the school's attention	.24
7. Knowledge of curriculum, instruction, & assessment	Is knowledgeable about current curriculum, instruction, and assessment practices	.24
8. Visibility	Has quality contact and interactions with teachers and students	.16
9. Contingent rewards	Recognizes and rewards individual accomplishments	.15
10. Communication	Establishes strong lines of communication with teachers and among students	.23
11. Outreach	Is an advocate and spokesperson for the school to all stakeholders	.28
12. Input*	Involves teachers in the design and implementation of important decisions and policies	.30
13. Affirmation	Recognizes and celebrates school accomplishments and acknowledges failures	.25
14. Relationship	Demonstrates an awareness of personal aspects of teachers and staff	.19
15. Change agent*	Is willing to and actively challenges the status quo	.30
16. Optimizer	Inspires and leads new and challenging innovations	.20
17. Ideals/beliefs	Communicates and operates from strong ideals and beliefs about schooling	.25

Leader responsibilities	The extent to which the principal . . .	Effect size (impact on student achievement)
18. Monitors/ evaluates*	Monitors the effectiveness of school practices and their impact on student learning	.28
19. Flexibility	Adapts his or her leadership behavior to the needs of the current situation and is comfortable with dissent	.22
20. Situational awareness*	Is aware of the details and undercurrents in the running of the school and uses this information to address current and potential problems	.33
21. Intellectual stimulation*	Ensures that faculty and staff are aware of the most current theories and practices and makes the discussion of these a regular aspect of the school's culture	.32

*NOTE: Larger effect sizes (impact) on student achievement

SOURCE: Marzano, Waters, & McNulty, 2005; Waters, Marzano, & McNulty, 2003.

Other principals indicated that to have maximum impact on instruction, their focus had to remain on teachers, students, and teaching during school hours, for the most part:

> On the practical side, you need to prioritize, make lists, and have backup dates. When there are children and teachers in the building, my time is spent with them. Every day, I am out in the building, and I don't let other tasks overtake that.
>
> —Elementary School Principal

Readings about "balanced leadership" and the notion of "purposeful community" (i.e., one in which the members share the collective belief that they can execute a course of action that makes a difference) are available for download from http://icee.isu.edu/Journal/JournalHome.html and in the book, *Balanced Leadership: What 30 Years of Research Tells Us About the Effects of Leadership on Student Achievement* (Waters, Marzano, & McNulty, 2003).

More recently, related meta-analyses have revealed that principal behaviors of *promoting and participating in teacher learning and development* have a strong influence on student outcomes (Robinson, Lloyd, & Rowe, 2008). Consistent with this research, principals in our study favored a professional-learning-community culture:

> I always prioritize things, and I always put the students first, so, for faculty meetings we don't do announcements; we do those on e-mail. Faculty meetings are for staff development, and that's what teachers wanted. I do staff development sessions myself, and I encourage our staff to do sessions on teaching strategies. Last year, for example, we all learned together about graphic organizers.
>
> —Elementary School Principal

SUMMARY

This chapter outlined the principal's responsibilities that research has shown have a substantial impact on student achievement including, for example, those with the greatest effect (i.e., culture building, using input, being a change agent, monitoring/evaluating, developing situational awareness, and enhancing intellectual stimulation). One should keep in mind that other responsibilities identified by Waters, Marzano, and McNulty (2003) are not unimportant vis-à-vis student achievement but simply have less of an effect on learning.

TIPS AND SUGGESTIONS

Maximizing Impact on Student Achievement

1. Self-evaluate the impact of your leadership on student achievement. Copy Figure 4.1 and then separate Marzano's 21 Research-Based Responsibilities (remove Effect Size) to create twenty-one separate slips of paper. Spread the responsibilities out to see all of them at one time. Next, put the responsibilities in the order in which you devote your time; the responsibility on which you spend the most time would be the first responsibility. After ordering all 21 responsibilities, record the order and replace the effect sizes. Determine whether you are maximizing your impact by emphasizing responsibilities with the greatest influence on student achievement. Also, determine if your leadership is balanced, with time spent on all leadership responsibilities. If not, develop a plan for getting your priorities in order to have the greatest possible influence on student achievement.

2. Ask faculty to evaluate your performance of leadership responsibilities. Create a survey using the middle column of Figure 4.1 and ask teachers to rate the extent to which you are accomplishing leadership responsibilities using a Likert scale of 1 to 10, with 1 as "not effective" and 10 as "very effective and accomplished." Utilize the results of the survey to increase your influence on student achievement.

3. Evaluate communication in your school continuously. Ensure that communication is timely, succinct, and clear; and, expect all communication to receive proper attention. Ensure that all communication reaches those who need to know and those who are responsible for dealing with the content of the communication.

4. Meet periodically with all students to explain discipline rules and consequences for infractions, focusing on the school as a learning environment and every student's right to learn. Bring rules to life by giving real life examples of infractions and consequences.

5. Rather than accept the status quo, lead for the improvement of teaching and learning, and create the subsystems that support teaching and learning.

Improving Instruction 5

Principals of high-performing schools work with teachers on the school mission: They engage in ongoing, collaborative study of schoolwide instructional improvement efforts.

The principals we studied were earnest about the need to build a knowledge base about schoolwide instructional improvement among all certified personnel, including assistant principals, instructional teacher-leaders, and teachers. They worked with others to form study groups and to create professional-learning opportunities, which included continuous dialogue and helped focus the efforts of various individuals and groups on student learning and improvement:

This year, we showed the Schools that Work tapes and got together and talked about them. We also studied elements of learning-focused schools, which have research embedded in them. We share articles, tapes, conversations, and information from visits to other schools.

—Elementary School Principal

Here, we talk about rigor, relevance, and relationships. I encourage teachers to build good relationships; I think good relationships with the kids are key—good relationships make kids want to stand up for you and do a great job because you're there for them, you're looking and watching.

—High School Principal

Over time, through conversations about such issues as inquiry and use of data, professional learning, and tools for school improvement, administrators and teachers developed a culture of teaching and learning.

Principals noted that pursuit of the mission was be viewed as ongoing and relentless work:

> *You have to develop the right focus and take the time to continuously work on achieving it. A lot of people develop goals that sit on the shelf when they should take the right vision and goals and relentlessly work on them.*
>
> —High School Principal

> *If you don't stay involved in getting results—which keeps me going—the school will get stale.*
>
> —High School Principal

Figure 5.1 provides information about resources and activities which principals will find helpful in their work on school improvement; this is a starting place for school improvement efforts.

Figure 5.1 Study Group Resources and Activities for Schoolwide Instructional Improvement

STUDY GROUP 1

Building a Foundation for School Improvement

Step 1. As a group of professional educators, divide into two study groups. One group should examine materials at the Web site, and the other should read the recommended book below.

Web site: "Tools for School-Improvement Planning," a project of the Annenberg Institute for School Reform (www.annenberginstitute.org/tools/index.php)

This comprehensive site has a range of FREE materials; it contains observation protocols, focus-group samples and questions, surveys, questionnaires, and techniques to help you examine your specific school-improvement concerns. In the Tools section, you will find a database of innovative tools used throughout the United States—tools for measuring school climate, leadership, professional development, and school improvement projects (racial justice report, school-equity survey, focus-group topics, etc.). The Tools in Practice section includes several important topics (i.e., student engagement) and presents an array of useful materials. See especially the School Improvement Guide, which provides a step-by-step process for successful school improvement, including worksheets and rubrics, how to create a school portfolio, how to prepare for an external review, a school inquiry process map, resources, and standards of practice. There is also a Using Data section in which schools across the country share types and uses of data, how to select and analyze data, and how to use data to drive your change efforts.

Book: Hale, S. H. (2000). *Comprehensive School Reform: Research-Based Strategies to Achieve High Standards.* San Francisco, CA: Comprehensive Assistance Center, Region XI WestEd. (Available free from www.wested.org/csrd/guidebook/pdf.htm)

Pay special attention to how to build a foundation for reform/school improvement; how to plan, implement, and sustain efforts; how to gather information for informed decisions; and useful tools and activities.

For your professional library: The following free items are also valuable instructional improvement resources.

Marzano, R. J. (2000). *A New Era of School Reform: Going Where the Research Takes Us.* Aurora, CO: Mid-continent Research for Education and Learning. Available free from McRel.org, This is a sophisticated meta-analysis of research on school-, teacher-, and student-level variables that affect student achievement.

Marzano, R. J. (2003). *What Works in Schools: Translating Research Into Action.* Alexandria, VA: Association for Supervision and Curriculum Development. This is the best book available on the school-, teacher-, and student-level variables that affect achievement.

PowerPoint: What works in schools: Translating research into action. This is a free PowerPoint and pdf download explaining the school-effects research, the 11 factors influencing student achievement, and the 9 instructional strategies that link to student achievement.
http://www.marzanoandassociates.com/documents/latest02.ppt#1
http://www.marzanoandassociates.com/pdf/latest02.pdf

Step 2. After completing the readings, meet at a convenient time and comfortable place to discuss what you have read. Consider whether the process and content of improvement in your school conforms to research-based strategies for improvement.

STUDY GROUP 2

Getting all Educators in a School Focused on Instructional Improvement and Committed to Advancing Student Learning

Step 1. Form a study group of professional educators.

Book: Glickman, C. D. (2002). *Leadership for Learning: How to Help Teachers Succeed.* Alexandria, VA: Association for Supervision and Curriculum Development.

This book provides helpful guidelines and materials to encourage a focus on learning and instructional improvement, including (1) how to provide teacher assistance through clinical supervision, peer coaching, critical friends, and action-research groups; (2) how to observe the teaching and learning process using teaching frameworks, open-ended questionnaires, samples of student work, and test scores; and (3) how to work with teachers using directive, collaborative, and nondirective approaches.

Step 2. Meet at a convenient time and comfortable place to discuss what you have read. Discussion questions might include, (1) How realistic are the scenarios in the book? (2) Would the approaches described in the book help teachers of diverse backgrounds and skill levels? (3) Which of the materials, checklists, forms, and examples can be adapted to your situation?

STUDY GROUP 3

Monitoring Our Performance Tasks for Rigor and Relevance

Step 1. Form a study group of professional educators.

Step 2. Read and study the materials on rigor and relevance, including the free materials listed below.

- www.icle.net/rrresources.html

    Click on the Research tab, then click on the Rigor and Relevance tab for a brief handout on rigor and relevance.

(Continued)

Figure 5.1 (Continued)

- www.leadered.com/pdf/Academic_Excellence.pdf

  Print out Daggett's (2005) article "Achieving Academic Excellence Through Rigor and Relevance."

- http://kmhs.typepad.com/rigor_relevance/

  Click on the PowerPoint Presentation. Look particularly at Using Rigor and Relevance Framework.

  Click on Handouts, click on Dyer's article "Introduction to Rigor and Relevance."

- www.ade.az.gov/

  In the search box, type in "teaching for rigor and relevance PPT"; then click on the "Do to Classroom to Do with Classroom PPT."

- http://www.natpd.com/present/files/rdj_icle_santarosa.pdf

  Hover over Dick Jones's Links, click on Presentation Slides, and scroll down to Rigor and Relevance Workshop; also explore other workshops and presentations.

Step 3. After members of the study group understand rigor and relevance as they relate to performance tasks, review a sample of randomly selected performance tasks assigned by teachers in your school. Assess them for Rigor and Relevance.

STUDY GROUP 4

Linking School Improvement, Inquiry, Professional Learning, and Governance

Step 1. Form a study group of professional educators.

Book: Joyce, B., Calhoun, E., & Hopkins, D. (1999). *The New Structure of School Improvement: Inquiring Schools and Achieving Students.* Maidenhead, Berkshire, UK: Open University Press.

Using the world's best research, this book links school improvement, inquiry, professional learning, and governance. The development of self-renewing schools in which students and faculty engage in ongoing inquiry has long been an elusive ideal in education. The "new structure of school improvement" described by the authors rests on the extensive corpus of research on effective and ineffective school improvement programs; this new structure of school improvement can be developed with a high probability of success by schools, school districts, local education authorities, and policymakers. At its core is an inquiry process centered on the continuous study of student learning and the development and continuous study of initiatives to enhance student achievement in academic, personal, and social domains. The practical strategies associated with this approach include study time for teachers, continuous professional learning, and building and organizing governance structures that include faculty, parents, community agencies, business partners, and district and education authority personnel.

Step 2. Meet at a convenient time and comfortable place to discuss what you have read. Consider the value of the research cited in the book and determine if any of the practical school improvement strategies discussed should be used at your school. Implement those strategies and study the results of implementation.

Our study clearly shows that high-performing principals do not let their egos stand in the way of what is best for student achievement and school improvement; they worked with and through other school leaders on the school mission. They deferred to the "best man [sic] for the job" in every aspect of school improvement. In the words of one principal:

> *One of the ways to get to instructional improvement is to make sure that you delegate, so you are not so consumed with the operational aspect of things. In addition, I have found that there are people who know more about instruction than I do, and even though I want to be the instructional leader and direct certain activities, I need to defer to their judgment at times, just as I have others handle the operational aspects of the school. You've got to have a lot of great people with a lot of different strengths, and then you make sure that both the push for instructional improvement and organizational efficiency and effectiveness are present.*
>
> —High School Principal

SUMMARY

Chapter 5 presented our findings on how high-performing principals work with teams of educators for instructional improvement. Structured activities for facilitating important aspects of schoolwide improvement efforts were described, and the best available books, PowerPoint presentations, and Web sites were listed.

TIPS AND SUGGESTIONS

Working With Teachers on the School Mission

1. Set your ego and personal needs aside when you approach school-improvement tasks, decisions, and activities. Always do what is best for student achievement.

2. Ask teachers to complete a professional-development-needs assessment at the end of each school year. Use school improvement goals and teacher-identified professional development needs and requests to guide professional development activities. To ensure that the whole school benefits from outside professional workshops and conferences attended by a few, require teachers who attend to present a summary and share valuable handouts at a faculty meeting.

3. Promote book studies by purchasing books for the participants. Be a participating member of book studies, but allow teachers to lead the studies. Provide participants with snack foods during the course of a study, and celebrate the end of a study with "dinner on the principal."

4. Require one book study per year for every teacher; book-study groups can be formed within teams, departments, grade levels, or among any teachers sharing a block of common planning time. Set dates for book study, establish norms for discussions (i.e., rotating discussion leaders, active participation in discussions, and dialogue about practical applications within the school), and ask groups to make presentations to the faculty.

6 Developing Systems

Principals of high-performing schools use a systems-development approach to dispatch with administrative/managerial responsibilities and to support instructional aspects of work.

All principals in our study stressed the importance of addressing administrative/ managerial responsibilities efficiently and effectively. This was crucial because it provided the necessary *foundation* (i.e., stable, predictable, supportive subsystems) for school-based instructional improvement. Put differently, principals disclosed that a failure to efficiently and effectively address administrative/managerial demands subverted school improvement efforts.

You have to take care of the managerial part; it's like the skeleton of the school because it supports instruction. But, you have to get a good handle on it or things will fall through the cracks, and you will have emergencies. You have to keep plugging away at it, get it organized and out of the way so it doesn't take away from your being involved with teachers, instruction, and students.

—Middle School Principal

I must balance my day between being the engineer—the managerial demands for running the castle—and being the architect, leading the development and implementation of effective classroom instruction that ensures every student's success.

—Elementary School Principal

Discipline, budgeting, public relations . . . are all managerial functions, just part of a principal's tool belt for making a school run forward and for supporting instruction.

—Middle School Principal

My first year as a principal, I ran around managing the school, but I have evolved into an instructional leader with management skills. Well, anybody can be a good manager, but [schools] are not little factories; we are dealing with the educational needs of children.

—Elementary School Principal

USE A SYSTEMS-DEVELOPMENT APPROACH TO CREATE EFFICIENT AND EFFECTIVE SELF-SUSTAINING STRUCTURES

As mentioned, our findings indicate that high-performing principals employed a bottom-up systems-development approach (a concept derived from our data) to systematically organize school-based administrative and instructional responsibilities in order to create structures that supported the school-improvement efforts. *In essence, this meant that principals collaborated with assistant principals, teachers, staff, and parents to create and maintain an integrated set of self-sustaining subsystems*—teams, policies, programs, and procedures—that, in concert, addressed all major administrative and instructional responsibilities at the school effectively and efficiently. Further, subsystems were not simply *developed* but were routinely *monitored* (for ways to improve), *coordinated*, and *integrated*. Concomitantly, principals facilitated the development of *cultures* or ecosystems (i.e., appropriate goals, values, beliefs, ways of thinking, behaviors) with those who participated in the work of their schools; this ensured that subsystems would respond efficiently, effectively, and flexibly to both internal and external factors. Said differently, principals, in collaboration with all relevant stakeholders, *reorganized* and *recultured* their entire schools; they took a big-picture perspective to address all major administrative/managerial and instructional components.

If you organize all the functions in the school competently, you don't have to spend all of your time dealing with details; this frees up time for you to deal with people and other more important things like supporting instruction. You've got to manage a lot of different aspects of the school, so you must understand your needs, understand what your priorities are, create a lot of structures, work with different people, emphasize the improvement of instruction, build instructional capacity, and, finally, you've got to understand how all that works together.

—High School Principal

We are highly organized, with systems in place, and we monitor those systems. Having systems and procedures, like teams and agendas, helps us clarify expectations for the year, check on them, and tweak them.

—Elementary School Principal

> *I've had lots of training in how to look at things with a wide-angle lens, from a systems perspective.*
>
> —Elementary School Principal

> *You need to put in place routines and procedures so everyone understands his or her part in the school. That takes care of the major part of business—not that it doesn't require some attention. For example, we have a comprehensive approach to discipline; there are still surprises but they don't get us too far off kilter.*
>
> —Middle School Principal

> *We have strong but controlled communication systems among our staff. We don't bombard teachers with e-mails during the week; instead, we put it all in one document called Staff Stuff at the end of the week. We do the same thing with parents by sending home a weekly newsletter.*
>
> —Elementary School Principal

> *This school was disorganized, like having things everywhere at home. You have to develop procedures and get things where they are supposed to be. It took five years to get this school organized into a professional learning community. Once we did that, life became much easier.*
>
> —Elementary School Principal

It is important to reiterate that although all principals of high-performing schools used a bottom-up systems-development approach to reorganizing and reculturing their schools, each principal created *unique* subsystems to organize administrative and instructional leadership responsibilities based on the characteristics and context of his or her particular school (e.g., level, population, resources, history).

> *It's not haphazard. We have procedures, policies, and guidelines that are our own, and everybody's got to do his part to make it all work together.*
>
> —Elementary School Principal

However, as the principals in this study reorganized their schools in unique ways for efficiency and effectiveness, they tended to reculture their schools *similarly*, sharing a common focus on instructional improvement and stressing trust, ownership, and collaboration as factors in the systems they developed and implemented:

> *Effective management, like effective instructional leadership, requires that you look for sources of strength around you. I can't be the expert in all these things, so I pull valuable and knowledgeable people together to share with each other. You can't do anything without good relationships.*
>
> —Elementary School Principal

> *To get where you want to be, whether it's about student gains or teacher pro-*
> *ductivity, professional development, or data interpretation, you have to be able to*
> *get out. Don't get locked behind your desk. You have to collaborate with the lead-*
> *ership team, work with the vertical teams, meet with the children, and find out*
> *the substance of the school—not get locked behind a desk.*
>
> —Elementary School Principal

USE TIME WISELY

According to extant research, school principals generally find it very difficult to "stick to the knitting" of instructional work; interruptions are myriad and a seemingly endless stream of administrative and unrelated matters take princi-pals away from their most important tasks of educating students, conducting ongoing diagnosis, and improving instruction. Consequently, in spite of the current emphasis on instructional leadership and school improvement, princi-pals often get trapped in safety, discipline, budget, and other administrative tasks that consume their time (Buckley, 2004; Cusick, 2003; Doyle & Rice, 2002; Kellogg, 2005; Lashway, 2002; McPeake, 2007). One principal in our study described the quicksand of ineffective and inefficient handling of man-agerial tasks this way:

> *What happens to a lot of principals is that they get caught up in distractions, not*
> *instruction, and let those distractions bog them down.*
>
> —Middle School Principal

In short, many principals who do not effectively employ a systems-development approach to organizing the school find themselves spending inordinate amounts of time and energy on repair and maintenance tasks (i.e., fixing things that should have been repaired or routinized long ago or keeping routine things functioning) rather than on school improvement and instructional growth tasks (e.g., building collaborative teams, developing teacher-leaders, analyzing student-assessment data, planning instructional improvements, and working with students).

Thus, a systems-development approach required that high-performing principals use time wisely to support teaching and learning and to prevent problems (e.g., pop-ups, "fires") from undermining such activities in their schools. The first triangle below depicts a condition in which the majority of a principal's time is being spent on repair and maintenance; precious little time is spent on growth (i.e., development). The goal for principals of high-performing schools and their administrative teams was, of course, to reverse this condition—to invert the triangle—as depicted in the second triangle, to spend much more time on growth and less on maintenance and repair.

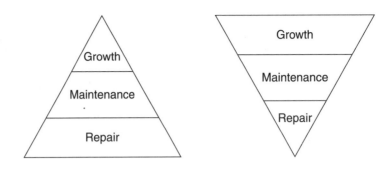

Overall, high-performing principals were successful at inverting the triangle, though, as noted earlier, there were fires (e.g., serious injuries, fights, physical plant and weather emergencies, and personnel matters) and other important situations that flipped the triangle from time to time. How did they invert it? Once again, they used a systems-development approach, which included systematic development of coordinated subsystems for administrative and instructional leadership functions, overlaid with critical thinking and reflection. Working at the higher, more complex levels of thinking about a task, they (1) broke the school apart into its parts or subsystems (e.g., teaching support, professional development, action research and use of data, curriculum development, group development, program evaluation, technical support, school plant and equipment, communication, constituent support); they examined each subsystem for strengths and weaknesses; (2) they looked at the interactions and relationships between the parts or subsystems; and, (3) they studied the impact of each subsystem on the others. Finally, they (4) reorganized the parts into a holistic synthesis of stream-lined subsystems that worked more effectively and efficiently toward school improvement. In other words, using a whole-school, bottom-up systems-development approach, principals in our study abandoned the "This is how we do it," framework and adopted the "What lends itself to stronger support of teaching and learning?" framework, with school improvement as the centerpiece.

> *There are a lot of bottom line things you just have to make sure happen and take care of—keep the school safe and secure, get a faculty who can work with students, get the instructional materials you need, keep the community constantly in touch with the school and informed about their children. So, you have to set up systems that work and continue to work no matter what comes down the pipe on a daily basis, and you have to continuously improve those systems so they function without constant concerns. You run the managerial pieces by putting the system in place, helping everybody to know how the whole machine works.*
>
> —Middle School Principal

Principals noted that although they implemented and routinely reviewed subsystems, occasionally a subsystem broke down; they then analyzed the breakdown, looking specifically for its cause. Then, rather than throwing the baby out with the bathwater or reinventing the wheel, they addressed the cause and tweaked the subsystem if it required adjustment.

To rephrase an idiom—and in contrast to how many principals function—high-performing principals saw the forest (the entire school) *and* the trees (the parts or subsystems within the school) and all the interacting relationships among them. To make a better forest, they planted new trees; they pruned unnecessary limbs; they shaped trees; they moved trees around within the forest; they watered, fed, and cared for the trees, thus maintaining and encouraging the "new forest;" and, when one tree was not doing well, they did not burn the forest down and start over: Instead, they addressed the issues with that tree.

We noted earlier that now, more than ever before, principals are generally investing increasing amounts of time and energy in their work in order to meet the competing and conflicting demands of administration (management) and leadership: Elementary school principals average 62 hours per week (Groff, 2001), and secondary principals spend even more time on the job (DiPaola & Tschannen-Moran, 2003). The principals who participated in our study worked an average of 65 hours per week. In other words, they did not necessarily work longer than other principals—they worked "smarter." Ironically, despite the No Child Left Behind Act (NCLB) and its requirement of greater emphasis on school improvement, most principals now spend even more time on accountability demands, including data management and analysis, and on volumes of paperwork related to compliance with NCLB (Thornton & Perrault, 2002). Indeed, it was no surprise that the high-performing principals we studied stressed the importance of using time wisely. They insisted that all school functions and processes be refined, reduced, or eliminated in order to protect administrators' and teachers' precious time for teaching and learning matters. One principal remarked,

> *There's no way to micromanage every piece of the job, so a principal really has to be the keeper of the process. You have to make sure the processes established in the school are understandable, work well, and don't impede getting to our mission: student achievement. We have to be the gatekeepers and get off of our plates and those of the [teachers] those things that would interfere with the teaching and learning process.*
>
> —Elementary School Principal

To state the problem differently, most principals and assistant principals typically find themselves spending inordinate amounts of time and energy on administrative stuff that is unrelated to instruction—what we call Level 0 and Level 1 (time wasting and time consuming) activities—*at the expense* of Level 2 and Level 3 (instruction and development—growth) activities (See Figure 6.1).

Figure 6.1   Time-Usage Activities

Level 3: Development (growth) and Instructional Focus Activities: Curriculum, Instruction, Technology, Data Use, Professional Learning, Talking about Instruction, Team Building

Level 2: Instructional Support Activities: Ordering Instructional Supplies, Managing the Budget, Hiring Personnel

Level 1: Time Consumers: Monitoring Busses and Cafeteria, Arranging Schedules, Managing Physical Plant

Level 0: Time Wasters: Filling Soda Machines, Cutting Paper, Making Repairs

In contrast, high-performing principals used the following time- and energy-saving strategies, which we offer as suggestions:

Some Time- and Energy-Saving Suggestions

1. Streamline administrivia as much as possible, making things function automatically and efficiently. This will help you avoid spending time and energy on Levels 0 and 1. If possible, personally avoid Level 2 activities, except involvement in hiring, so you can focus on Level 3.

2. Put every possible notice or communication in mailboxes or e-mail (not on the public address system).

3. Use meeting times for discussions about instruction, not for directives and discussions about administrivia.

4. Reorganize and train the school's administrative team to increase involvement in instruction-related activities.

5. Prioritize (and reprioritize) constantly, always trying to increase the school's emphasis on instruction rather than on administration.

6. Design meaningful professional development.

7. Encourage parent, community, and student volunteers to help with any task possible (routine administrative tasks, teacher support, student tutoring, help with activities and athletics, clerical support, staff appreciation).

8. Empower and delegate; do not "parent" or micromanage faculty and staff.

9. Deal effectively with external influences, including parents and central office personnel.

10. Reorganize, balance, and streamline your personal life to focus on what really matters to you and your family.

Testing Ourselves

Here are two activities designed to test your use of time:

1. Consider your faculty meetings. To what degree do faculty members and administrators focus on items that have a significant influence on learning (i.e.,

core and/or comprehensive impact—see Figure 6.2)? Do you waste time on issues that have little or no influence on learning? If so, brainstorm ways to make better use of valuable meeting time as well as ways to deal efficiently with administrative (managerial) responsibilities.

Figure 6.2   What We Talk About During Meetings and Its Influence on Learning[*]

Zero Impact on Learning	Minimal Impact on Learning	Core Impact on Learning	Comprehensive Impact on Learning
• Parking spaces • Lunchroom supervision • Faculty lounge • Sunshine fund • Adult recreation • Bus duties • Refreshments	• Textbook adoption • Inservice days • Small budget items • Discipline	• Curriculum • Staff development • Supervision • Peer coaching* • Instructional programs • Student assessment • Action research • Program evaluation • Instructional budget	• School budget • Hiring of personnel • Deployment of personnel • Personnel evaluation • Parent programs*

*NOTE: Some aspects of this original (1991) figure should be considered in the context of new research on high-performing schools. For example, parent programs traditionally had little impact on learning; however, much has been done to involve parents in meaningful ways in the educational work of the school, which has the potential of producing a greater impact on learning. Similarly, current approaches to the supervision of instruction frequently include peer coaching in addition to principals' observations, with core impacts on learning.

SOURCE: Adapted from the League of Professional Schools (1991).

2. Evaluate the assignment of duties at your school and focus on whether key people are wasting valuable time on noninstructional duties and responsibilities. Using Figure 6.2 as a guide, consider major categories of job duties or responsibilities performed at your school. On a whiteboard or on chart paper, using the column headings provided in Figure 6.2, arrange each job duty in Figure 6.2 under the appropriate column heading, based on the group's belief regarding the duty's impact on learning; add other significant job duties that are not included in Figure 6.2.

When the group is satisfied with the lists in the revised Figure 6.2 table, make four 3-column tables (on a whiteboard or chart paper): Copy the first column from your revised Figure 6.2 in the first column of one of your new tables; label the second column, *Who performs the duty/responsibility now?* Label the third column, *Who could/should perform the duty/responsibility?* As a group, identify who currently performs the job duty or responsibility. Next, brainstorm who could do the job and who should do the job, keeping in mind that the school's key instructional personnel should be devoting the bulk of their time to instructional activities. Continue to develop tables, using the process described above, by placing each of the remaining columns from your revised Figure 6.2 in the first columns of your new tables. Then, answer Column 2 and Column 3 questions.

PLAN WELL

Once a system of policies, programs, and procedures was in place and time for instructional work was protected, principals of high-performing schools relied heavily on *continuous-planning processes* to provide "direction and focus" and to eliminate "a lot of the fluff" that usually consumes large amounts of time and energy in many schools. In essence, principals, in collaboration with assistant principals and teachers, constructed plans that targeted academic goals. Regular meetings were a necessary element of good planning, and establishing healthy norms for meetings (e.g., publishing an agenda in advance, setting time limits for items, having a gatekeeper monitor adherence to norms, ensuring that all who want to participate are heard) kept meetings efficient and effective.

> We meet weekly as an administrative team, monthly with both the administrative and the instructional leadership team (counselors and the grade-level and department chairpersons), and grade levels typically meet at least weekly, on Thursdays. The assistant principals and I eat lunch together every day. That's how we coordinate the whole program.
>
> —Middle School Principal

Generally, planning in high-performing schools relied heavily on use of instructionally relevant data, identification of weaknesses, working with teachers, and provisions for feedback. Such planning derived from shared goals and grew out of multiple opportunities for input and the development of faculty ownership. One principal asserted, "I start out telling teachers that I am not going to accept any target unless it represents a significant instructional gain, and that they must have a say in the process because they are going to have to do the work." Indeed, teachers' ownership (as defined earlier) was viewed as critical to the successful implementation of plans for school improvement ("It's the big thing that makes the connection.").

Principals also reported that they provided assistant principals and department and grade level chairpersons with formal training in planning; department chairpersons were usually responsible for ensuring that teachers understood the planning process. In support of shared instructional goals and consistent with the professional learning community concept, principals required teachers to hold grade-level and department meetings to address relevant teaching strategies, evaluate student work, and ensure delivery of curricula. One elementary principal shared the teaching and learning issues addressed at his school during grade-level meetings:

> *It's one of the first few things we do at weekly meetings: How are you doing? What are the kids doing in math, reading? Teachers bring student work and we talk about it.*
>
> —Elementary School Principal

Further, benchmark testing was conducted and test results were analyzed and discussed periodically during department and grade-level meetings as well as during whole-school faculty meetings. Teachers were also invited to attend leadership-team meetings to discuss progress and plans.

Routinely, principals made available summaries of the school's plans to school and community individuals and groups. As noted earlier, they shared "the work" and workings of the school through whole and specialized group meetings and through a variety of oral and written forms of communications.

The following sections of this chapter highlight high-performing principals' systematic approaches to dealing with two major administrative/managerial functions, *budgeting and handling the physical plant.* The importance of hiring competent individuals, clarifying expectations, building inclusive and collaborative relationships, encouraging ownership, communication, coordination, and oversight are described in relation to creating and sustaining viable budgetary and physical plant subsystems in support of teaching and learning.

MANAGE THE BUDGET EFFICIENTLY AND EFFECTIVELY

All principals involved in our study reported strict compliance with district policies and procedures regarding development and implementation of the school-level budget. Although school bookkeepers had no formal involvement in the budget development process, it was their competence, efficiency, and consistent and careful efforts that kept school-level finances running smoothly.

> *You must have a good bookkeeper; they can make or break you in a heartbeat.*
>
> —Middle School Principal
>
> *Budgeting and finances scare new principals to death. The budget always has to be done right, and the number one ingredient in getting the budget right is the right bookkeeper. At my other school, we had a faltering bookkeeper who was irritable and defensive and always fumbling. Now I can sleep at night because our [current] bookkeeper has a notebook with every policy, knows the appropriate contact person if she has a question, and she runs the budget beautifully.*
>
> —Elementary School Principal

Principals indicated that district offices provided most of the formal training related to school budgets, periodically updated school staff members, and provided timely information via meetings. In addition, principals directed book-keepers to conform to their particular expectations (e.g., with regard to reviews of statements, paying vendors, check signing) and their leadership style. On a day-to-day basis, bookkeepers typically ran the budget; that is, they technically implemented the budget. These procedures helped school principals to efficiently monitor budgetary processes.

> *Our bookkeeper generally writes the checks (I'll be honest with you, I don't even know where the checks are at school.), I sign them (Our assistant principal can also sign.); and every month, I review the bank statement. I look to see what the money was spent on, and I make sure it's my signature.*
>
> —Middle School Principal

> *The principal before me didn't know how to budget, put the school in debt, and left it to me to get the school out of debt and to create a cushion. In the beginning of my tenure as principal, I did all the books, and that's where I learned how to budget, but now I just direct the bookkeeper, who is trained by the county office. She runs the budget and keeps me "out of jail."*
>
> —Elementary School Principal

> *You want to have checks and balances, and I am it. The bookkeeper keeps the checkbook and writes the checks, and I sign them. I might get 50 checks at one time to sign, and I look to see if there is money there. I have a system for looking at the statements, but you don't want to do that every time; you want a good bookkeeper.*
>
> —Elementary School Principal

To ensure that school budgets focused on instructional needs, high-performing principals used an inclusive-leadership approach to creating subsystems that centered on development of teams (e.g., leadership, advisory, technology teams; assistant principals, grade-level heads, and department chairpersons) and the development of viable communication links between and among teams. Invariably, leadership teams created a preliminary budget that emphasized school improvement; other teams provided input. Such input was seriously considered and incorporated into the school budget.

> *Planning the budget includes the leadership team, the school advisory council, and the faculty advisory council. We get a lot of feedback from everyone. Most of the hard labor comes from the leadership team; other teams review their work and make sure it is consistent with our school improvement plan.*
>
> —Middle School Principal

> *Here, we share leadership. By working together in quality teams, teachers figure out how money should be spent to enhance student achievement.*
>
> —Middle School Principal

I tell teachers, committees, and teams, "Okay. We have this much money. Tell me what you need." Once in a while, I will let something run out just to see how long we can teach without it, to shake things up and make us think.

—Elementary School Principal

Principals strongly believed that the involvement of all stakeholders was essential for identification of needs and development of deep levels of ownership necessary for successful implementation of the budget in the context of school improvement.

Budgeting is critical because money makes things go around. The trick is that you have to correctly identify your needs, and that takes time and a lot of people's involvement.

—Middle School Principal

At the beginning and end of the year, we find out from teachers what their needs are; this is usually derived from quarterly impact checks and benchmarks which link to standards, initiatives, or testing results which indicate strengths and weaknesses, which all tie to our school improvement plan.

—Elementary School Principal

Initially, I go through the building budget to see what's been cut and what's been added, and I think about how I think the money should be spent to impact student achievement. I get input from the administrative team and then present it to the leadership team. I get input from parents and teachers by way of their representatives. Having everyone involved creates buy in, which keeps everyone working to improve student achievement—we see where we are going, and we see the impact. This process gives me the opportunity to not be the person in charge.

—Elementary School Principal

You get input helping to build the budget, which gives others the primary responsibility for managing the budget so it accomplishes what you have all agreed on. It helps others have a great deal of ownership in the process and the program, it motivates them, and it makes them look for improvements. It's 10 or 15 people thinking about how to improve an area as opposed to only me trying to figure out how to improve it.

—High School Principal

Further, summaries of final budgets were posted on schools' computer networks for faculty review and were distributed to parent groups. Copies of the budget were also bound and made available for review in school lobbies.

According to our findings, as individuals and teams developed ownership and competence in their respective areas of responsibility, principals (and assistant principals) gradually removed themselves from day-to-day involvement in implementing the budget.

> *I give the per-child expenditure to the grade-level leaders and they choose how to spend it. The first couple of years, I really checked on what they spent it for, but I don't check any more, because they know what to spend it for.*
>
> —Elementary School Principal

Principals of high-performing schools explained that correct use of a school budget had a dramatic impact on teaching and student achievement; correct use also enhanced teacher development.

> *Our superintendent would probably tell me that the budget is the most critical thing "I" do—because of legal issues—but I disagree. In this school, how the money is spent is teacher driven; it's the right budget that has a major impact on the classroom.*
>
> —Elementary School Principal

> *Our money goes to improve instruction for our students. Most of it goes toward staff development for teachers and providing an extended day program for kids, and we are always looking at student test data to see if those students are improving.*
>
> —Elementary School Principal

> *We use whatever money we can get to fund our school improvement plan in the areas of reading, writing, and math achievement, as well as staff development and materials for those areas.*
>
> —Elementary School Principal

> *To prepare for next year's implementation of math standards, we've made funds available to train teachers and to purchase kits now so teachers can begin using them, knowing that next year there will be full implementation.*
>
> —Elementary School Principal

> *If we don't have children at the heart of it, then I think we are missing something. I don't want teachers to want for anything they can use with students to improve student achievement, so we buy big-ticket items like math manipulatives and science kits.*
>
> —Elementary School Principal

> *We are newly implementing an SAT program [college entrance exam preparation program], and we will have to budget for it, including two teachers in math and language arts.*
>
> —High School Principal

> *Our scores have dropped in math, so we went through a lot of money for math in the past four years; out of local funds, we are paying for two math coaches who work two days a week.*
>
> —Elementary School Principal

> *The last thing you get to is materials; you fill your classrooms with teachers first. I have to look at classified and support staff, see if we can collapse and save a position or use parts of two pots of money to buy another teacher. We also cut back on field trips if we need instructional materials. What goes on in the classroom is what drives the budget, and it all trickles down from there.*
>
> —Middle School Principal

> *We tie results to the budget, and if we see that results were not impacted by resources, then we look at the teaching in that area.*
>
> —Middle School Principal

During difficult financial times, principals supplemented insufficient budgets by writing grants, soliciting funds from community groups (e.g., business partners, parents), and creative and legal use of different budget lines.

> *Trying to provide the same level of support with fewer dollars has become a major challenge. Our district had a reduction in force for the first time, and the reduced budget is going to have a dramatic impact on programs and delivery of services. This summer, we are going to search for some grants for work that is linked to our school improvement plan, and faculty will talk about tightening our belts on materials and supplies. We're gong to have to rethink what is important.*
>
> —Middle School Principal

> *My role is to get the most for the dollars that I have; and with the severe cutbacks we have had this year, I have tried to bring back the things that have a more direct impact on students, not staff. Our situation has been dramatically impacted, and we will just have to limp along and do what we can do. When I am forced to make choices, I make them for the folks who directly touch kids. It's going to be a difficult year.*
>
> —Middle School Principal

> *The teachers look to me because I have good money-management skills, and I can usually generate funds or finagle moving money from one place to another legally in order to get what they need. We even look like a rich school because we never throw anything away; teachers value that model.*
>
> —Elementary School Principal

We found that many high-performing principals believed that school principals generally fail to make implementation of school improvement the centerpiece of the budget.

> *I think a lot of principals will make a school improvement plan and a separate budget plan and then put the plans off to the side.*
>
> —Middle School Principal

In contrast, as noted earlier, principals recognized that the school budget should be "consistent with our school improvement plan," that allocation of money in the budget should "fund our school improvement plan," and that money should be spent "to improve instruction for our students" and "to enhance student achievement."

MANAGE THE PHYSICAL PLANT EFFICIENTLY AND EFFECTIVELY

Principals reported that proper maintenance of the school plant was integral to teaching and learning. They hired competent custodians, designed routine subsystems that operated "in the background," and expected *all* school personnel to support maintenance functions. High-performing principals pointed out that their school's physical appearance was concretely and symbolically important to the public as well as to the staff, the teachers, and the students.

> *We make sure that building management happens in the background and happens so smoothly that you don't even notice or have a question about the safety, cleanliness, or state of repair of the building.*
>
> —Elementary School Principal
>
> *The main thing to understand is that your public—parents, teachers, students, administrators—are really aware of the appearance of the building.*
>
> —High School Principal
>
> *For the maintenance staff, the outside is probably the number one focus, but the commons area or entry to the school, where you see the floors and walls and lighting, sets the tone, gives the first impression. One thinks, "Is this a school where kids are safe and nurtured, or is it a cold, stark place?"*
>
> —High School Principal
>
> *It doesn't seem that toilet paper and paper towels would make a difference, but they do, and people need those things, too.*
>
> —Middle School Principal

As with the hiring of bookkeepers and other personnel, all principals we studied attempted to hire excellent (e.g., competent, hardworking) head custodians, and worked to build respectful, appreciative, and open relationships to maintain standards, to enhance professional pride, and to build *ownership*. Principals indicated that such head custodians and their employees would not only go the extra mile on a day-to-day basis, but they could also be relied upon to fill in the gaps when the school was shorthanded and during emergencies. In fact, principals believed that showing respect and appreciation for school custodians and district maintenance personnel (who routinely worked on designated tasks and in emergency situations at the school) were essential to securing efficient ongoing service.

> *We have a custodian appreciation day; we send the custodians to lunch and give them most of the day off.*
>
> —High School Principal
>
> *Knowing and calling system-maintenance people by name is a big thing. Knowing who cuts the grass, does the plumbing, painting, or electrical work is important, and I work to build that professional relationship. I encourage them to enjoy lunch with us, on me. You want to offer them that respect and appreciation, because they are experts in their fields, of course.*
>
> —High School Principal
>
> *Every December, we have a big holiday dinner for all the county maintenance men, and they remember that. If we have a broken pipe in the freezer and it's 6:00 P.M., they get out here fast because we have built a relationship with them.*
>
> —High School Principal

High-performing principals were acutely aware of the high cost, literally and personally, of poor hiring practices. Several principals indicated that problematic head custodians with whom they had worked in the past required large amounts of their time and energy and thus reduced their efficiency and effectiveness as instructional leaders.

> *Prior to this, the person who was head custodian did not see things the way I did; I was constantly having to point out things that needed to be done, areas that needed improvement, and everyday cleaning needs, and that was really frustrating. At this point, I have a wonderful head custodian whom I trust. He takes pride in the building, knows what needs to be done, and knows what it should be like when finished.*
>
> —Middle School Principal
>
> *We had a custodian who turned out not to be a good hire. Working with him on his issues took a lot of time, and he finally moved on. Now we have a lady who is doing an awesome job, and we all just love her.*
>
> —Middle School Principal

According to our data, principals created well-organized subsystems to deal with routine maintenance issues. Typically, an assistant principal was responsible for the custodial staff, and both the assistant principal and the head custodian were empowered to handle all operational and personnel matters; principals were consulted only when necessary. Collaboration and staff training produced maintenance plans, clear job expectations, and detailed procedures (e.g., a front office secretary was "point person" or initial contact for reporting problems; schedules, checklists, time sheets, and work orders were standard) which, in turn, produced effective maintenance teams.

> I am responsible for every single thing that occurs in and around our building, including safety, attractiveness, and cleanliness. However, I don't get to school at 5:00 in the morning and walk around the building; I very much rely on other people, clear policies, and specific procedures.
>
> —Elementary School Principal

> Make sure your administrative team is diverse, and look for somebody that has some background in facilities, especially if you don't have experience dealing with custodians or cafeteria workers or the maintenance department.
>
> —High School Principal

> This year, we were shorthanded on custodial crew members, and the remaining staff was not able to clean every classroom every day, which made teachers very unhappy. We simply reminded them to be flexible and patient and gave them a form on which they could let us know if they were satisfied or had concerns we needed to address.
>
> —Middle School Principal

In all respects, principals designed subsystems that were thoroughly embedded in the school's culture to ensure that the physical plant operated smoothly, unobtrusively, and in a taken-for-granted way to prevent negative effects on teachers and students and their learning.

> I don't want kids to worry about anything. I want the plant to be clean and functioning so students don't think twice about whether the building is filthy or we are out of something when they go to the restroom, or worry about bugs, light bulbs, or leaks. So, I make sure this old building is clean, inviting, and as nurturing as possible. They come here to learn, and that's what I want them to concentrate on.
>
> —Middle School Principal

> The state of the building definitely impacts instruction, and its environment must be comfortable and safe; but more importantly, this needs to feel like an important place to everyone. We always receive a score of 97 or 98 from county maintenance inspections.
>
> —High School Principal

> One of our most important jobs is to make the building safe, clean, and healthy. Students who come into this building do not have to concern themselves about going to a dirty restroom; that's a phobia that's really out there, and it's very difficult on a student's biological system. If they are uncomfortable, it's like being hungry: They're not able to concentrate.
>
> —High School Principal

To facilitate direct two-way communication among faculty, administrators, and custodians, principals at times asked head custodians to attend faculty and administrative team meetings to learn about school improvement.

> *We have no secrets and we are all in this together, so I encourage the custodial team to question things; it also helps a lot when they understand what we [administrators and teachers] are doing.*
>
> —High School Principal

Further, high-performing principals encouraged *everyone* to play a part in school maintenance. While custodians "kept a general eye looking out" for problems, teachers were asked to carefully monitor their classrooms, playgrounds, and other areas throughout the campus to address problems before they mushroomed into major problems that required additional time and resources to correct.

> *We communicate clear procedures in the form of a simple, step-by-step process to all the staff, and it has become embedded in the daily work of the school; this approach removes barriers to instruction. A safe and clean school means a barrier-free school. If a teacher sees a tree limb hanging over the fence, she needs to report it only one time and it is taken care of; she doesn't need to worry about a child getting hurt.*
>
> —Elementary School Principal

Principals also routinely solicited formal feedback (e.g., surveys) about the physical plant from parents, teachers, students, and staff, which, along with district-level inspections, was taken seriously and used to improve the school's maintenance operations. In addition, high-performing principals encouraged individual students, student government groups, and other student leadership clubs to participate in brainstorming and problem-solving meetings about the repair, maintenance, and development of the physical plant, particularly when problems were student-generated or when students had a vested interest in the problem. Principals pointed out that, in addition to giving the students a voice, their involvement gave them an authentic opportunity to practice critical thinking, develop problem-solving skills, develop and implement self-governing rules and norms for the student body, and encourage student buy-in to decisions and solutions.

Several principals reported that special projects (i.e., major building renovations) often required large commitments of time and energy and considerable coordination efforts on their part, despite efforts to share this responsibility with others.

> *I have built very collegial and respectful relationships with all the district maintenance departments; now, when we are dealing with major construction projects,*
>
> *(Continued)*

(Continued)

they are willing to move mountains for us. I never demand anything; rather, I request things, and I thank them profusely every time.

—Elementary School Principal

In this county, it is part of the principal's responsibilities to play an active role in building initiatives; so when a three-story tower was added to our building, I was directly involved in every step. I organized and orchestrated the whole process. And after the beautiful new facility was completed, little flaws showed up and teachers started getting sick from dust and chemicals; so, I spent another year dealing with that.

—Elementary School Principal

This summer, the carpets in all the classrooms are being replaced, the inside of the building is being painted, and we are moving into twelve new classrooms; the school looks like a war zone, and the cafeteria looks like a refugee camp. For me, its constant interaction with the county office people and the subcontractors. It's just crazy.

—Middle School Principal

The county is converting our interior classrooms to science labs, so I have become almost like a project manager, making sure that the interests of the campus are always guarded and that staff and students are not shortchanged. It takes so much of my time, going from the original drawings to determining the best location for things, determining how we should proceed, and going to all the meetings. This has monopolized my time.

—Middle School Principal

In a couple of cases, problematic buildings (e.g., hazardous materials) presented ongoing challenges to principals.

There's always something wrong with this building.

—Elementary School Principal

Dealing with this building is a continuous issue; it's constant coordination with the district office and contractors who are doing the work.

—Middle School Principal

We are not very far above the water table at the bottom of a little basin, so we just have lots of mold! We are pulling out this nasty eight-year-old carpet, and it's going to make everything a lot cleaner and brighter and more sanitary, which I think means we're going to have better attendance and keep kids awake and alert a little bit longer.

—Middle School Principal

> *This building has been very difficult to deal with. I would say that, over my eight years here, I have spent two years' worth on the physical plant. Even for daily cleaning (custodial work). I became so weary of the battle to find quality workers that I finally opted to subcontract the work out. They clean only certain rooms and hallways and my small crew takes care of the rest.*
>
> —Middle School Principal

PREVENT PROBLEMS FROM BEGETTING PROBLEMS

All principals who participated in our study stressed the importance of creating effective subsystems for the administration of tasks, including hiring teachers, organizing the custodial team, and working together to solve problems; and all stressed that such an approach to administration was the "only path" to achieve the school's instructional and learning goals. To be sure, principals were acutely aware that, in the end, ineffective administration consumed inordinate amounts of everybody's time and energy, exacerbated problems, and created additional problems. Ineffective administration of student discipline problems, for example, could produce secondary problems including interference with classroom instruction, critical parents, and intervention by district-level administrators. Principals explained that secondary problems were frequently more time consuming and more difficult to manage than the initial, primary problem. Therefore, they attempted to create protocols to reduce or eliminate the potential of such problems arising.

> *You have to put procedures in place very carefully. For example, a suspension letter has to be correct, has to follow policy and do exactly what it is supposed to do; if it is not done properly, it will cost you many, many hours of your time. I think that a recommendation letter for a student is 10 times more important than a suspension letter, and I try to put my energy on what is more important, but things must be effective, thus efficient.*
>
> —High School Principal

> *You must follow through so that small issues, small situations, don't mushroom.*
>
> —Elementary School Principal

> *If a parent comes in and wants to talk with me, I try to stop, listen, and take care of the situation right then, so it doesn't become an enormous issue that takes an inordinate amount of time.*
>
> —Elementary School Principal

SUMMARY

This chapter opened with a discussion of research that reveals how administrative (i.e., managerial) responsibilities frequently dominate school principals' work and, as a result, many principals fail to provide effective instructional leadership. The chapter also described high-performing principals' approaches to time usage. Finally, the chapter described how high-performing principals used a systems-development approach to deal with several major administrative responsibilities including planning, budgeting, and handling the physical plant. In sum, principals created well-organized and deeply-embedded subsystems in concert with appropriate school cultures. This chapter also emphasized how problems that are not dealt with effectively and in a timely manner frequently spawn additional and more challenging problems.

THE HEXAGON EXERCISE*

**Review of Our School's Subsystems and
Their Impact on Student Achievement**

(This exercise is for administrative teams, all instructional personnel, or all instructional and support personnel in your school.)

Consider the possible administrative and instructional subsystems in your school.

1. Make two lists of as many administrative and instructional subsystems you can name (see sample lists below). Note particularly that the same subsystems appear on both lists but with different emphases; this indicates that administrative and instructional subsystems are linked and that subsystems impact and are impacted by other subsystems.

2. Choose six core (or critical) subsystems from the lists.

3. Arrange the six core subsystems from the lists on the points of a hexagon.

4. Draw lines between subsystems that impact each other.

5. Determine how well you develop, monitor, coordinate, and integrate each of your school's subsystems.

6. Discuss ways to improve the effectiveness and efficiency of subsystems to maximize student learning opportunities. (It may help to organize information in broad categories such as goals, tasks, people, tools/resources, and structures.)

Examples of Administrative Subsystems

Physical plant (custodial, playground)

Budget (operating building, supplies)

Communication (in-school, newsletters, parents)

Media and public relations (interviews, news releases)

School organization (scheduling, meetings, calendar, emergencies)

Technology (resources, maintenance)

Student services (health and safety, special education, extracurricular activities, counseling, records and information, discipline and attendance)

Personnel (hiring and retention, legal issues, duties)

Assessment (testing, procedures reviews)

Advisory groups (meeting plans)

Examples of Instructional Subsystems

Physical plant (instructional needs, grouping, special needs)

Budget (instructional supplies, field trips)

Communication (teacher collaboration, parent involvement)

Media and public relations (academic reports, instructional volunteers)

School organization (coteaching, diversity needs)

Student Services (diversity needs, portfolios, outside agencies)

Personnel (group development, professional development, performance evaluation)

Assessment (data collection/analysis, action research, curriculum development)

Advisory groups (instructional involvement)

*NOTE: We acknowledge William Greenfield's conceptualization of this exercise.

TIPS AND SUGGESTIONS

Using a Systems-Development Approach

1. Establish subsystems for effective and efficient handling of administrative/ managerial and instructional leadership tasks. When subsystems break down, do not reinvent the wheel. Instead, analyze the breakdown and tweak the subsystem to prevent future breakdowns. When subsystems are tweaked, ensure that changes are communicated to all need-to-know individuals.

2. Talk with other school principals about their subsystems for handling administrative/managerial and instructional leadership tasks. Incorporate the best of their subsystems into your whole-school system.

3. At the beginning of each year and periodically during the year, meet with teachers to list and discuss obstacles to teaching and learning. Respond to teachers' concerns, brainstorm solutions with them, and implement subsystems to protect teaching and learning time and opportunity.

4. Share your emphasis on and commitment to the instructional aspects of school leadership with all stakeholders. Share approaches for keeping teaching and learning front and center at all times. Welcome all suggestions.

5. Establish for yourself a sacrosanct time each day for instructional activities; allow only emergencies to interrupt that time. Communicate this to parents and other stakeholders at the beginning of the year and ask secretarial staff to inform visitors and callers that you are in classrooms, engaged in instructional matters, and unavailable.

(Continued)

(Continued)

6. Make your time count. To ensure the most effective use of your time, periodically conduct a time-usage and efficiency study. Document what you do for each 15-minute increment of a day. At the end of the day, analyze where your time was spent. Determine patterns that inhibit efficiency and effectiveness. Develop action steps to better use your time.

7. Establish guidelines and norms for meetings. For instance, keep meetings short by developing an agenda and a beginning and ending time frame. Begin and end punctually; stick to the published agenda. Utilize a gatekeeper to enforce norms of meeting behavior.

8. When relinquishing administrative/managerial or instructional leadership duties to other administrators, teach them about the subsystem that deals with the particular duty. Explain the subsystem and your expectations for handling it; model how it is to be handled; guide others until they are comfortable in what to do and how to do it; then, be a resource to them and monitor for compliance with the correct way. However, be open to suggestions for a better way of handling the duty.

9. Let one question guide budget decisions: Does the budget support school improvement and increased student achievement?

10. Work with building or central office level supervisors to develop checklists for evaluating the quality of custodial, maintenance, and food service work. Discuss evaluation results with the immediate supervisors of personnel. Use ongoing checklists to track quality improvement.

Empowering 7

Principals of high-performing schools take an empowering (team) approach to almost everything and create learning communities in their schools.

Earlier, we pointed out that high-performing principals hired only qualified administrators, teachers, and, in most cases, noncertified personnel, whom they believed were team players (i.e., collaborators, problem solvers, people capable of ownership who were committed to team and school goals). In this chapter, we describe another dimension of the systems-development approach, that is, the principals' empowering orientation to administrative teams, leadership teams (cross-personnel advisory and decision-making groups), and instructional teams (various configurations of teacher groups) in high-performing schools. We emphasize that although the principals we studied were considered very sophisticated administrators as well as instructional and school improvement leaders, they did not believe that they alone possessed sufficient knowledge and skill to create and sustain an instructionally effective school. *Virtually all of these principals believed that empowered teams (i.e., various combinations of key stakeholders including assistant principals, teachers, instructional technology personnel, noncertified staff, other support personnel, and parents) had the greatest potential to produce viable approaches to continuous school improvement.*

Building the capacity of teachers to lead and influence instruction has the greatest payoff for learning. There's no way to improve a school faster than to involve people in important processes like hiring, with a clear idea of what you want to accomplish. Get the right people doing the right jobs and give them the tools they need. If the principal doesn't provide leadership in that area, you're going to have an underperforming school.

—High School Principal

One time, my mentor principal told me, "Don't think you have all the answers because if you believe that you'll shortchange the staff, the school, and yourself." Teamwork is the best approach to instructional leadership; the more heads you have working together, the better ideas you get. A principal can't do it alone.

—Middle School Principal

Everybody has to be a partner in the education of the youth of this country: the custodian, the cafeteria worker, the bus driver, the guidance counselor, the media specialist, the bookkeeper, the teachers, the principals—all are involved in graduation day because for four years they have all been directly involved in the students' learning. It's very important that we all realize that whatever service or responsibility one has in the building on a daily basis, it is absolutely necessary for the students to meet their goals. I don't teach English, but I enable them to go to a clean and comfortable classroom or to get to school on time or have breakfast before class. The entire staff comes on board as part of the instructional team.

—High School Principal

I'm doing a lot of teambuilding at this school, and one of the notions I had to work on was that it's not the teachers against the administration. Teachers' experience with the prior principal was very negative, and it took me a while to get the staff to understand that I wasn't in the office all alone and disconnected from the teachers out there with students—we are all here together.

—Elementary School Principal

Prior to my coming to this school, teachers were working hard but they were working alone. I started a lot of initiatives to get them involved in working on teams and involved in the school as a whole. I gave them time to plan and to do staff development, and I rewarded them for their collaborative work.

—Elementary School Principal

If we are going to improve education, we have to be about something that everyone, at every level, buys into. It has to be a "we," with everybody committed to the same goal.

—High School Principal

High-performing principals realized that the collective mindset and synergy of groups in collaboration was a win-win situation for teachers and their teaching and for students and their learning:

You get the best of everybody's thinking when you encourage collaboration on teams, not competition and isolation.

—High School Principal

Creating teams is a pulling together of people's minds. Once they see the gains that can be derived from a team strategizing for children, they realize it's a good thing.

—Elementary School Principal

> *In my first principalship, I didn't have an administrative team; I was a one-man show for school leadership. I learned to draw on teachers and staff, to tap into their strengths. Now, the administrative team also bounces ideas around, which has helped us to mesh. We are a really good team.*
>
> —Elementary School Principal

> *Together, everybody achieves more.*
>
> —Middle School Principal

Consistent with the research on professional learning communities, principals in our study had groups develop meeting agendas wherein the group thinking was devoted to scrutiny of what matters in teaching and learning: data analysis, collegial inquiry and dialogue, research-based learning strategies for student achievement, demonstration and modeling of what's new and effective, analysis and study of student work, problem solving, and other related items.

> *We have faculty and grade-level meetings, a faculty-advisory council, a school-advisory council, and an instructional support team focused on student behavior; the latter works to find positive, prosocial ways to communicate with the kids about their behavior.*
>
> —Middle School Principal

> *The quality teams are based on content areas, and they take part in the school-improvement planning; their job is to keep the mission and the vision of the school alive in their particular content area, whether it's media, technology, science, math, language arts, or social studies. They are all focused on moving our mission and vision forward.*
>
> —Elementary School Principal

In implementing a systems-development approach, principals also facilitated collaboration and support within and between teams and relevant others as well as the development of standard protocols and procedures related to team operations.

> *A lot of teachers were very protective of and very devoted to doing well with children in their own classrooms, but by using our data in our strategy discussions and by using each other's brains and skills, we have all become accountable to the entire grade level and then the entire school; thus, we are becoming a true community of learners.*
>
> —Elementary School Principal

> *We live and breathe as teams, which gives us a great advantage because each group has a support network, whether it is your home base team, your grade-level team, or your subject-level team. You are always connected to someone who knows what you are going through and who can help.*
>
> —Middle School Principal

> *Our committees and teams change from year to year based on what our needs are. We've worked on building these teams, and they are much more effective than they were in the past. They all look at our shared vision, our values, and our goals. This year, we have grade-level team leaders, a data-management team, the PTA representatives committee, the school-advisory council, an antibullying program team, a writing committee, a technology committee, a student study team, and the curriculum leaders' team.*
>
> —Elementary School Principal
>
> *We developed team protocols this year wherein each team decided their own procedures and protocols, their commitment to agendas, use of time, and procedures and commitment to giving respect in conversations and ways to appreciate everyone. We then spread those protocols into the 10 vertical teams' conversations.*
>
> —Elementary School Principal

Principals frequently reported that "teaming" produced teacher-leaders throughout their schools.

> *As a result of what we are doing in committees, the teachers are taking on leadership responsibilities. It's great, because administrators shouldn't be the only instructional leaders in the school. In the past, some committee chairs didn't know how to get their committees together, but our work in building community has made them far more effective. They have agendas ahead of time and minutes are published.*
>
> —Elementary School Principal

High-performing principals used walk-throughs to inform their work with teachers; but when walk-throughs revealed weaknesses, principals required peer coaching, observations of proficient teachers, and/or observations by and feedback from peers. Principals created ways to accommodate such teacher-to-teacher support by hiring a substitute teacher to provide coverage for several teachers' classes, creating an open period for lead teachers to provide coaching, recruiting nonworking certified teacher-parents for volunteer teaching, and encouraging teachers to occasionally volunteer to cover a class during planning time. Principals acknowledged that occasionally individuals failed to accept the team approach, which created time-consuming work for the principals and, at times, indicated a need for such individuals to work elsewhere:

> *If one person is not [committed to the shared mission and vision], then that person becomes a weak link in the teaching and learning environment; then, usually an administrator has to stop what she is doing to take care of the problem. We call that putting out fires.*
>
> —High School Principal

> *One of our assistant principals was effective and efficient, but she did not have the cooperative spirit. She worked hard, but she worked for herself, and she wasn't supportive of others. I helped her get another job elsewhere.*
>
> —High School Principal

THE LEADERSHIP TEAM

Decidedly, all principals in our study designed "inclusive" leadership teams consisting of themselves, assistant principals, and relevant others who were drawn from all areas of the school; members were collaborative, problem-oriented, and unrelentingly focused on instruction. Leadership teams met regularly, established communication protocols, and coordinated work with other teams when necessary.

> *Our school-leadership team begins every year with a daylong retreat in the summer, where we look at test scores, talk about what we could be doing better, and set goals for the year. This group is all about instruction, to give our children the best education we can.*
>
> —Middle School Principal
>
> *Our leadership team represents every area and grade level in the building and it meets weekly. The team does a lot of gathering information, doing reports, some paper pushing, and making decisions that are truly shared.*
>
> —Middle School Principal
>
> *Every group in the school is represented on our Leadership Team. People send agenda items through their representatives, team members all feel they have a voice, notes are taken, and the whole staff is copied. No one has to worry that the team will do something like take away something needed.*
>
> —High School Principal
>
> *I have a very strong belief in shared leadership. I have a competent leadership group that meets once a week, including the assistant principal, instructional leaders, the technology specialist, the media specialist, the bookkeeper, our cafeteria manager, our custodian, and my secretary. Everybody knows what's happening, who needs to do what, and where we need to be. We all know, for example, not only what part of the curriculum is addressed but also how lunch is handled when the children go on a field trip.*
>
> —Elementary School Principal
>
> *The first point about our leadership team's collaboration is that we truly understand our curriculum standards, what students need to learn and be able to do. Second, we must be truly able to provide support to teachers in the forms of instructional strategies as well as instructional materials. We also try to stay on the forefront of research and local, state, and federal initiatives. It's a meshing, a coordinating of individual needs with the*
>
> *(Continued)*

(Continued)

broader picture. We make sure teachers have time to meet and that they have everything they need, and we take away barriers that would keep them from being able to focus on what's important. It's about supporting people who are gung ho and enticing people who are not, and it is a constant balance of support and challenge for teachers. It's fostering critical and independent thinking among the staff.

—Elementary School Principal

My vision is that kids come first. So, all decisions the leadership team makes are kid focused, whether we're talking about managerial or instructional parts of the job. Each administrator has a managerial and an instructional piece; no one has so many of those mundane pieces that would prevent them from getting into the classroom where the kids are.

—Middle School Principal

In different ways and in varying degrees, leadership team members contributed significantly to team decisions. Principals observed that such involvement increased members' ownership of decisions, and this, in turn, substantially increased proper implementation of decisions.

Leadership team members conducted site visits to other schools with block schedules, and they came back and developed the block schedule they wanted to see in our building. Having them determine the structure for our school was very, very important; their ownership and buy-in was critical because they are the ones who implement the decisions. If teachers aren't comfortable with a decision, you're not going to see the benefits you're looking for in the classroom.

—Middle School Principal

Most high-performing principals either implied or directly stated that their goal in creating empowered collaborative teams (and teacher-leaders, as well) throughout their schools was to establish a school culture that was inclusive and deeply embedded; these cultures reflected elements of a professional learning community (DuFour, Eaker, & DuFour, 2008; see Chapter 14 for details about professional development and professional learning communities) in which all leaders and teachers work together to continuously grow and are, in effect, lifelong learners in the service of student achievement:

Over time, I can help them unearth and discover the realities of best practices and move collectively toward them. My style of being collaborative and rewarding but responsible is a little disguised right now, but I am wise enough to assess the culture and the community and to plant seeds of opportunity for personal growth so that I can enable them to find ways, resources, and opportunities to see a better way and implement it in the classroom; this is not me making them better.

—Elementary School Principal

> *I consider myself a consensus builder for the leadership team. Some people would say that is wishy-washy or, "he doesn't want to make a decision when he has to," but I really believe people have to internalize things, so I try real hard to float ideas out to the faculty. I find out more and more what the faculty can and can't do. And some decisions aren't made in a day . . . it may take a week or two to involve people.*
>
> —Middle School Principal

A number of principals stated that ideally their goal was to build a configuration of teams that together would enable the school to run smoothly without dependence on the principal.

> *My greatest accomplishment is in knowing that I can be gone for a week and the building is not going to miss a beat. The office staff is cross trained, the teams are in place, we have a system and policies and procedures. People know what to do and how to do it. If they have a question, they know where to get the answer. Internal grooming has reaped tremendous benefits.*
>
> —High School Principal
>
> *I want to know that the ship sails beautifully whether I am present or not. For that to happen, leadership must exist throughout the entire building.*
>
> —Elementary School Principal

Administrative leadership for school improvement as a dimension of the systems-development approach included empowering others, establishing regular meeting times and communication protocols between and among teams, developing reasonable and clear policies and procedures, and creating school culture as a learning community. It did not mean that principals were no longer an integral part of the instructional leadership picture. To the contrary, principals routinely met with teams to facilitate their individual and collective work (e.g., share information, make suggestions, provide resources, monitor progress).

> *Everything is done here as a team effort, and an administrator is covering part of everything that's going on, but the principal has to stay in touch with all of it; it's a fine line between micromanaging and staying involved.*
>
> —High School Principal
>
> *Grade-level teams have common planning time and they meet once a week. I meet with them once a month to give them information and to ask them if they need any assistance.*
>
> —Elementary School Principal

> *I have a three-prong approach to leadership: I meet with three teams, including the lead teachers, who work with me on day-to-day functions; the curriculum team; and the data-management team, which makes suggestions to the curriculum team. I will ask, "Okay, how is this going to change student achievement?" and they sell the rest of the faculty on it.*
>
> —Elementary School Principal

Principals also trained assistant principals to promote instructional improvement and teacher leadership (embedded leadership) to increase the efficacy of teams and to extend instructional improvement efforts in the school.

> *All of our administrators were outstanding teachers, and all of them understand the academic classroom [good teaching and learning] and have responsibilities attached to instruction and participation in curriculum meetings. Their responsibilities are not just doing discipline, bus call, and cafeteria duty; rather, they each work with a grade level and must be knowledgeable about what teachers are teaching, what we are looking for in observing teachers, and what we are trying to reinforce with teachers. Even though they are not each responsible for issuing the textbooks or coordinating staff development, they are all a part of instruction, which I hold high on their list of responsibilities.*
>
> —Middle School Principal

> *I am also nurturing future principals among the assistant principals (APs), so the APs have to see the big instructional picture, know that they can't let discipline, for example, take them away from all that. You can't let the bus duty or the parent phone calls consume you, even though they are very time consuming. So, there's a lot of discussion among the administrative team members about teaching and learning. We meet weekly and talk about curriculum things we need to be focused on for the upcoming week, staff development needs, teachers who need extra support. We talk about the nuts and bolts, too, the toilet leaking, but our conversation is about instruction as our major focus.*
>
> —Middle School Principal

> *Right off the bat, you have to decide whether you're going to focus on being a leader or a manager. In reality, you need to train excellent assistant principals, teach them to lead, delegate to them, keep an eye on them so they don't burn out. That's the key.*
>
> —Middle School Principal

> *My leadership style is to enable leaders to emerge throughout the school, and I am training the assistant principals to do this with our instructional teams; we slowly bring people around to the reality that this is a good thing.*
>
> —Elementary School Principal

> *You can get so bogged down as a principal, with the politics and the everyday stuff, so a lot gets funneled to everybody else. One assistant principal knows what's being taught as well as I do, and he also is doing the master schedule. Another is in charge of strategic planning and does the school profile. The key is that it's all a team effort.*
>
> —High School Principal

> *Every day, with one or both of the assistant principals, I go back and think about what went well during the day, what didn't go so well, what is left unattended . . . so I begin the next day with a plan, as opposed to "Okay, we got through the day. I'm going home. That's it."*
>
> —Elementary School Principal

Principals' involvement with any particular team tended to vary according to a team's maturity (i.e., its level of experience, competence, and efficiency); by devoting less time to more mature groups, principals were able to free time for involvement in other instructional improvement activities.

> *As the grade-level managers became more skilled in their leadership, I stopped going to their meetings.*
>
> —Elementary School Principal

Further, principals explained that teams at their schools were not considered fixed or static entities; thus, principals routinely scrutinized teams to determine if changes were necessary to improve a team's effectiveness.

> *We add committees and we take committees away every year; we don't want to have a committee just to have a committee. So, we look at how well they are functioning. Now, the writing committee is always a work in progress, so we will probably always have that, as well as the technology committee. The curriculum- and data-management committees will change a bit.*
>
> —Elementary School Principal

> *Next year, our leadership team is going to change a little bit; I am going to start bringing in some of the younger folks who have potential and train them to be leaders.*
>
> —Elementary School Principal

> *I tell each team, "You're going to work together, and we're going to be one big happy family." I don't like pettiness, baby stuff, which can ruin a faculty. If there is a problem we need to talk about it, work it out, and get over it. If teachers are happy, the kids are happy, and the parents are happy.*
>
> —Elementary School Principal

> *In a school I visited, the leadership team had gotten out of control; there was divisiveness, people were not team players, there was no collegiality, there was unnecessary competition, and they didn't focus on instruction. Here, it's different.*
>
> —Middle School Principal

SUMMARY

Chapter 7 provided a description of high-performing principals' empowering orientation to school-based leadership teams. As another dimension of the systems-development approach, an empowering orientation means including stakeholders in the development of policies, standards, procedures, and programs; coordination between and among members of relevant teams; regular, productive meetings; support for teacher leadership; and oversight by the principal; and all elements of this orientation are focused on school improvement. It is important to remember that all high-performing principals began their careers with control-oriented approaches; however, they learned through trial and error that they could not create instructionally effective schools without involving all stakeholders.

TIPS AND SUGGESTIONS

Taking an Empowering Approach to Create Learning Communities

1. Adopt a mantra (e.g., "Who has the strength?" "Who knows this best?"), and apply it when approaching all administrative and instructional tasks; let the answer to the mantra/question guide your or the group's choice of leaders to spearhead new endeavors and to perform tasks. Take care, however, not to overload the strongest teachers and best teacher-leaders.

2. Invite parents to participate in learning activities. For instance, at the elementary level, a group of teachers might sponsor a Parent-student Writing Workshop; high school students could invite parents with various types of expertise to demonstrate and share their knowledge and talent in classes. Ask parents to present at career fairs in which students learn about different careers and have opportunities to ask questions.

3. Develop a schoolwide standard for writing, and inform students and parents that any writing that does not meet the standard will have to be redone. Ask all teachers to attend training on how to score essays and other written responses to questions using the schoolwide standard.

4. Require teachers to use a balanced approach to assessment (i.e., do not rely solely on recognition test items such as true/false or multiple choice questions). Remind teachers that production test items (e.g., essay questions) require higher-order thinking. For example, mandate the use of at least one essay question on every assessment and worksheet used in the classroom.

5. Ensure that teachers are teaching to the standards, not the textbook. Encourage activities such as (1) teacher collaboration on lessons that engage the students and incorporate the use of technology, and (2) a division-of-work approach, wherein each teacher takes one unit and develops a state-of-the-art teaching plan for the unit (this makes teachers the beneficiaries of the work of their colleagues). Consistency in planning can be accomplished by the establishment of planning guidelines.

6. Expect teachers and other staff members to develop norms of professionalism for their roles and job duties. Encourage self-governance and adherence to the established norms.

Hiring 8

Principals of high-performing schools hire strong people for administrative, faculty, and staff positions.

Overwhelmingly, our data point out that high-performing principals used a systems-development approach to school leadership; with respect to hiring personnel, they carefully developed subsystems to hire new faculty and staff and always did so with the help of others. They argued that a systematic hiring process could be very time consuming, but that it was critical to hiring the right people. For example, principals asserted that hiring the best teachers was essential to student achievement and, when done properly, resulted in more efficient use of their own time over the long run.

Hiring is one of the most important things principals do. Teachers are the front line, and having good people in classrooms and making sure they have what they need is 80% of your job.

—Middle School Principal

Human-resources management is one of your most important responsibilities. The success of your entire program, meeting your goals, and attaining what's in the school improvement plan are based on the people you hire.

—High School Principal

What I know best about hiring is that there are no shortcuts, and you hire very, very carefully; I feel that if I hire desperately, I will be desperate forever. You check references carefully, you listen carefully, and you take your time.

—Elementary School Principal

There's no doubt that a higher-quality teacher means higher student achievement, but it's hard getting the right people. It takes lots of hours, but we invest the time, and it's worth it.

—Middle School Principal

I have few problems because I hire the right people with the right goals and expectations. It helps students to have someone who knows how to help them raise that bar and achieve, and it makes my job easier.

—Elementary School Principal

KNOW WHO YOU NEED

Principals of high-performing schools understood the characteristics of teachers essential to successfully educating children.

Those are the kinds of teachers I want, the good teachers who are constantly looking at what they are doing, evaluating student achievement, looking at ways to improve units or change strategies, always revising, always adapting. And, I want people who care about their students and who can communicate their caring to students.

—Middle School Principal

Teachers make it happen for students; they unlock whatever barriers to learning they have. They've got to be able to find the key and to keep going.

—Middle School Principal

We screen the candidates for high-caliber instruction by including people who really know the content area and have actually taught the courses, and we see if the candidates fit into the department.

—High School Principal

Some of our students can be very unlikable, and anyone we hire, from the instructional paraprofessional to the media person to the data clerk to the teacher, has to understand who we are serving, and they have to like them.

—Middle School Principal

High-performing principals shared the mission and vision of the school as well as their (and the teachers') expectations of new hires:

Our hiring process includes talk about the vision and the mission of our school. If you're going to add someone to the faculty, she needs to buy into the school and be able to be a productive member of the faculty.

—Elementary School Principal

We let candidates know our expectations ahead of time. I always tell interviewees, "Whatever you tell us during this interview, I'm going to hold you to it."

—Elementary School Principal

Clearly, our findings indicate that processes put in place to hire teachers were informed by a research-based definition of good teaching; accordingly, principals and others created interview questions consistent with the elements of teaching (see, for example, Danielson's, 2007a, framework for teaching, which articulates these elements, and Marzano, Pickering, and Pollock's, 2001, description of research-based instructional strategies that affect student achievement; both of these publications are discussed in detail in Chapter 13 of this book). More generally, we found that principals and teams of assistant principals and teachers worked to hire teachers who exemplified the same broad qualities of effective teaching articulated by Stronge (2007) (see Figure 8.1); a protocol for teacher selection based on these qualities can be found in Stronge and Hindman (2006).

Figure 8.1 Six Qualities of Effective Teachers

1. Teacher has the prerequisites for effective teaching (e.g., subject matter knowledge, communication abilities, certification)

2. Teacher is a quality person (e.g., positive attitude, reflective style)

3. Teacher is expert at classroom management and organization (e.g., behavior expectations, use of materials, classroom in order)

4. Teacher is organized for instruction (e.g., planning, use of time, transitions, high expectations for student achievement)

5. Teacher can effectively implement instruction (e.g., instructional strategies, questioning strategies, maintaining student engagement)

6. Teacher monitors student progress and potential (e.g., use of homework, use of data from testing, differentiation for diverse needs)

SOURCE: Adapted from Stronge (2007).

In addition, high-performing principals only hired teachers who they believed would be team players, highly motivated teachers with appropriate knowledge, skills, teaching style, personality, interests, and a willingness to fit into the school's collaborative system and team structure.

You have a team in place with certain teaching styles and personalities; you need to hire someone who fits in with that team and in that spot.

—Middle School Principal

I don't care how strong a teacher is instructionally if he isn't a team player. We don't have a team if we don't have team players; instead, we have everything from petty dynamics to problems with parents.

—Elementary School Principal

We use the research on effective practices in our school, so when we interview as a team we ask candidates some important curriculum and instruction questions, which gives us a really good idea of the teaching strategies the candidate knows and uses. That's how we know if they'll fit in and feel comfortable here.

—Elementary School Principal

A couple of bad hires in one department can hurt you for years. You have to find someone who will blend in with the department, be a team player, and bring out the best in the kids.

—Middle School Principal

As discussed earlier, principals also looked for potential teacher-leaders.

We really look for the kind of person to be our future leaders. The leader of the school is not necessarily just the principal or the assistant principal, but the teacher-leaders; they help other teachers on their team be leaders.

—Elementary School Principal

In fact, our data indicate that principals believed that team players and teacher-leaders were essential to the successful implementation of a systems-development approach.

INVOLVE EVERYONE IN HIRING

All of the high-performing principals we interviewed were directly and fully involved in hiring faculty, and, although they were very responsive to input from others, they always insisted that they make final hiring decisions.

The principal needs to take a great deal of ownership over the hiring process.

—High School Principal

Huge amounts of time can be taken up with hiring, particularly when you have some 30 people to hire, which might represent three hundred interviews. We put in place procedures to do this as efficiently as possible, but we understand that this is probably the most critical thing an administrator does: Put the right people in the classrooms with the children.

—Middle School Principal

> *I can tell you that on many issues I'm not the bottom line, but I am the bottom line in hiring teachers. I want that say-so. I am still mindful that the whole thing is still my responsibility.*
>
> —Elementary School Principal

Principals of large high schools we studied reported that effective hiring systems necessarily empowered department heads to interview job applicants (i.e., department heads had not only primary interviewing responsibility but also considerable training), though not without their occasional involvement.

> *Department heads and the associate principal for instruction take the leadership role in hiring; I only get involved sometimes. We have 170 staff members, and I need to rely on others to make a lot of decisions.*
>
> —High School Principal
>
> *When we hired new department heads, we did extensive training in leadership skills, techniques, teaching requirements, certification matters, and approaches to hiring.*
>
> —High School Principal
>
> *Our other administrators generally meet with candidates, talk with them, ask detailed questions, see if they meet our criteria, and determine the top choices; then, I meet the top two or three candidates.*
>
> —High School Principal

Many principals reported that teacher involvement in the hiring process significantly contributed to greater teacher ownership in the school, subsequent support of teachers they helped hire, and development of teacher-leaders who, in turn, mobilized others for sustained instructional improvement.

> *Teachers are more supportive of new teachers when they are on the hiring team. They really help the new teacher transition, and it really builds their relationships.*
>
> —Elementary School Principal
>
> *If they have input in hiring a teacher, they take that teacher under their wings and help that teacher get acclimated. They stay after school with them, they work with them in the morning, they teach them how to do things, they stand right behind them; and if they fall, they're going to pick them right up, and they make sure the new teacher has a fighting chance at success.*
>
> —High School Principal

> *Once a teacher is hired, we do formal observations, but we also have curriculum-support teachers who go into classrooms to do practice observations that the teacher feels good about. We also have subject-area support personnel, grade-level representatives, and team buddies.*
>
> —Middle School Principal

> *Teacher teams have to use data to determine their effectiveness, and they really don't want teachers on the team who aren't going to pull their weight. There's peer pressure on that team. So if you don't get input from the teachers when a teacher is hired and you then have issues with the new hire, you won't have the teachers' support.*
>
> —Elementary School Principal

ESTABLISH HIRING PROTOCOLS

Principals of high-performing schools began as early as possible in the school year to determine their school's hiring needs, and this frequently included moving existing faculty to new positions.

> *Every time I observed one teacher, I felt she was very, very strong in the area of math; she just stood out. I thought she might do better with older students, so I asked her if she'd be interested in moving; she took the challenge and now says, "Why didn't I do this 10 years ago?" She has found her forte, is very happy, she likes to teach, and she communicates better with those older students.*
>
> —Elementary School Principal

Principals also required teachers to complete letters of intent, not as pro forma district notices, but to communicate early in the school year their interest in a new position in their current school, transfer to another school, or pending retirement. Principals explained that this was a symbolic way for teachers to highlight their commitment to the school.

> *As soon as I know there might be some openings, I start looking. If I am fortunate, it might be January or February; but at least by March, I begin thinking about changing some folks around, given my classroom observations and if I think they may be better suited for a different grade level or different type of student.*
>
> —Middle School Principal

> *The letter of intent is not binding, but they give me a wealth of information. I ask what type of team they want to work on (two-, three-, or four-member team), what grade level, and which teammates they would like to work with.*
>
> —Middle School Principal

> *Our intent form asks them for a commitment to support the total school program for performance in such a way as to instill excellence in academics, arts, and athletics. We expect a lot.*
>
> —High School Principal

To determine staffing needs, principals, in collaboration with relevant individuals and teams, used a range of data sources in hiring, including teacher evaluations, student achievement data, candidate qualifications, and documented strengths and weaknesses of current team members as well as projected instructional budgets.

> *When we have a vacancy, we clearly define our needs, the previous teacher's talents, what we'd like to see continued or implemented, and what new skills we'd like to have the new person come in with.*
>
> —High School Principal
>
> *These are tough decisions, and you have to have a master plan. How many teachers will we have at a grade level? Which teachers want to move or stay? Which teachers need a change? We also look at test data and the dynamics, including personalities, of the instructional team.*
>
> —Elementary School Principal

Sources of names for faculty recruitment included district lists of candidates, colleges and universities, job fairs attended by principals alone or in teams with other administrators and teachers, and recommendations from other teachers (i.e., word of mouth).

> *I have not hired very often at the job fair; but once in a while, you find that magical fit. If I see a good teacher there, I ask him or her to visit the school, meet the faculty, and really get into the nuts and bolts of the job.*
>
> —Elementary School Principal
>
> *It's often word of mouth, the family-team approach. It makes my job easier when teachers have a say in whom their colleagues are, and it makes the school more successful.*
>
> —Elementary School Principal
>
> *We try never to hire anyone who isn't known at least by someone who knows someone here, because we have found that you can interview a person for four hours or four days and still be surprised by their performance. So, we try to find people who know them and are comfortable telling us what the situation is.*
>
> —High School Principal

Typically, principals and their assistant principals carefully examined applicants' qualifications. Principals insisted that they alone make calls to candidates' previous principals to obtain "truthful" feedback.

> *As a principal, when another principal calls me directly, I am much more open to that conversation. It's confidential information, so I wouldn't share it with assistants; in other words, I treat those teachers like I want to be treated.*
>
> —Middle School Principal

Principals usually worked with their administrative teams and relevant teachers to determine an appropriate approach to interviewing teaching candidates; as many individuals as possible were included on the interview teams and structured interview protocols were developed by these teams.

> *When we have a vacancy, we convene a meeting of all teachers who would love to work with us on the hiring. Everyone around the table participates in outlining our value system and determining what we want to know about potential candidates; for example, we want to know how they use technology and how collaborative they are. We don't just go on the Internet and find some interview questions.*
>
> —High School Principal

> *I involve as many people as possible—the assistant principal, the literary-support specialist, paraprofessionals, and teachers—though it's sometime difficult to find people during the summer. We ask the candidates the same questions, which is a fair way to assess everyone.*
>
> —Elementary School Principal

> *We have had good luck by including everybody in the interviewing system; we get a lot of people in on the act. People see different things, and it's also a matter of matches with our school and our teams. Even so, every year we have one to three nonrenewals because, even with this process, we get people who just aren't able to provide the quality we want.*
>
> —High School Principal

> *The teachers and I meet to decide what information we'd like to collect from candidates. During the interviews, each person has some time to dialogue with the candidate. Everyone has equal input in hiring decisions, as well, and I think that when the teachers are so involved they also commit to helping the person we hire to become successful.*
>
> —High School Principal

> *We make every interview as informal as possible, so candidates feel more relaxed and so we get a truer picture of the person. It sounds a bit like a trick, but we want to see what's on both sides of the coin. Some people are very enthusiastic and energetic when first in a job, but we want to know if they will become complacent.*
>
> —Elementary School Principal

Principals indicated that they and their administrative teams stood behind hiring decisions by investing in and supporting new personnel:

> *We go over all of it in our team meeting when we start each year: How are those we hired doing? How are they scheduled? What are we going to do to help them, and how?*
>
> —Middle School Principal

They also indicated that they reviewed hiring decisions throughout the year and at the end of the year to determine the efficacy of their hiring process; reviews included such data as parent comments and/or complaints, input of other teachers, attendance, classroom walk-through comments, and student-achievement results.

CORRECT HIRING MISTAKES

High-performing principals assumed full responsibility for dealing with problematic teachers they hired. Usually, they began by providing constructive support to a new teacher having problems, but if constructive approaches failed, principals initiated procedures to document and, if necessary, terminate the employment of such teachers.

> *I feel that if I hire you, it's my responsibility to be part of your progress and help you grow, to support you with a mentor or resources. If it doesn't work out, I have to help on that end as well; I have to be the one to say you're not fitting in. Before I recommend probation or recommend that we not offer another contract to a teacher, I want to know that I have been a part of the process.*
>
> —Middle School Principal
>
> *If I have messed up in hiring someone, I am going to take responsibility and either help them improve or take care of what needs to be done, so the students are not paying the price for my not hiring well; those teachers are not going to be here.*
>
> —Middle School Principal

High-performing principals unfailingly followed up on new hires and weak teachers; these teachers were targeted for additional support and for frequent walk-throughs to monitor growth. When growth was not evident within a reasonable period of time, principals moved expeditiously into a standardized process:

> *I always start with an undocumented conference, because a lot of times all someone needs is a little direction, like, "This is not going well. What's going on here?"*
>
> —High School Principal

If a nudge and additional support did not provide the expected results, principals moved to the documentation phase:

> *If they don't improve, we begin to document it, hold conferences with the appropriate chairperson and assistant principal and, with notice of the agenda in advance, talk about the topics of concern and get them on an improvement plan, arrange for them to observe three other teachers, and have them write reflections on what they saw, and whatever else we want them to do. We offer staff-development courses, and we give them plenty of opportunities to improve.*
>
> —High School Principal

If those opportunities produced no fruit, principals met with the teacher to share results of the ongoing observations and to explain the next course of action:

> *We . . . tell the problematic teacher that she will receive an unsatisfactory evaluation and that we will recommend nonrenewal [or dismissal].*
>
> —High School Principal

High-performing principals continued their efforts to salvage such a teacher, but support was followed by frequent written documentation of failure to improve and with frequent conferences in which evidence of unsatisfactory performance and the plan of nonrenewal was reiterated to the teacher. Principals noted that such a process is good practice, is fair to the teacher, and eliminates drama at the time of nonrenewal:

> *A recommendation to dismiss is never a surprise because we have been telling them [problematic teachers] that they will receive an unsatisfactory evaluation and we will recommend nonrenewal. It's never drama because for months prior there have been conferences. It's fine, wonderful, if they correct it, and they realize we really don't want them to go, that we were not trying to "get" them.*
>
> —High School Principal

Several principals reported that principals generally shy away from dealing with problematic teachers.

> *A lot of principals are just not involved in the observation and evaluation process, and that's why a lot of bad teachers are not "documented out" of the profession. If you're not jumping on a potential termination early, you're going to miss the deadlines. But, it is something you have to manage for the benefit of the students.*
>
> —Elementary School Principal

It was evident from our data that mistakes in hiring were very costly not only for students and their learning but also for the principal and the teachers in a school.

If you hire great teachers, you've won! You're on top! But as a true instructional leader, if you see that instruction is not happening and students are not learning, then you are constantly spinning your wheels trying to help, trying to get the teacher to where she needs to be.

—Elementary School Principal

I was desperate for a coach, so I hired him, but he has a very high opinion of himself, which doesn't always enable him to get along with others. I paid for it.

—High School Principal

She's a good worker, but she's not a team player, and I'll tell you what: I paid for that hire. She was a viper who tattled on everybody. She would always be here on time and always do her job, but she would not do one thing more than that. She took a delighted glee in reporting on everybody, and, god, did she drive me crazy.

—High School Principal

For every time that you don't get those references, you will pay, pay, pay, and pay.

—High School Principal

It takes about 10 pounds of documentation to fire a teacher and 15 pounds to nonrenew or fire an administrator.

—High School Principal

A number of principals included parents in interviews, and this was usually a positive experience; nevertheless, some principals described situations in which parents were so attuned to teachers' qualifications or performance that they attempted to block hiring teachers or were involved in running people off.

When you work in a school, you're in a fish bowl. The good thing about working here is that the parents notice. The bad thing about working here is that the parents notice. If someone is not up to the standard, you have something akin to a feeding frenzy, where parents just pick at the teacher. They've been known to run teachers off if they didn't deem them competent; most of the time they were right... they're very astute. It's not always fair, but it's astute. So, we have to deal with that.

—High School Principal

Our parents are reluctant to hire brand new teachers; they know that they are inexperienced and might be weak, and they don't want their children in a first-year teacher's classroom.

—Elementary School Principal

SUMMARY

In Chapter 8, high-performing principals' systems-development approach to hiring strong teachers and its importance to school improvement was discussed. Principals hired teachers who were team players, and they sought individuals who had the potential to become teacher-leaders, both of whom were essential elements of the systems-development approach. They used the best research-based literature on teaching effects as a guide to interviewing and hiring teachers, included all relevant stakeholders in the hiring process, and established hiring protocols. If a hiring mistake was made, principals worked with problematic teachers in a timely, constructive, and professional manner to remediate their teaching or, if necessary, terminate their employment.

TIPS AND SUGGESTIONS

Hiring Well

1. Encourage each member of the faculty to examine Stronge's (2007) *Six Qualities of Effective Teachers* and to complete a 1-through-10 Likert scale on his or her effectiveness on each quality. Encourage teachers to develop growth plans for areas of weakness and report the results of such efforts in annual evaluations.

2. Ask candidates for open teaching positions to prepare written responses to a generic essay question at the time of their interviews, and score the written responses for spelling, grammar, responsiveness to the question, and writing skill. Because incorrect use of written and spoken standard English has a negative impact on student learning (and, understandably, creates parental concerns), use the results of this test to exclude candidates with poor written communication skills.

3. When walk-throughs reveal a failure to implement the school's adopted best-teaching practices, act swiftly. Notify mentors and other potential coaches of a teacher's failure and brainstorm action steps. Use effective strategies to help teachers improve, including peer observations and peer coaching.

4. When feasible, involve teachers and relevant others in interviews. However, train teachers and others about questions that should and should not be asked.

Using Data 9

Principals of high-performing schools insist on using data
to inform instructional decisions.

At the beginning of the new millennium, Elmore (2000) noted that school administrators' instructional leadership responsibilities were changing dramatically, shifting from using limited amounts of internally-generated data to building a culture of "organizational capacity" in which teachers are engaged in improving instructional practices based on emerging information provided by external accountability systems. Principals in our study agreed.

> *Years ago, we didn't use data in schools to make decisions; now we are truly immersed in data. With current technology, you can pull up data on any child, and teachers can use that data to make decisions and plans for the student's learning.*
>
> —Elementary School Principal

In fact, the No Child Left Behind Act (NCLB, 2002) ignited an unprecedented move to data-driven decision making in America's schools: generating, analyzing, and using student-achievement data had become increasingly keyed to external accountability demands (i.e., content standards, policies, and testing requirements). Schools faced a vast change in their already-challenging work that required administrators and teachers to design feedback-rich, data-driven instructional systems to improve student learning.

A quality-oriented, data-driven approach is designed to systematically improve student learning through an ongoing, repeated process of measuring student achievement to improve instruction (i.e., to adjust learning goals, experiences, materials, approaches, and support) (see Deming, 2000; Halverson, Grigg, Prichett, & Thomas, 2007). This is a *formative* rather than a summative approach to using data (i.e., measuring achievement only at the end of the school year is a summative approach to using data) (see Halverson, Prichett, & Watson, 2007, for an explication of formative feedback systems). Leaders in a DDIS (data-driven instructional improvement system) maintain the focus on student achievement and teachers engage in a variety of activities to disaggregate data, interpret data, and to initiate improvements in teaching and learning. In a DDIS, data are the information, and they are used in an interactive way by teachers and leaders to plan for appropriate adjustments to improve teaching and learning. Note that in a DDIS teachers are teaching for the test, but not to the test. Figure 9.1 shows the six component functions of a model DDIS.

The high-performing principals we interviewed stated that the collection and use of school-related data had increased significantly in recent years, and many viewed data management as a critical job function and an essential aspect of the systems-development approach to school leadership. Principals used professional literature as well as state certification standards that called for the increased use of data in conjunction with the use of technology in

Figure 9.1   A Framework for Data-Driven Instructional Improvement Systems

1. *Data acquisition:* seeking out, collecting, and preparing information to guide teaching and learning. Data include standardized student-achievement test scores, student placement and behavioral records, grades, observation of teacher personnel, community survey data, and technological capacity. This function also includes data warehousing and reporting capabilities.

2. *Data reflection:* processes developed to make sense of student learning data that result in goals for improving teaching and learning. This includes structured opportunities for teachers and leaders to collaboratively interpret data.

3. *Program alignment:* processes to make the school's instructional program congruent with relevant content and performance standards and with the actual content taught in classrooms to meet student needs and to improve learning. Program alignment also includes noncurricular initiatives such as guidance and support programs, professional development, and community outreach, all of which require further planning and program evaluation.

4. *Program design:* creating or adapting curricula, pedagogies, student service programs, and instructional strategies to improve student learning. This includes addressing policies, programs, procedures, and financial capacity.

5. *Formative feedback:* learner-focused evaluation cycles designed to create ongoing timely flows of information to improve both student learning and instructional program quality across the school. This includes information on student learning and teacher practice; it is utilized to improve program design efforts.

6. *Test preparation:* activities designed to motivate students and to develop strategies for improving their performance on state and district assessments. Test preparation topics can include test format, test-specific skills, test areas in which school or district students are demonstratively deficient, and habits shown to improve test scores. Such efforts are not intended to "game" the testing system; rather, test preparation is intended to help make children comfortable with increasing testing time and pressure.

SOURCE: Adapted from Halverson, Grigg, Prichett, and Thomas (2007).

decision making for school improvement purposes. Typical databases included standardized and teacher-generated test results, school climate, volunteerism and parent involvement, technology use, attendance, and discipline. In all schools, principals collaborated with other administrators, teachers, and stake-holders to create subsystems, including teams to collect, analyze, and interpret data and to implement data-based action plans.

We measure just about everything, which gives us information about what we are doing and what we need to continue or discontinue. We collect data for state reporting, achievement, parent involvement, and technology use; and for each data piece, there are different people who handle different parts of the process. For instance, teachers gather local achievement data such as reading inventories, writing assessments, and standardized tests of reading and math.

—Elementary School Principal

My role as an instructional leader is to build a performance culture that is based on data-driven decisions that affect the quality of instruction and even the professional learning in our school as a whole.

—Elementary School Principal

We try to make improvements based on longitudinal studies of our data. That includes academics and attendance and any other areas we choose to work on. It's important to look at not only how you did in the past year but also two or three years before.

—Middle School Principal

You need to study the school data, and you need to involve other people in learning about the data. There are 100 other fine people around you who should do these tasks with you, who can gain an understanding of what the data look like; then, you always move in the same direction.

—Elementary School Principal

We probably get more data in schools than in any other business, and we share our data at the level of implementation. For example, we analyze end-of-course data by teacher and by student, graduation-test and SAT data by department, and vocabulary data by student (for all teachers to use). The questions we always ask are, What does this tell us about our students? Did we make improvements? What have we done differently this year?

—High School Principal

Once we get scores on standardized tests back, we make copies of the scores, and then grade-level committees dissect them. We note strengths and weaknesses for individual teachers, grade levels, and the whole school. This analysis is fed back into the work of the curriculum team for decision making. The teams buy into what they are doing, and it makes me a stronger instructional leader. Everybody's got to do their thing to make it all work together.

—Elementary School Principal

> *Last year, our kids didn't do well at all on math tests, so we had a need and a duty to find out what strategies we needed to use to strengthen those kids' math skills, with the result that we embedded opportunities for kids to apply algebraic concepts in the instructional units across the curriculum.*
>
> —Middle School Principal

Principals believed that there was a strong link between proper use of data and improvement in teaching.

> *The whole purpose of the testing program is to improve the instructional program. We lose sight of that because test scores are often used for everything except that. But I encourage teachers to use test data, not to ensure good grades but for mastery of skills; this must be firm in teachers' minds.*
>
> —Middle School Principal
>
> *I encourage teachers to reflect what they learned from their analysis of test data in their subsequent lesson plans, and they give me a copy of it.*
>
> —High School Principal

In all schools, high-performing principals relied heavily on technology to assist in data collection. Moreover, principals reported that they and designated others supervised data collection and made timely modifications to data-collection systems.

> *Our technology team monitors the integrity of the data we use.*
>
> —Elementary School Principal
>
> *A lot of data management is done with technology.*
>
> —Elementary School Principal
>
> *We have a good, clean system in place, and we don't micromanage it, but we also don't assume that when something new comes on board it won't need to be adjusted; if it makes sense to change something, we do it.*
>
> —Elementary School Principal

Principals also created effective forms of communication between and among data-gathering teams with related responsibilities.

> *We get data from different groups, pull it all together, and communicate it to others including the leadership team and teachers and other stakeholders. I am involved at the big-picture level; I don't do the gathering as much as I oversee the analyzing, interpreting, and decision making.*
>
> —Elementary School Principal

Significantly, principals worked vigorously to provide systematic proper training for all personnel in data collection, analysis, interpretation, and use. While data reports for school improvement purposes were compiled by data management teams, data coaches, or other data specialists, principals recognized that the value of data collection lies in its analysis, interpretation, and use by the generating teacher; thus, principals refused to accept the "I'm not good at math or crunching numbers" excuse. High-performing principals expected teachers to take responsibility for all classroom-level data analysis; thus, teachers who viewed themselves as poor at data analysis received extra instruction as well as periodic refresher courses.

> *We started working on data use by having about a year's worth of training with a person from the Center for Performance Assessment. Our big effort this year is on collaborative-team data analysis.*
>
> —High School Principal

> *Teachers are well versed in how to use data, and we make decisions as a group. We do a two-day retreat in June, a full day in September, and a full day again in January, as well as meeting every month to go through data. We don't spend a lot of time on "We need rolls of toilet paper" or other small things; instead, we deal with school improvement.*
>
> —Elementary School Principal

> *A lot of our teachers don't know how to work with data because some teacher preparation programs didn't teach it, so all our teachers are being trained in data use through professional development sessions.*
>
> —Elementary School Principal

In all cases, subsequent to creating teams to deal with different types of data, principals provided oversight at the school level.

> *We use data to help people see our current reality, we compare it to our vision, and we have checkups along the way. We have planning days for going through data with teachers and other stakeholders such as our local school council and our area instructional directors.*
>
> —Elementary School Principal

> *I must be instructionally oriented, the driving force that sets the expectations for the development of curricula, ensures frequent assessments, and monitors children's progress while tweaking and improving classroom effectiveness. I am the one for setting the tone and putting a face on data so that we see the data as it reflects the children we serve.*
>
> —Elementary School Principal

> *Our teachers feel we live or die by data, and that's a good thing. I pull back to look at the big picture, to consider weaknesses and strengths, to see trends and make adjustments.*
>
> —Elementary School Principal

Several high-performing principals reported that they valued hard data, but such data were not a replacement for effective communication with people, including parents. In other words, qualitative data were also highly valued.

From where I sit, I think data don't tell us everything about children, but they do give us important information.

—Elementary School Principal

I'm old fashioned, so I'd rather have people tell me what's happening than see it on a computer, so we make our data more meaningful by meeting four times a year with teachers, media specialists, assistant principals, and reading and math specialists. We call it WOW, or Working On the Work. Every aspect of the data is analyzed and used for improvement, growth, and achievement. Data help us move on to the next step and improve, but the main way I manage data is by talking with people.

—Elementary School Principal

Some people spend too much time looking at data, and they don't hear the children; they need to look at the children first and then use data to help them.

—Elementary School Principal

When we meet with parents, we expect to talk about data; the use of data is ingrained in us, never isolated from conversations.

—Elementary School Principal

QUESTIONS ABOUT DATA USE IN YOUR SCHOOL

Consider the following questions about the use of data in your school.

1. Do faculty members participate collectively in planning for data use and/or action research (i.e., a systematic approach to collecting, interpreting, analyzing, and using data to improve instruction and learning with instructional goals in mind)? What are the mechanisms for such participation?

2. What are some examples of data use and/or action research that have been carried out in your school (e.g., use of computer-based instructional programs, cross-curriculum instructional units, parental involvement, student-activity involvement, climate assessments)?

3. Are teachers allowed opportunities for professional interaction, discussion of ideas for instructional improvement, and reflective and collective thinking? How are such opportunities provided?

4. How do you rate the effectiveness of data use in your school? What improvements can you suggest?

Figure 9.2 identifies excellent Web site links for principals and teachers who want to improve their use of data.

Figure 9.2 Links to Support the Use of Data in Schools

Using Data to Improve Student Achievement

- http://www.classroomdata.org/index.cfm
  This site presents eight lessons for educators, including handouts and video clips.

Data-Driven Instructional Systems

- http://ddis.wceruw.org/index.htm
  This site describes how to develop systems for translating test data into information to improve teaching and learning.

Decision Making Using Data

- http://www.setda.org/web/guest/datadrivendecisionmaking
  The site provides instruments and tools for data collection, storage, analysis, and use.

- http://datause.cse.ucla.edu/
  This site includes a process guide for using data to make decisions, describes how to map data-use capacity, provides tools, and presents a research library.

- http://edadmin.edb.utexas.edu/datause/
  This site describes how to make decisions using data and provides reviews of software for analyzing data.

Data and Accountability

- http://privateschool.about.com/gi/dynamic/offsite.htm?site=http://3d2know.cosn.org/publications.html
  This site describes how to collect, analyze, and report data to respond to accountability mandates.

ADDITIONAL HELPFUL MATERIALS ABOUT DATA USE

Explore the many excellent materials related to data use listed below including books, workbooks, tools, kits, interviews, study guides, Web sites, and related videos, many of which are available free; some, at cost. Many of these can be found in your school or colleagues' professional libraries, at your nearest university, or on the Web. What you explore depends on your knowledge, interests, career plans, and the state of your professional library.

Data Use and Action Research: Basic How-To Materials

- *The Action Research Web Site of Madison (WI) School District:* This Web site includes guidelines, phases, techniques, and how-to tutorials. www.madison.k12.wi.us
- *Data Primer, North Central Regional Educational Laboratory (NCREL):* This is an instructional Web site designed to help educators become more

proficient at thinking about and using data for the purposes of instructional decision making. The Data Primer is organized around four modules. Each module provides practical questions that educators can ask when developing school improvement plans. Each module also contains three sections: (1) The Tutorial section uses different graphing techniques to show how putting data in graphical form increases readability, illuminates patterns, and elicits questions about meaning. (2) The Practice section lets users apply their own data to the graph type used in the Tutorial section. (3) The Going Further section acts as a bridge between the sample scenario and actual tools, resources, and services that users can access and implement to address more thoroughly some of the questions and issues that arise throughout the instructional portion. http://www.ncrel.org/datause/dataprimer/

- Bernhardt, V. L. (2006). *Using Data to Improve Student Learning in School Districts.* Larchmont, NY: Eye On Education. (This book is one title in the Using Data series published by Eye On Education; others focus on elementary, middle, and high schools.)
- Calhoun, E. (1994). *How to Use Action Research in the Self-Renewing School.* Alexandria, VA: Association for Supervision and Curriculum Development. (This book is clearly written and user friendly, an excellent how-to guide for educators, but can be hard to find [try used book retailers]).
- Creighton, T. (2007). *Schools and Data* (2nd ed.). Thousand Oaks, CA: Corwin. (This book is an easy primer on how to use quantitative data for school improvement.)
- Cotton, K. (2003). *Principals and Student Achievement: What the Research Says.* Alexandria, VA: Association for Supervision and Curriculum Development. (This report summarizes significant research findings about schools which demonstrate effects on student learning.)
- Depka, E. (2006). *The Data Guidebook for Teachers and Leaders.* Thousand Oaks, CA: Corwin. (This guidebook includes information on data collection, item analysis, rubrics, classroom assessment, and change.)
- Glanz, J. (1998). *Action Research: An Educational Leader's Guide to School Improvement* (2nd ed.). Norwood, MA: Christopher-Gordon. (This book provides a number of tools for administrators and leadership teams as they study school effectiveness and student performance.)
- Hopkins, D. (2002). *A Teacher's Guide to Classroom Research* (3rd ed.). (2002) Buckingham, England: Open University Press. (This book emphasizes changes in classroom practice through careful study by individual teachers as researchers.)
- Mertler, C. A. (2006). *Action Research: Teachers as Researchers in the Classroom.* Thousand Oaks, CA: Sage. (This is a helpful guide, particularly for individual teachers studying their classrooms.)
- Sagor, R. (2005). *The Action Research Guidebook: A Four-Step Process for Educators and School Teams.* Thousand Oaks, CA: Corwin. (This is a useful guide for all-school improvement projects.)

Diversity and Data

- Johnson, R. S. (2002). *Using Data to Close the Achievement Gap.* Thousand Oaks, CA: Sage. (This is the best of a handful of existing books that address data collection, analysis, and use when special populations are being assessed.)

Using Data for Change

- *Asking the Right Questions: A School Change Toolkit.* (This toolkit provides multiple lenses through which to conduct school improvement, with helpful tools.) Available free from McREL: http://www.mcrel.org/topics/products/139/
- *Using Data to Improve Schools.* (2002). American Association of School Administrators. (This guide from the American Association of School Administrators explains how to use data to promote whole-school change. It also provides tools and insights to help schools cultivate an inquiry culture that recognizes the power of data to guide educators' decision making and improvements to teaching.) Available online at http://aasa.files.cmsplus.com/PDFs/Publications/UsingDataToImprove-Schools.pdfSame.
- *Data-Driven School Improvement Series.* (2006). (This series includes six workbooks available through ets.org—see Pathwise Series or Leadership Resources. These workbooks deal with training to create a framework for collecting and assessing data to drive school improvement, meeting NCLB challenges, and improving instruction in the classroom. See especially Workbook 3: *Engaging in Action Research.*)
- *Improving Education Practice Through Data Use: Data-Driven Decision-Making.* (n.d.). (This Web site provides resources on data-driven decision-making, including reviews of software for analyzing student data. The site contains a variety of resources to help educators and other researchers advance the practice of data-driven decision making including state-level databases, student work analysis, and current research publications.) http://edadmin.edb.utexas.edu/datause/index.htm
- Anderson, G., & Herr, K. (2007). *Studying Your Own School* (2nd ed.). Thousand Oaks, CA: Corwin. (This book describes how to collect, analyze, and use qualitative-research data for school improvement.)
- Schmuck, R. A. (2006). *Practical Action Research for Change.* Thousand Oaks, CA: Corwin. (This comprehensive book includes definitions, models, steps, phases, methods, tools, and information about cooperative research.)

Teacher Collaboration and Protocols for Examining Data

- Cushman, K. (1996). Looking Collaboratively at Student Work: An Essential Toolkit. *Horace, 13*(2), 1–12. Read this article at http://www

.essentialschools.org/cs/resources/view/ces_res/57. (This article describes how groups of teachers can examine student work and how they can use specific *protocols* to focus their discussion on the qualities of the work; it also describes what they can learn about their students and themselves from student work. Cushman describes a "tuning protocol" that creates a ritual of presentation and response and provides a structure for conversations among teachers.)

- Holcomb, E. L. (2004). *Getting Excited About Data: Combining People, Passion, and Proof to Maximize Student Achievement* (2nd ed.). Thousand Oaks, CA: Corwin. (This is a clearly written how-to guide for educators embarking on research projects.)
- Murphy, C., & Lick, D. W. (2005). *Whole-Faculty Study Groups: Creating Professional Learning Communities That Target Student Learning* (3rd ed.). Thousand Oaks, CA: Corwin. (This is the best available publication about study groups for educators.)
- Annenberg Institute for School Reform: http://www.annenberginstitute.org/
- Critical Friends Groups at the National School Reform Faculty (a professional development initiative of the Harmony School Education Center in Bloomington, Indiana): http://www.harmony.pvt.k12.in.us/www/cfg1.html

Assessment

- Sparks, D. (1998). Making Assessment Part of Teacher Learning. *Journal of Staff Development, 19*(4), 33–35. Read this article at http://www.nsdc.org/library/publications/jsd/joyce194.cfm. (This is an interview of Bruce Joyce by Dennis Sparks regarding his advocacy for staff development that improves student learning. Joyce discusses the importance of continuous adult learning, studying implementation, assessment as part of instruction, formative evaluation, and barriers to implementation of educational innovations.)
- Marzano, R. (2006). *Classroom Assessment and Grading That Work.* Alexandria, VA: Association for Supervision and Curriculum Development. (This is arguably the best book available about assessment. Drawing from years of in-depth research, Marzano provides guidelines and steps for designing a comprehensive program that ensures that assessments and grades lead to timely, accurate feedback on specific, standards-based learning goals.) Purchase at ASCD.org. Also available as an e-book. See also the *Study Guide* at http://www.ascd.org/portal/site/ascd/template.chapter/menuitem.6b8e5ca7dd1e8e8cdeb3ffdb62108a0c/?chapterMgmtId=a5e68b0047730110VgnVCM1000003d01a8cORCRD.
- See the Web site library for assessment materials from the National Center for Research on Evaluation, Standards, and Student Testing (CRESST), http://www.cse.ucla.edu/

SUMMARY

Chapter 9 reviewed high-performing principals' approaches to the use of data to improve instructional decision making. This chapter covered the use of different types of data, the role of technology in instruction, available data-use programs, and professional development for use of data. An overview of excellent Web sites and resources that address related topics such as action research, diversity, change, and teacher collaboration were also presented in this chapter. The importance of proper data use in schools for instructional improvement cannot be overstated; thus, all school administrators and teachers must take advantage of the numerous opportunities available for developing expertise in data collection, analysis, and use.

TIPS AND SUGGESTIONS

Using Data to Inform Instructional Decisions

1. Remember that data must guide the school improvement process and that the school improvement process must guide budgetary decisions (e.g., professional development and instructional materials expenditures).

2. Talk data with teachers. Expect teachers to know what their data reveal about student learning in their classrooms. Ask teachers probing questions about data to help them draw proper conclusions.

3. Publish results that enable teachers to compare their data with those of others, and remove any stigma from comparing data among teachers. Encourage teachers to identify teachers with the best results and encourage them to ask those teachers questions about how they taught specific concepts.

4. When analyzing and interpreting data, ask teams and departments to use graphic organizers (e.g., fishbone, cause/effect) to get to the bottom of their results. Ask them to develop specific plans for improvement based on their analysis and interpretation.

5. Analyze attendance and discipline data, looking for patterns related to student achievement. Show the data at PTA/PTSA meetings to impress upon parents their child's need for regular attendance and good behavior.

6. Use data to inform annual teacher evaluations (e.g., teacher attendance data, state-mandated test results, classroom management, and discipline referrals).

7. Ask teachers to establish achievement goals for students and to compare test results with the goals, including a narrative analysis of that comparison.

8. If benchmark test results raise concerns about teaching and learning in a specific classroom, ask for an explanation and a plan of action to address concerns. Provide help as needed.

Part I

Suggested Reading for Further Learning

Administrative Leadership

A Research Base on Leadership for School Improvement

Danielson, C. (2002). *Enhancing student achievement: A framework for school improvement.* Alexandria, VA: Association for Supervision and Curriculum Development.

Elmore, R. (2003). *Knowing the right thing to do: School improvement and performance-based accountability.* Washington, DC: National Governors Association (NGA) for Best Practices. Retrieved October 14, 2009, from http://www.nga.org/cda/files/0803knowing.pdf.

Joyce, B. R., Calhoun, E., & Hopkins, D. (1999). *The new structure of school improvement: Inquiring schools and achieving students.* Maidenhead, Berkshire, UK: McGraw-Hill Education.

Marzano, R. J., Waters, T., & McNulty, B. A. (2005). *School leadership that works: From research to results.* Alexandria, VA: Association for Supervision and Curriculum Development.

McNulty, B., & Bailey, J. (2004). McREL's balanced leadership framework: School leadership that works. *Journal for Effective Schools, 3*(1), 17–33. Retrieved October 14, 2009, from http://icee.isu.edu/Journal/JournalHome.html.

Mid-continent Research for Education and Learning (McREL). (2001). *Leadership for school improvement* (rev. ed.). Aurora, CO: Author.

Mid-continent Research for Education and Learning (McREL). (2005). *The future of schooling: Educating America in 2014.* Aurora, CO: Author.

Waters, T. (2006). *The balanced leadership framework: Connecting vision with action.* Denver, CO: Mid-continent Research for Education and Learning.

Waters, T. J., Marzano, R. J., & McNulty, B. A. (2003). *Balanced leadership: What 30 years of research tells us about the effect of leadership on student achievement.* Aurora, CO: Mid-continent Research for Education and Learning (McREL).

Waters, T., & Grubb, S. (2004). *Leading schools: Distinguishing the essential from the important.* Aurora, CO: Mid-continent Research for Education and Learning.

Waters, T., & Grubb, S. (2004). *The leadership we need: Using research to strengthen the use of standards for administrator preparation and licensure program.* Aurora, CO: Mid-continent Research for Education and Learning.

Leadership for Effective Change

Gray, S. P., & Streshly, W. A. (2008). *From good schools to great schools: What their principals do well.* Thousand Oaks, CA: Corwin.

Kruse, S. D., & Seashore-Louis, K. (2008). *Building strong school cultures: A guide to leading change.* Thousand Oaks, CA: Corwin.

Wagner, T., Kegan, R., Lahey, L., Lemons, R. W., Garnier, J., Helsing, D., et al. (2006). *Change leadership: A practical guide to transforming our schools.* San Francisco: Jossey-Bass.

Assistant Principals

Bloom, G., & Krovetz, M. L. (2008). *Powerful partnerships: A handbook for principals mentoring assistant principals.* Thousand Oaks, CA: Corwin.

Marshall, C., & Hooley, R. M. (2006). *The assistant principal: Leadership choices and challenges* (2nd ed.). Thousand Oaks, CA: Corwin.

Hiring

Stronge, J. H. (2007). *Qualities of effective teachers* (2nd ed.). Alexandria, VA: Association for Supervision and Curriculum Development.

Stronge, J. H., & Hindman, J. L. (2006). *The teacher quality index: A protocol for teacher selection.* Alexandria, VA: Association for Supervision and Curriculum Development.

Stronge, J. H., Tucker, P. D., & Hindman, J. L. (2004). *Handbook for qualities of effective teachers.* Alexandria, VA: Association for Supervision and Curriculum Development.

Wald, P. J., & Castleberry, M. S. (2000). *Educators as learners: Creating a professional learning community in your school.* Alexandria, VA: Association for Supervision and Curriculum Development.

Teacher Leadership

Blase, J., & Blase, J. (2006). *Teachers bringing out the best in teachers: A guide to peer consultation for administrators and teachers.* Thousand Oaks, CA: Corwin.

Crowther, F., Ferguson, M., & Hann, L. (2008). *Developing teacher leaders: How teacher leadership enhances school success* (2nd ed.). Thousand Oaks, CA: Corwin.

Danielson, C. (2006). *Teacher leadership that strengthens professional practice.* Alexandria, VA: Association for Supervision and Curriculum Development.

Katzenmeyer, M., & Moller, G. (2001). *Awakening the sleeping giant: Helping teachers develop as leaders* (2nd ed.). Thousand Oaks, CA: Corwin.

Mentoring

Brock, B. L., & Grady, M. L. (2007). *From first-year to first-rate: Principals guiding beginning teachers* (3rd ed.). Thousand Oaks, CA: Corwin.

Daresh, J. C. (2003). *Teachers mentoring teachers: A practical approach to helping new and experienced staff.* Thousand Oaks, CA: Corwin.

Jonson, K. F. (2002). *Being an effective mentor: How to help beginning teachers succeed.* Thousand Oaks, CA: Corwin.

Sweeny, B. W. (2007). *Leading the teacher induction and mentoring program* (2nd ed.). Thousand Oaks, CA: Corwin.

Peer Coaching

Allen, D. W., & LeBlanc, A. C. (2004). *Collaborative peer coaching that improves instruction: The 2+2 performance appraisal model.* Thousand Oaks, CA: Corwin.

Observing and Teacher Talk

Achinstein, B. (Ed.). (2005). *Mentors in the making: Developing new leaders for new teachers.* New York: Teachers College Press.

Allen, D. W., & LeBlanc, A. C. (2004). *Collaborative peer coaching that improved instruction.* Thousand Oaks, CA: Corwin.

Blase, J., & Blase, J. (2006). *Teachers bringing out the best in teachers: A guide to peer consultation for administrators and teachers.* Thousand Oaks, CA: Corwin.

Clark, M. C. (2001). *Talking shop: Authentic conversation and teacher learning.* Alexandria, VA: Association for Supervision and Curriculum Development.

Danielson, C. (2009). *Talk about teaching! Leading professional conversations.* Thousand Oaks, CA: Corwin.

Fisher, D., Frey, N., & Rothenberg, C. (2008). *Content-area conversations: How to plan discussion-based conversations for diverse language learners.* Alexandria, VA: Association for Supervision and Curriculum Development.

Hall, P., & Simeral, A. (2008). *Building teachers' capacity for success: A collaborative approach for coaches and school leaders.* Alexandria, VA: Association for Supervision and Curriculum Development.

Johnson, T. (2002). *Improving instruction through observation and feedback.* Alexandria, VA: Association for Supervision and Curriculum Development.

Knowles, M. S., Holton, E. F., & Swanson, R. A. (1998). *The adult learner: The definitive classic in adult education and human resources development.* Alexandria, VA: Association for Supervision and Curriculum Development.

McGuire, V. J., & Duff, C. (2004). *Conversations about being a teacher.* Thousand Oaks, CA: Corwin.

Mezirow, J. (2000). *Learning to think like an adult.* Alexandria, VA: Association for Supervision and Curriculum Development.

Nieto, S. (Ed.). (2005). *Why we teach.* New York: Teachers College Press.

Sherin, M. (2000). *Viewing teaching on videotape.* Alexandria, VA: Association for Supervision and Curriculum Development.

Tileston, D. W. (2005). *Ten best teaching practices: How brain research, learning styles, and standards define teaching competencies.* Thousand Oaks, CA: Corwin.

Beginning Teacher Assistance

Gordon, P., & Maxey, S. (2000). *How to help beginning teachers succeed.* Alexandria, VA: Association for Supervision and Curriculum Development.

Teachers' Work

Hargreaves, A. (1994). *Changing teachers, changing times: Teachers' work and culture in the postmodern age.* New York: Teachers College Press.

Lieberman, A., & Miller, J. (1999). *Teachers—Transforming their world and their work.* New York: Teachers College Press.

Data Use and Action Research (Includes Data-Driven, Whole-Faculty Planning for School Improvement)

Calhoun, E. M. (1994). *How to use action research in the self-renewing school.* Alexandria, VA: Association for Supervision and Curriculum Development.

Clauset, K. H., & Lick, D. W. (2008). *Schoolwide action research for professional learning communities: Improving student learning through the whole-faculty study groups approach.* Thousand Oaks, CA: Corwin.

Clauset, K. H., Lick, D. W., & Murphy, C. U. (2008). *Schoolwide action research for professional learning communities: Improving student learning through the whole-faculty study groups approach.* Thousand Oaks, CA: Corwin.

Goldring, E. B., & Berends, M. (2008). *Leading with data: Pathways to improve your school.* Thousand Oaks, CA: Corwin.

Gray, S. P., & Streshly, W. A. (2008). *From good schools to great schools: What their principals do well.* Thousand Oaks, CA: Corwin.

Langer, G. M., Colton, A. B., & Goff, L. S. (2003). *Collaborative analysis of student work: Improving teaching and learning.* Alexandria, VA: Association for Supervision and Curriculum Development.

Lauer, P. A. (2004). *A policymaker's primer on education research: How to understand, evaluate, and use it.* Aurora, CO: Mid-continent Research for Education and Learning (McREL) and Denver, CO: Education Commission of the States (ECS). Available from: www.ecs.org/researchprimer.

Leithwood, K., Aitken, R., & Jantzi, D. (2006). *Making schools smarter: Leading with evidence* (3rd ed.). Thousand Oaks, CA: Corwin.

Neal, P. M., & Watts, G. (1994). *Action research, inquiry, reflection, and decision making.* Alexandria, VA: Association for Supervision and Curriculum Development.

Ontario Principals' Council. (2008). *The principal as data-driven leader.* Thousand Oaks, CA: Corwin.

Poetter, T., McKamey, C., Ritter, C., & Tisdel, P. (1999). *Emerging profiles of teacher-mentors as researchers: Benefits of shared inquiry.* Alexandria, VA: Association for Supervision and Curriculum Development.

Robertson, J. (2000). *The three R's of action research methodology: Reciprocity, reflexivity, and reflection-on-reality.* Alexandria, VA: Association for Supervision and Curriculum Development.

Sagor, R. (1993). *How to conduct collaborative action research.* Alexandria, VA: Association for Supervision and Curriculum Development.

Sagor, R. (2000). *Guiding school improvement with action research.* Alexandria, VA: Association for Supervision and Curriculum Development.

Sagor, R. (2005). *The action research guidebook: A four-step process for educators and school teams.* Thousand Oaks, CA: Corwin.

Technology

Brooks-Young, S. (2006). *Critical technology issues for school leaders.* Thousand Oaks, CA: Corwin.

Instructional Leadership

Blase, J., & Blase, J. (2004). *Handbook of instructional leadership: How successful principals promote teaching and learning* (2nd ed.). Thousand Oaks, CA: Corwin.

Teacher Empowerment

Blase, J., & Blase, J. (2001). *Empowering teachers: What successful principals do* (2nd ed.). Thousand Oaks, CA: Corwin.

Effective Communication

Schmuck, R. A., & Runkel, P. J. (1994). *The handbook of organizational development in schools and colleges* (4th ed.). Prospect Heights, IL: Waveland Press.

Group Development

Martinez, M. C. (2004). *Teachers working together for school success.* Thousand Oaks, CA: Corwin.

Wheelan, S. (2004). *Faculty groups: From frustration to collaboration.* Thousand Oaks, CA: Corwin.

Developing Trust

Bryk, A. S., & Schneider, B. (2002). *Trust in schools: A core resource for improvement.* New York: Russell Sage.

Caring in Schools

Beck, L. G. (1994). *Reclaiming educational administration as a caring profession.* New York: Teachers College Press.

Noddings, N. (1992). *The challenge to care in schools: An alternative approach to education.* New York: Teachers College Press.

Pellicer, L. O. (2007). *Caring enough to lead: How reflective practice leads to moral leadership* (3rd ed.). Thousand Oaks, CA: Corwin.

Working With Parents and Other Stakeholders

Boult, B. (2006). *176 ways to involve parents: Practical strategies for partnering with families* (2nd ed.). Thousand Oaks, CA: Corwin.

Epstein, J. L. et al. (2008). *School, family, and community partnerships: Your handbook for action* (3rd ed.). Thousand Oaks, CA: Corwin.

Glasgow, N. A., & Whitney, P. J. (2008). *What successful schools do to involve families: 55 partnership strategies.* Thousand Oaks, CA: Corwin.

Part II

Instructional Leadership for School Improvement

Goals of High-Performing Principals

INTRODUCTION TO PART II OF THE *HANDBOOK*

Thus far, we have described what is referred to as *administrative leadership for school improvement.* High-performing principals used a systems-development approach to administrative leadership that consists of nine action foci; these action foci, which are consistent with relevant research and the professional literature, provide a foundation for instructional leadership and school improvement. In Part II of the *Handbook,* we examine the *instructional leadership for school improvement* of high-performing principals, which, according to our data, also illustrates a bottom-up systems-development approach (e.g., consisting of policies, practices, programs, protocols, routines, teams, standards) and rests on the principals' five central goals:

Goal 1. To maintain a *focus* on teaching and learning

Goal 2. To develop a schoolwide *culture* that supports and sustains instruction

Goal 3. To establish a *context* (i.e., a specific set of practices and routines) for dialogue about instruction

Goal 4. To reference *research-based instructional elements* when observing instruction and talking with teachers

Goal 5. To provide ongoing, effective *professional learning* (staff development)

These goals are discussed in the following five chapters.

Teaching and Learning 10

Principals of high-performing schools maintain a focus on teaching and learning.

In contrast to the practices of principals generally (Murphy, 2003), the principals we studied developed and maintained the school's (i.e., administrators', teachers', staff members', and parents') focus on teaching and learning. Our data demonstrate that high-performing principals were committed, determined people who successfully used a systems-development approach to create subsystems to address administrative/managerial and instructional leadership responsibilities. Nevertheless, they were constantly challenged to sustain the school's focus on instructional improvement activities due to unrelenting threats, especially from interruptive managerial responsibilities (i.e., "pop-ups," "putting out fires") which, according to research, sideline (bog down or distract) most well-intentioned but less-successful principals. Furthermore, high-performing principals keenly felt the need for relevant expertise, so they diligently developed and updated their own knowledge of effective teaching and learning:

> *I am very close to the other principals who are high fliers in our county, and they're absolutely brilliant. Those affiliations have helped me tremendously. We meet very informally every week, and we talk about the issues we have in our schools. Much of it is about professional learning, which is the one thing that has moved me along the farthest professionally.*
>
> —Elementary School Principal

Principals' ongoing growth, in turn, enabled them to maintain their focus and to support and encourage teachers in their work.

As a principal, you have to have a clear focus, a personal focus that you go back to when you make decisions. You've got to have a bottom line, a grounding, whether it's hiring, how you put strategies in place, how you organize the building or the managerial part of the job, how you maintain your schedule; no matter what you are doing, you've got to have a grounding for all decisions. Mine has always been teaching and learning. Then, you need to build the culture internally and externally with your committees, so everyone begins to realize what the focus of the school is. Principals who have gone into the position without knowing what their grounding is get sidetracked into all the managerial issues.

—Middle School Principal

I keep a very strong focus on instruction, what's best for students and student learning. It's not easy because of the great number of things that come into play for principals, and we can lose sight of instruction when there are so many other factors that weigh on us, but school leaders have to decide that instruction is the bottom line and all decisions and all that we do have to somehow come back to that.

—Middle School Principal

I try not to let myself get bogged down in managerial things. I'll think, "This is not important right now. More importantly, I need to talk with teachers."

—Middle School Principal

You have constant interruptions, and you have to flow with that, but then you have to pull yourself back. You have to stay extremely organized, set your priorities for each day, and focus on what's important. I remind other leaders to never lose sight of the eyes of children and the unlimited stories those eyes tell us. Every day, I make a conscious effort to keep the pendulum out of the managerial realm and in the instructional realm; I owe that to our staff and our children.

—Elementary School Principal

I try to keep instruction and kids first. Every single day, I ask myself, "Is what I am doing going to impact instruction in some way?" The answer is not always yes—because I may be dealing with a threat or a food fight in the cafeteria; I don't spend a lot of time on that kind of thing, but there are alligators and my job is to drain the swamp, which basically improves student achievement.

—High School Principal

Paperwork can wait. If I miss a deadline, it's not going to be the end of the world. I do try to keep on top of the paperwork, but the kids are the priority, and I have to keep that focus. I know principals who never come out of their offices to help teachers and kids. There are too many bad principals out there, and they give us a bad name.

—Elementary School Principal

> *If you don't keep your focus, it doesn't take long for a couple of weeks to go by and then, all of a sudden, whoops, I've been paying too much attention to those little fires, and I haven't focused on getting into the classrooms. Managerial things come up—the custodian, the cafeteria, the heating and air conditioning, the vendor who wants to show you something, student supervision, hall duty, lunch duty, and the ever-popular student discipline—and those things eat away at your day.*
>
> —High School Principal

Principals of high-performing schools believed that they devoted more time and energy to instructional leadership than their less-effective counterparts; nevertheless, most struggled to increase the time they spent on this key responsibility. Most of the principals we studied spent between 50 and 55% of their time on instructional leadership; a few, however, were not as successful.

> *I would love to have at least 50% of my day focused on instruction; I think the reality is thirty to forty percent.*
>
> —Middle School Principal

Moreover, principals insisted that key school-level teams (e.g., administrative, leadership, and in-school improvement teams) focus on teaching and learning and instructional improvement.

> *When I first came to this school, I realized that the Leadership Team was focusing on things like people's job descriptions, things that aren't really appropriate for a leadership team. I started out with the notion that this group was going to be about instruction and that we were going to talk about what we were going to do to give these children the best education we could; we were going to talk about instructional goals, instructional needs, and other things that help us do a better job with the children. We changed our mission statement from "All Kids Can Learn" to "All Kids Can Learn and We Can Teach All Kids Together."*
>
> —Middle School Principal

> *You need to build a collaborative administrative team and a faculty that works with you and believes that the sole and most important thing we do is be involved in student learning. Part of each assistant principal's responsibilities is clearly attached to instruction.*
>
> —Middle School Principal

> *Our leadership team doesn't spend time on small things; rather, it deals with school improvement. The management team (the head custodian, secretary, media specialist, technology coordinator, and cafeteria manager) look at the school's infrastructure.*
>
> —Elementary School Principal

> *At our leadership-team meetings, we share best practices and challenges. For example, we looked at our clientele coming in, where the deficiencies were, and we developed what we needed to do in the classroom, the preparation course, and so forth. We had big improvements in our SAT scores.*
>
> —High School Principal

> *Our school improvement plan is a living document. We spent an entire day with the school improvement team, encouraging representation from the different areas, figuring out what were the most important things we need to do for the kids, and focusing on things that can really improve instruction.*
>
> —High School Principal

High-performing principals used a variety of methods to ensure that everyone—including themselves—maintained a focus on school improvement, teaching, and learning.

> *Our entire school is focused on student achievement and continuous improvement. During preplanning, we have a big push. We celebrate successes of the previous year and we launch into the goals of the current year. Last year, we used Max Thompson's model,* Good to Great! *Part of my role is to get teachers the resources they need, so it's not piecemeal or extra effort on their part.*
>
> —Middle School Principal

> *I have signs all over my office, and they just kind of remind me and others what we are all about. We have our mission and beliefs statement, signs about teams like "Together we achieve more," signs about discipline; I even take signs to faculty meetings.*
>
> —Middle School Principal

> *We use time for collaboration among teachers to keep everyone aligned with the focus of the school.*
>
> —Elementary School Principal

> *Every year, I am trying to improve, looking for ways to help teachers be more effective with student achievement. Even during my down time at home, I am thinking about things. I never let it go; it's not a job, it's my life.*
>
> —Elementary School Principal

In addition, school vision statements were always created collaboratively by all stakeholders; they were designed to emphasize school improvement, teaching, and learning; and they were routinely reinforced by principals. For instance, several principals in our study inserted school improvement goals in a footer at the bottom of personal e-mails.

> *Our school leaders are expected to enact the school instructional mission and vision, so it becomes pretty much ingrained in who we are. These are living documents rather than something talked about in August and then put away in a notebook. We even have laminated cards that we keep with us, so our mission and vision are just part of our normal dialogue; quite often, in faculty, grade-level, and committee meetings, we go back to those statements.*
>
> —Elementary School Principal
>
> *Each department sets forth a vision and shows how their vision supports the school vision; all of this comes out of the planning we do.*
>
> —High School Principal

(See "Suggested Reading for Further Learning," Leadership for Learning, at the end of Part II.)

SUMMARY

Chapter 10 described some of the methods used by high-performing principals to maintain the school's focus on teaching and learning. This chapter also revealed that despite principals' ability to create subsystems to deal with major administrative and instructional leadership responsibilities, maintaining a school improvement focus was by no means an easy task; in fact, it was a constant struggle for principals—one that overwhelms many principals. The chapter also described some methods used by high-performing principals to maintain the school's focus, included devoting significant, uninterrupted time to instruction; continuously upgrading one's knowledge of teaching and learning; insisting that all key teams devote time to instructional matters; establishing collaborative processes and shared school vision statements; and consistently reinforcing school goals. Needless to say, although a systems-development approach was essential to maintaining the school's focus, principals' continuous reflection and action were also necessary.

TIPS AND SUGGESTIONS

Maintaining the Focus on Teaching and Learning

1. When students and teachers are in the building, emphasize instructional leadership. Use the time before students arrive and after they leave for administrative duties.

2. Showcase student work on a Principal's Pride Wall, in a display case, or on hallway walls. Give credit by taking pictures of students with the principal and teachers standing in front of the honored work.

(Continued)

(Continued)

3. Use a faculty meeting to tour the building (halls and classrooms) for evidence of best practices. Break into small groups, assign a specific wing or area to each group, establish a time limit, describe the purpose of the tour (i.e., to identify specific artifacts or evidence that teaching and learning is the focus in the school and in the classroom), and ask groups to take notes about their findings. Reconvene after the tour to share results.

4. When planting the seed for a possible change, divide teachers into two groups and assign a pro side and a con side. Ask each side to brainstorm its position on the change and to develop and record reasons to support its positions as well as data to use in persuading others to its side. Reconvene the group to share the pros and cons of the change. Table further discussion of the change until a later date, so faculty members have time to reflect on the change and to conduct further independent research on the change. To nudge teachers to be open to a potential change, share research that demonstrates the value of the change.

5. Share brain research with teachers to explain and support best practices. Use brain research to help students develop effective learning strategies and study habits.

6. Ensure that teachers teach test-taking strategies to students and share test-taking strategies with parents for reinforcement at home.

7. Ask teachers to instruct students about metacognition; one exercise would be to ask students to write essays about how they know what they know.

8. Regularly discuss teaching strategies with teachers (e.g., ask, What strategy are you using? Why? What evidence do you have of student learning?).

9. Regularly look for evidence of differentiation during walk-throughs (e.g., what is being done for the struggling students, culturally different students, and high achieving students?).

10. Regularly look for evidence of accommodation and modification for all special education students during walk-throughs.

11. Use a standardized process for special education data collection throughout the school (e.g., ask special education teachers and others serving such students to create data collection notebooks, using forms they have collectively created for that purpose; alternatively, use commercially created programs to track and coordinate such information).

12. During walk-throughs, regularly look for evidence of appropriate interventions for students in the response to intervention process.

Culture 11

Principals of high-performing schools develop a schoolwide
culture that supports and sustains instruction.

We have reiterated throughout the *Handbook* that principals in our study employed a bottom-up systems-development approach to address both administrative and instructional leadership responsibilities. This approach included all stakeholders and was designed to systematically build school cultures based on deeply internalized values, beliefs, ways of thinking, and routine behavior that emphasized school improvement, teaching, and learning. This approach (i.e., creating systematic approaches to hiring strong people, empowerment, modeling, use of data, professional development, and resource allocation) is remarkably consistent with Edgar Schein's (2004) pioneering work on how leaders generally create organizational cultures. In his book, *Organizational Culture and Leadership*, Schein describes how leaders—like the high-performing principals we studied—embed and transmit culture, including what they pay attention to, measure, and control; how they react to critical incidents; how they model, teach, and coach; criteria by which they allocate rewards; criteria by which they recruit, select, promote, retire, and dismiss people; and how they use secondary culture-reinforcement mechanisms (e.g., organizational structure, systems, and procedures; rites and rituals; use of space; formal creeds and charters; and stories about important events and people).

> *School improvement is really important to us, and it is part of every conversation, not just isolated to the days we set aside for it. It is part of everything we do, like talking with parents. It's ingrained in every conversation.*
>
> —Elementary School Principal

Everything has to be prioritized, with teaching and learning at the forefront. We just keep reminding everybody of that, making sure transportation people understand the important role they have because every minute kids miss instruction is detrimental to student achievement. Maintenance people need to look at preventative work as well as repair and remodeling, and everyone needs to do more without being told by the principal, which takes away from instructional leadership. Teaching and learning has to be something that the entire staff and faculty buy into; if we are to improve education, it has to be a we, with everybody committed to that goal. If not, that becomes the weak link and the principal or other administrators have to invest more time putting out fires that could have been prevented.

—High School Principal

I am an educator but, in this role, I am also an architect, an artist, an engineer, even an explorer. My job as a building-level instructional leader is to build a performance culture based on data-driven decisions that affect the quality of instruction and even professional learning as a whole.

—Elementary School Principal

My role as a new leader on this campus is one of getting to know and understand the culture rather than immediately reforming the culture. I have to be clever, to move simultaneously parallel to the culture, slowly, carefully, and then very artistically integrate a new beginning to build a new culture. I need to set the tone and gain the commitment for directions that may not yet be in the thoughts of everyone in the building. It's the planting of the seed. I have come in as an appreciative individual, looking to learn from the existing culture, not one to overwhelm or overtake it. I take time to assess and reflect, and I am mindful of my role as a leader and my expectations, but I have only the right to inspire them, not overwhelm them.

—Elementary School Principal

To change the culture means to change the daily habits of people. So, as an instructional leader, you have to find out what's going on every day in the classroom.

—High School Principal

High-performing principals disclosed that principals generally failed to understand the importance of developing a culture focused on school improvement.

I've seen too many people ignore the culture of an organization; they change something, and it doesn't result in improvement. As long as we move systematically along the improvement continuum, I am willing to move slowly, take time to create consensus, and get the stakeholders committed to the organization. Getting there will take different rates of speed depending on the consensus-building capabilities of the people.

—High School Principal

Rewards were used to support school cultures focused on school improvement:

> *As an instructional leader, one of my goals is to improve student attendance at our school. At the end of every month, the four classes with the best attendance get a pizza party, so now students put pressure on classmates to come to class, and that puts pressure on the parents. Now parents are saying, "My child wants to come to school."*
>
> —Elementary School Principal
>
> *We do little things as rewards. For example, every time a student made a goal on a practice test for the criterion-referenced standardized test, he got a balloon. Now every grade level has some form of poster about little rewards, and I always say to students, "Look at the poster and see how your classmates are doing; if they don't have a balloon, encourage them."*
>
> —Elementary School Principal
>
> *I have ways to recognize faculty and staff. It's really corny, but I give them certificates of achievement, which I also use for students who receive nominations for college scholarships or scholarships. It helps create our school culture.*
>
> —High School Principal

SUMMARY

Chapter 11 reminds the reader that high-performing principals' approach to both administrative and instructional leadership was designed to create deeply embedded school cultures devoted to school improvement. It was noted that principals' approach to creating high-performing schools is consistent with the approach discussed in Schein's (2004) highly regarded book on organizational culture; in other words, all *action foci* and *goals* described throughout the *Handbook* will, in varying degrees, enhance both organizational and cultural components consistent with school improvement.

TIPS AND SUGGESTIONS

Developing a Culture That Supports and Sustains Teaching and Learning

1. Encourage teachers to provide rubrics and exemplars for assignments and projects. Rubrics allow students to get the grade they want, and exemplars allow students to see what the assignment looks like when completed.

(Continued)

(Continued)

2. Implement a rewards-for-reading program to encourage reading as a lifelong habit; similarly, create a rewards-for-hard-work program. Purchase spirit wear and other school-related products to reward excellence. For a no-cost or minimal-cost reward, consider creating a Hard Work Café where students who have excelled are rewarded with a special dining experience; when the budget permits, provide special treats.

3. Reduce homeroom time to a minimum; take the saved minutes to create a miniperiod for "double-dipping" instructional support: tutoring, conferencing, remediation and reteaching sessions.

4. Create voluntary academic lunches during which the top gun (or best of the best) teachers reteach difficult concepts.

5. Assign students to homeroom teachers in accordance with their academic needs; for instance, place students struggling in math in a math teacher's homeroom to provide support during homeroom.

6. Encourage teachers to confer with students to facilitate learning, set individual goals, and check progress on goals. Also encourage student-led conferences with parents.

7. Monitor student placement with teachers from one year to the next. Never place a student with a weak teacher two years in a row. (Naturally, weak teachers should be given an opportunity to improve, but failure to do so must be carefully documented and followed by dismissal within a reasonable amount of time.)

Dialogue 12

> Principals of high-performing schools establish a context (i.e., a specific set of practices and routines) for dialogue about instruction.

A recent study of effective principals' instructional leadership published in *The Handbook of Instructional Leadership* (Blase & Blase, 2004) revealed characteristics of principals who had successfully built a school *context* for collaboration, equality, and lifelong study of teaching and learning (see Figure 12.1). Such principals blended an unremitting focus on instruction and the development of a functional context (i.e., concrete practices and routines) centered on instruction. They promoted, for example, a specialized form of teacher thinking—reflection—that arises from a teacher's questions about perplexing classroom experiences and leads to purposeful inquiry and problem resolution (Dewey, 1933; Schon, 1987). Specifically, in their interaction with teachers, effective principals encouraged inquiry, reflection, exploration, experimentation, and problem solving, which enabled teachers to build repertoires of flexible alternatives rather than collections of rigid teaching procedures and methods (Blase & Blase, 2004; Schon, 1987).

We found that high-performing principals engaged in many of the same instructional leadership behaviors as those described above. For example, to reinforce the school's focus on school improvement, principals conveyed high expectations for teaching and learning and encouraged support, oversight, and assessment of students' academic progress. They did this in a variety of different ways, including modeling, rewarding, supporting, and encouraging—not simply by mentioning this expectation or including it in the school's vision statement.

Figure 12.1   Establishing a Context for Principal-Teacher Dialogue About Instruction

Theme	Principal's Behaviors
Talking with teachers	Building trust
	Developing the group
	Fostering collaboration
	Supporting peer coaching
	Observing in classrooms
	Conferring with teachers about teaching and learning
	Empowering teachers
	Maintaining visibility
Promoting teachers' professional growth	Studying the literature and proven programs
	Supporting new skills practice, risk taking, & innovation
	Providing effective staff development options
	Applying principles of adult development to staff development program design
	Praising, supporting, and facilitating teachers' work
	Providing resources
	Giving feedback and suggestions
Fostering teacher reflection	Developing teachers' reflection skills
	Collaboratively constructing professional knowledge and social insights
	Developing action-research skills (critical study skills)
	Modeling an inquiry orientation
	Using data to question, evaluate, and critique teaching and learning
	Extending autonomy to teachers

SOURCE: Adapted from Blase and Blase (2004).

> The main focus of our school is student learning and respect, and our goal is that students (and teachers) exceed at everything. If we expect that teachers spend one to two hours a day on math, they need to do that or go somewhere else. And every day we talk about students' acceptable behavior, what it looks like and what it doesn't look like. I also communicate in a monthly newsletter what parents can do to help their child at home with reading and math.
>
> —Elementary School Principal

> *Bottom line, we're here for the kids. What I have done is to offer the teachers more instructional support than they could ever imagine, and it's been very positive for them as well as for the kids, because teachers are the most effective instrument for getting to kids.*
>
> —Elementary School Principal

We also found that high-performing principals used published research to analyze their performance. In fact, a number of principals created Likert scale self-evaluations based on research. To illustrate, principals could use Figure 12.1 to create a self-survey of their effectiveness in dialogue with teachers, and they could subsequently develop action plans to address their shortfalls.

Principals also encouraged teachers to take risks (i.e., try new things) in the classroom. According to our data, principals associated risk taking with effective teaching.

> *I suggest we try new things, and before you know it, it's working. And, teachers say, "See, we can do this!" It's my job to try to expose myself to new things, to motivate others to try new things.*
>
> —Elementary School Principal
>
> *Professional learning is so important here; that's why we are as good as we are. We are willing to take risks and try new things. I'm not surprised when new things work, because they are based on the research.*
>
> —Middle School Principal

FACULTY MEETINGS: A SEA CHANGE

To enable teachers to talk about instruction, most principals we interviewed eliminated traditional schoolwide faculty meetings (i.e., principal-dominated meetings that emphasized one-way communication about general school business or announcements). In contrast, they insisted that all meetings routinely stress the improvement of teaching and learning and focus on three things: curriculum, instruction, and technology.

> *We don't have "old-time" faculty meetings; we have professional development meetings. We do things teachers need to implement in their classrooms. Everything we do, we make sure it's benefitting teachers and then getting the most out of their time.*
>
> —Middle School Principal

High-performing principals also turned over faculty meetings to teachers for research-based presentations (e.g., book studies, topics of inquiry taught in jigsaw presentations).

ENCOURAGING FREQUENT TEACHER DIALOGUE AND COLLABORATION

Despite the complexity of teaching and the challenge of continuous professional growth, research indicates that many teachers work in isolation, barred from support and assistance from those who know and understand their experiences and needs in the classroom (Glickman, 2002). Blase and Blase (2006) found that teachers themselves recognized the value of peer consultation (i.e., informal, naturally occurring, spontaneous, timely assistance and support that teachers give teachers). These researchers also found that practical reasoning, when joined with experiential knowledge and adapted to the school context by way of dialogue among teachers, results in instructional innovation and improvement (see Figure 12.2). Furthermore, peer collaboration among teachers builds teachers' morale and influences their teaching skills and professional growth; specifically, peer collaboration among teachers builds healthy relationships through communication, caring, and trust; helps teachers structure learning experiences; facilitates effective planning and organizing for instruction; fosters sharing of techniques and materials; and improves teachers' classroom management. Not surprisingly, we found that high-performing principals also encouraged teachers to routinely help their colleagues improve teaching and learning.

> *There are certain things teachers can do better than others, based on their strengths, and we are trying to share those strengths. Last year, I selected three teachers for training in learning-focused schooling; this was a huge commitment as they were out of the school for four days. This year, those teachers will train others in each grade level. Even young teachers have new ideas, and we encourage them to share. We are building our little community, our little family.*
>
> —Elementary School Principal

Our study of high-performing principals also shows that dialogue and collaboration were not limited to teachers; they also included principals, assistant principals, and even parents.

> *As a learning-focused school, we try to do five walk-throughs a day, not for evaluation but for feedback. We administrators gather and discuss what we see and deliver general feedback at grade-level meetings, and that makes it nonthreatening. Next year, we will give feedback to individual teachers from the walk-throughs.*
>
> —Middle School Principal

In addition, high-performing principals indicated they were members of informal groups of school leaders within and across county lines who met to

Figure 12.2 Teachers' Perspectives on Teacher-To-Teacher Assistance (e.g., Peer Consultation, Teacher Conversations)

Because teaching

- Is dynamic, situated, complex, contextualized work;
- Is about working with diverse learners;
- Unfolds in practice; and
- Requires continuous decision making and problem solving;

We must

- Develop trust;
- Create opportunities to discuss experiences and knowledge;
- Foster dialogic discourse;
- Develop a culture of shared learning rather than a culture of isolation;
- Engage in continuous learning from each other;
- Engage in critical collaborative processes;
- Engage in social sharing;
- Nurture sharing;
- Develop a recursive, problem-based collaboration of practitioners;
- Become an interdependent learning community of informal, self-constituting, naturally-occurring, spontaneous relationships among practitioners;
- Help each other fill the gaps in knowledge; and
- Prevent being discounted, diminished, inhibited, or marginalized by others;

So we can

- Access teachers' expertise;
- Access unarticulated knowledge learned in work;
- Move from tacit knowledge to explicit knowledge;
- Generate improvisational knowledge;
- Adapt knowledge;
- Mobilize knowledge;
- Amplify knowledge throughout our school;
- Solve problems of teaching and learning;
- Ask new questions;
- Search for new perspectives;
- Craft new explanations;
- Design innovative solutions;
- Spontaneously solve problems; and
- Do what works.

Thus, spontaneous forms of collaboration among teachers

- Contain innovative knowledge; and
- Are critical to school innovation and improvement.

SOURCE: Blase & Blase (2006); Brown & Duguid (1991); Bryk & Schneider (2002); Daft & Weick (1984); Fullan (2003); Lave & Wenger (1991); Nonaka (1994); Shellard (2003).

"talk school." Figure 12.3 describes some instructional improvement activities and resources for teachers, principals, and parents interested in growing professionally and developing a culture of dialogue about instruction.

Figure 12.3 Instructional Improvement Activities for Teachers, Principals, and Parents

ACTIVITY 1

Building a Culture of Ongoing Dialogue About Instruction

Step 1. Plan a meeting in which you discuss the ways you talk about teaching. Consider any ongoing informal dialogue between and among teachers, leaders, and parents of your school. Consider whether such dialogue (1) is sufficiently frequent; (2) improves classroom instruction; (3) raises student achievement; and (4) promotes a school culture of support, inquiry, and growth.

Step 2. Plan a meeting to discuss and develop a list of meaningful questions, vocabulary, and talking points related to teaching and learning that can be used during team, grade, and content-area meetings to generate dialogue. At regularly scheduled meetings, each group can explore the same question and/or talking points, make a bulleted chart of key points based on their dialogue, and submit their chart. Hang the charts from all of the groups together in a centralized location; use the charts to develop a master list combining feedback from all groups.

Helpful Resources

- See Danielson's (2009) book, *Talk About Teaching: Leading Professional Conversations*, which discusses (1) the importance of conversations among teachers for ongoing professional learning, (2) leadership and power as they relate to teaching and learning, (3) conversational skills needed by teachers and leaders to address instruction, and (4) sample topics, activities, and "mental maps" for conversations among educators.
- Visit the Web site of the Lesson Study Research Group to learn how Japanese educators collaborate to reflect on their teaching behaviors. http://www.tc.edu/centers/lessonstudy/lessonstudy.html

ACTIVITY 2

Peering in on Peers (for Two or More Teachers)

Visit each other's classrooms and observe your colleagues' teaching and the students' learning. Meet to discuss, analyze, and reflect on each lesson with respect to (1) unit design, (2) the use of instructional strategies related to student achievement, and (3) meeting the needs of diverse students (i.e., culturally, linguistically, at-risk, rural, Native American, and/or low-performing students).

Helpful Resources

- Review the collegial work of peer-consultant teachers studied by Blase and Blase in *Teachers Bringing Out the Best in Teachers* (2006). (Peer consultation is characterized by the teachers' collective belief in five guiding principles for designing learning experiences: (1) addressing every child's needs, (2) individualizing and contextualizing learning, (3) engaging students in cooperative learning, (4) developing interdisciplinary approaches to learning, and (5) using technology in learning.)
- Visit the Web site of the Critical Friends Groups: http://cesnorthwest.org/cfg.php; and read Deborah Bambino's article about critical friends: http://www.harmonyschool.org/nsrf/articles_bambino.html
- See "Suggested Reading for Further Learning" (Walk-Throughs and Observing in Classrooms) at the end of Part II of this book.

ACTIVITY 3

Enhancing Collaboration

(This exercise is for one or more teachers or instructional leaders, including principals and assistant principals.)

Learn about protocols. Visit the Web site, *Looking at Student Work,* by the Annenberg Institute for School Reform, www.lasw.org, or read the book identified below to learn more about structured conversations (i.e., protocols), about classroom instruction, including expectations, goals, outcomes, procedures, tips, questions, and steps about conducting protocols for teachers, instructional coaches, principals, and students:

- Blythe, T., Allen, D., & Powell, B. S. (1999). *Looking Together at Student Work: A Companion Guide to "Assessing Student Learning."* New York: Teachers College Press.

Learn about portfolios. Study classroom, teacher, and principal portfolio design in the following books:

- Danielson, C., & Abrutyn, L. (1997). *An Introduction to Using Portfolios in the Classroom.* Alexandria, VA: Association for Supervision and Curriculum Development.
- Rolheiser, C., Bower, B., & Stevahn, L. (2000). *The Portfolio Organizer: Succeeding With Portfolios in Your Classroom.* Alexandria, VA: Association for Supervision and Curriculum Development.
- Wyatt, R. L., & Looper, S. (2004). *So You Have to Have a Portfolio: A Teacher's Guide to Preparation and Presentation.* Thousand Oaks, CA: Corwin.

Compare information gleaned from the materials identified above with your district's or school's use of protocols and portfolios.

Learn about collaborative parent involvement. Visit the Web site of the National PTA and read about parent involvement related to helping improve a school, teaching, and learning (e.g., standards for parent involvement, assessment of parent involvement, and parent involvement and schools of excellence certification): http://pta.org.

A NOTE ABOUT THE NEED FOR COMMON PLANNING TIME AMONG TEACHERS

Principals of high-performing schools noted that common planning time and collaborative work on scheduling were essential elements in maintaining the school's focus on teaching and learning. Accordingly, principals did not do scheduling alone; rather, they created teams composed of administrators, teachers, and support personnel who had specific planning skills. Proper scheduling produced common planning time for teachers to reflect on instructional improvement, maximize instructional time, and collaborate with administrators about instructional and resource needs. Scheduling was seen as a continuous process, and schedules were routinely monitored and tweaked to ensure their viability and efficacy from semester to semester and year to year.

Our people on the scheduling team know how to create scheduling cycles that really work, yet it takes literally hundreds of hours to create a schedule that works.

—High School Principal

Ours is one of the district's few elementary schools to have developed a schedule including common planning time for teachers every day. Now, rather than begrudging the fact that they have to stay late, teachers have planning time during the day. Some teachers have said they would give up their paraprofessional before giving up their common planning time.

—Elementary School Principal

The preparation and planning and the decisions made about a good schedule can create so many opportunities for students and teachers. It's amazing how students benefit from our doing creative things like bundling courses and linking teams of teachers.

—High School Principal

Scheduling is the nuts and bolts of curriculum delivery, and it takes a master planner to lead it, someone who is innovative and who is not just doing the same thing but is thinking outside the box. You need thoughtful and analytic planning.

—Elementary School Principal

By working together, the kindergarten faculty figured out how to increase instructional time from 270 minutes to 330 minutes each day.

—Elementary School Principal

With the right people in the right positions, you empower them. Our assistant principal and the reading-support specialist spread all of the scheduling data, the variables, out on the floor and say to teachers, "Okay, we need to do this, we need to fit this in here…"

—Middle School Principal

We don't have a schedule set in stone, and we are already talking with people about next year; in fact, we're always getting input about it from teachers, department chairs, students, and parents.

—High School Principal

If you don't give people the opportunity to plan together with the tools and resources and to make academic decisions and then be accountable, how will they ever grow or become instructional leaders? They're going to look around and say, "Oh, my God, what do I do now?"

—High School Principal

SUMMARY

Chapter 12 demonstrated that high-performing principals engage in specific activities (i.e., talking with teachers about instruction, promoting teachers' professional growth, and fostering teachers' reflection about teaching and learning) to build a context for dialogue about instruction. In addition, communicating high expectations, modeling, rewarding, encouraging risk taking, scheduling common planning time, emphasizing teaching and learning at all meetings, and encouraging teacher-to-teacher assistance were described. Chapter 12 also included an array of instructional improvement activities for collaborative work among administrators, teachers, and parents.

TIPS AND SUGGESTIONS

Establishing a Context for Dialogue About Instruction

1. Give teachers responsibility for faculty meetings. Set expectations and guidelines for meetings and support faculty presentations by providing needed resources and being present. Divide meeting responsibilities among teams and departments.

2. Facilitate teacher development through the creation of structures for peer observations, peer coaching, and peer consultations; use Figure 12.2 to guide the process of creating these structures. Ensure that these structures are "safe zones" for teachers and allow professional growth to occur in a supportive, protected environment.

3. Stagger department meeting times so that you can attend all department meetings. Encourage dialogue about teaching and learning in all department meetings.

4. Recognize and reward teams or department members who achieved the highest results on state-mandated tests. For instance, allow the highest-scoring team to pick its planning time or recess time.

5. Engage teachers in discussions about the use of technology to enhance learning. Create shared computer folders of units and lesson plans that incorporate technology and lists of interactive technology Web sites for each content area.

6. Arrange continuing-education credits through your district for in-house book studies and other studies of teaching and learning based on research. Discuss best practices.

13 Research

Principals of high-performing schools reference research-based instructional elements when observing instruction and when talking with teachers.

In conducting classroom observations, the high-performing principals systematically focused on many of the same elements discussed in the best extant educational research; in fact, 11 such elements clearly emerged from a comparative analysis with our findings:

1. Factors influencing achievement
2. Planning for instruction
3. Standards-based instructional units
4. Components of instruction
5. Student abilities that teaching strategies should enhance
6. Effective teaching practices across content areas
7. Ordering and pacing of content and instructional strategies
8. Addressing diverse students' needs
9. Using technology
10. Models of teaching
11. Classroom management (discipline)

ELEMENT 1: FACTORS INFLUENCING ACHIEVEMENT

High-performing principals were well-informed about instructional matters, including theoretically derived school-, teacher-, and student-level practices and factors that influence achievement. As noted in Part I of this book, principals in our study insisted that school policy and decision-making (school-level factors) focus on teaching and learning and instructional improvement and that teachers be accountable for teacher-level practices, such as using effective teaching strategies, curriculum, and discipline approaches that contribute to student achievement.

> *Last year, we learned that two social studies teachers teaching the same course got very different results on the same test, so the teacher whose students performed poorly observed the multiplicity of approaches the other teacher used in classes; the first teacher then made a big departure from lecturing and overuse of worksheets.*
>
> —High School Principal

For ease of reference, we reproduce Figure 3.1 here (see Figure 13.1; the full report of the research underlying this figure is contained in R. J. Marzano's (2000) paper titled "A New Era of School Reform: Going Where the Research Takes Us." This is available free from www.mcrel.org/PDF/SchoolImprovementReform/5002RR_New EraSchoolReform.pdf). In many cases, the principals we studied required all-school study of this research and discussion of its implications for the school and its classrooms. See Figure 13.1 below.

Principals reported that, in order to close the achievement gap, they employed systematic, step-by-step implementation examples of other high-performing

Figure 13.1 School- and Teacher-Level Practices and Student Factors Influencing Student Achievement

School practices	1. Guaranteed and viable curriculum
	2. Challenging goals and effective feedback
	3. Parent and community involvement
	4. Safe and orderly environment
	5. Collegiality and professionalism
Teacher practices	6. Instructional strategies
	7. Classroom management
	8. Classroom curriculum design
Student factors	9. Home environment
	10. Learned intelligence/background knowledge
	11. Motivation

SOURCE: Marzano, Pickering, & Pollock (2001); Marzano (2003).

schools such as the 90/90/90 schools in Milwaukee and the Brazosport schools in Texas, in which research-based factors influencing achievement are emphasized (see Figure13.2). In 90/90/90 schools, for instance, more than 90% of the students are eligible for free and reduced lunch, more than 90% are from ethnic minorities, and more than 90% met or achieved high academic standards. Characteristics of these schools include a focus on academic achievement, clear curriculum choices, frequent assessment of student progress and multiple opportunities for improvement, an emphasis on writing, and external scoring. These schools have closed the achievement gap and significantly raised student achievement (Reeves, 2000). Similarly, the Brazosport Independent School District has implemented an approach in its schools to successfully close the achievement gap based on these same school characteristics (Davenport & Anderson, 2002). In short, schools that have closed the achievement gap and have enhanced student achievement, like schools led by the principals in our study, deliberately emphasize school and teacher factors that research has linked to school improvement. See Figure 13.2.

Figure 13.2   Factors Emphasized in 90/90/90 (Milwaukee) and Brazosport (Texas) Schools

School/Teacher Factors	90/90/90 Schools	Brazosport Schools
Guaranteed and viable curriculum	X	X
Challenging goals and effective feedback	X	X
Parent and community involvement	*	X
Safe and orderly environment	X	X
Collegiality and professionalism	X	X
Instructional strategies	X	X
Classroom management	*	*
Classroom curriculum design	X	X

Key: X = primary emphasis

 * = secondary emphasis

SOURCE: Adapted from Reeves (2000); Davenport and Anderson (2002).

ELEMENT 2: PLANNING FOR INSTRUCTION

High-performing principals also indicated that noteworthy accomplishments of schools using formal models of school improvement significantly contributed to their determination to implement research-based strategies consistent with learning and brain research and designed to keep the focus on student learning. The dimensions of learning model (Marzano et al., 1997) and learning-focused schools model (Thompson & Thompson, 2000) are two such approaches. (See Figure 13.3.)

Basically, the dimensions of learning model is a structure for planning units of instruction; in this approach, "planning for learning" addresses five issues related to instructional effectiveness: content to be covered, student assessment, grading, sequencing instruction, and conference use. See Figure 13.4 for an outline of the eight-step process used in planning for learning in the Brazosport Schools.

Figure 13.3 Research-Based Models Cited by Principals Who Created High-Performing Schools

Marzano et al.'s *Dimensions of Learning Model* (5 dimensions of thinking essential to successful learning)	Thompson's *Learning-Focused Schools Model* (focus on achievement, curriculum choices, frequent assessment, multiple opportunities for improvement; emphasis on writing and external scoring; instruction using essential questions, concept maps, and rubrics)
Dimension 1: Positive attitudes and perceptions about learning	
Dimension 2: Thinking involved in acquiring and integrating knowledge	Level 1: Acquisition
Dimension 3: Thinking involved in extending and refining knowledge	Level 2: Extending and refining
Dimension 4: Thinking involved in using knowledge meaningfully	Level 3: Authentic, meaningful use and mastery
Dimension 5: Productive habits of mind	

SOURCE: Marzano et al. (1997); Thompson and Thompson (2000).

Figure 13.4 Eight-Step Process for Planning for Learning in Brazosport Schools

1. Disaggregate data (by district, campus, subject, grade level, classroom, and student)

2. Develop timeline of skills and topics to be taught

3. Deliver instructional focus

4. Administer assessment

5. If no mastery, provide tutorial

6. If mastery, provide enrichment

7. Provide ongoing maintenance

8. Monitor

SOURCE: Adapted from Davenport and Anderson (2002).

See "Suggested Reading for Further Learning" (Planning and Organizing for Teaching) at the end of Part II of this book.

ELEMENT 3: STANDARDS-BASED INSTRUCTIONAL UNITS

The principals we studied recognized that different types of standards address learning in different ways (see Figure 13.5), and they were keenly aware of the range of curriculum standards (i.e., what students should know and be able to do).

Therefore, high-performing principals assisted teachers in developing standards-based instructional units by asking pertinent probing questions (see Figure 13.6) and by requiring teachers to identify state standards (and, in some

Figure 13.5 Different Types of Standards

1. *Content standards* cover what students are to learn in various subject areas, such as mathematics and science.

2. *Performance standards* specify what levels of learning are expected.

3. *Opportunity-to-learn standards* state the conditions and resources necessary to give all students an equal chance to meet performance standards.

4. *World-class standards* indicate content and performances that are expected of students in developed countries. This term is used by groups in the United States working to bring U.S. students' academic achievement and knowledge on par with students' accomplishments in the other industrialized countries.

SOURCE: McBrien and Brandt (1997).

cases, world-class reading and math standards), operational descriptors, assessment targets, and implementation resources. (For more on educational reforms in the United States and state standards, see Myron Lieberman's 2007 book, *The Educational Morass.*)

Figure 13.6 Questions for Teachers Developing Standards-Based Instructional Units

To teach in a comprehensive, standards-based manner, teachers should consider the following questions about their classroom teaching. How well did you

1. Communicate to students what the learning was (outcomes of the lesson or activity)?

2. Align instruction and activities with communicated outcomes?

3. Vary activities and/or materials for students?

4. Assess and monitor students to adapt instruction?

5. Provide feedback to students about their work?

6. Engage students in learning activities?

7. Manage the classroom to maximize learning?

8. Impart meaningful content?

9. Promote understanding and exploration of meaning across disciplines?

10. Promote student interest in the learning content?

SOURCE: Adapted from Hansen, Schalock, McConney, and Rudd (2001).

Moreover, some principals involved in our study were familiar with and referred teachers and other administrators to three particularly useful online documents:

1. The Compendium of Standards

The *Compendium of Standards* (Kendall & Marzano, 2004) synthesizes information from more than 137 documents, reports, and other materials compiled by professional education organizations for the following content areas: language arts, mathematics, science, geography, foreign language, history, arts, economics, civics, health, physical education, behavioral studies, life skills, and technology. *The Compendium* is an online database (available free from http://www .mcrel.org/standards-benchmarks/) that presents a coherent set of standards for primary, upper elementary, middle school, and high school levels in a number of content areas. The online edition also has browsable topics, pre-K through 12 benchmarks, revised vocabulary terms, and knowledge and skill statements for each of the benchmarks. McREL (The Mid-continent Research for Education and Learning, producer of *The Compendium*) is a nationally recognized leader in standards-based education. McREL works with educators to review, revise, and develop new standards; to prioritize standards to ensure balanced and realistic curricula; to design classroom activities and assessments aligned with standards; and to integrate performance standards into classroom instruction.

2. The Process for Developing an Integrated Standards-Based Instructional Unit

Dean and Bailey (2003) put out a document describing a process to help teachers design standards-based units of instruction; it incorporates knowledge gleaned from professional practice and research on learning and instruction; it is based on the belief that careful attention to classroom curriculum design—the sequencing and pacing of learning experiences—decreases the likelihood of breakdowns in student learning. Their report, "A Report Documenting the Process for Developing an Integrated Standards-Based Instructional Unit," is available free from http://www.mcrel.org/PDF/Standards/5031TG_DevelopingaStandards-basedUnit.pdf.

3. Models of Standards Implementation: Implications for the Classroom

This monograph (Marzano, 1998), which is free from http://www.mcrel.org.topics/products/92, describes the three basic approaches (external tests, performance tasks, and portfolios) that a school, district, or state might take to implement standards. Emphasis is on careful planning for standards implementation to ensure that the effects on classrooms are a function of design rather than happenstance. Each approach is reviewed and implications for classroom teachers are discussed. The explication of the three general skill areas which are frequently embedded in performance tasks and student portfolios is thought provoking, and includes the following:

Skill Area 1: Thinking and Reasoning Skills

- Utilizing mental processes that are based on indentifying similarities and differences
- Applying problem-solving, troubleshooting, and decision-making techniques
- Understanding and applying basic principles of argumentation, hypothesis testing and scientific inquiry, and logic and reasoning

Skill Area 2: Communication Skills

- Expressing ideas clearly
- Effectively communicating with diverse audiences in a variety of ways and for a variety of purposes

Skill Area 3: Lifelong Learning Skills

- Demonstrating the ability to work toward the achievement of group goals and demonstrating effective interpersonal skills
- Restraining impulsivity
- Seeking multiple perspectives
- Setting and managing progress toward goals
- Persevering
- Pushing the limits of one's abilities

See Apthorp and colleagues' (2001) free article (available from http://www.mcrel.org/topics/products/103) for a detailed synthesis of research findings about standards-based education practice (particularly with respect to literacy and mathematics).

- Apthorp, H., Dean, C., Florian, J., Lauer, P., Reichardt, R., Sanders, N., & Snow-Renner, R. (2001). "Standards in classroom practice research synthesis." Aurora, CO: Mid-continent Research for Education and Learning.

Also see "Suggested Reading for Further Learning" (Maintaining High Expectations and Developing Critical Thinking Skills) at the end of Part II of this book.

ELEMENT 4: COMPONENTS OF INSTRUCTION

Several principals we studied have used Danielson's (2007, 2008) *Framework for Teaching* (see Figure 13.7) to define the components of teachers' professional practice. This framework (i.e., rubric) of teaching tasks, which has been documented through empirical studies and theoretical research, focuses on improving student learning. It is a research-based set of instructional components (divided into four domains consisting of 76 smaller elements), aligned to instructional standards, and grounded in a constructivist view of learning and teaching (i.e., emphasis is on development of personal schemas and ability to reflect on one's experiences as well as on the social nature of learning; students construct meaning from values, beliefs, and experiences; and multiple outcomes are expected). The framework serves as a basis for conversations with teachers, as principals work to improve teaching. In fact, the framework has been adopted and adapted for use in principal and peer observations and teacher evaluation in several of the districts of principals we studied. Principals stated that they and their teachers used the framework in their mentoring, coaching, professional learning, and teacher-evaluation processes. (Note: Software that codes/aligns observation notes with the framework's rubric and facilitates interpretation and teaching-pattern discovery over time and in different situations is available from www.charlottedanielson.com.)

Figure 13.7 The Framework for Teaching: Components of Professional Practice

Domain 1: Planning and Preparation	Domain 2: The Classroom Environment
❏ Demonstrating knowledge of content and pedagogy ❏ Demonstrating knowledge of students ❏ Setting instructional outcomes ❏ Demonstrating knowledge of resources ❏ Designing coherent instruction ❏ Designing student assessments	❏ Creating an environment of respect and rapport ❏ Establishing a culture for learning ❏ Managing classroom procedures ❏ Managing student behavior ❏ Organizing physical space
Domain 3: Instruction	Domain 4: Professional Responsibilities
❏ Communicating with students ❏ Using questioning and discussion techniques ❏ Engaging students in learning ❏ Using assessment in instruction ❏ Demonstrating flexibility and responsiveness	❏ Reflecting on teaching ❏ Maintaining accurate records ❏ Communicating with families ❏ Participating in a professional community ❏ Growing and developing professionally ❏ Showing professionalism

SOURCE: Danielson (2007).

ELEMENT 5: STUDENT ABILITIES THAT TEACHING STRATEGIES SHOULD ENHANCE

Research has confirmed that teachers can make a substantial difference in student achievement. (For a brief review of this body of research, see Blase & Blase, 2004). Therefore, many school-reform efforts (e.g., the No Child Left Behind Act), have focused on enhancing the quality of teaching. Accordingly, we found that high-performing principals expected teachers to design classroom instruction that develops specific student abilities, thereby reliably improving student achievement. We also found that these principals specifically referenced the school-effects research that undergirds the use of instructional strategies linked to developing student abilities, especially that of Marzano (2000) and Marzano, Pickering, and Pollock (2001). As mentioned earlier, this research includes a meta-analysis of more than 30 years of research on instruction and student achievement. (See Figure 13.8.) Our analysis indicates that principals encouraged the use of the following 10 instructional practices associated with higher levels of student achievement, and they supported extensive professional learning opportunities based on these instructional practices for all instructional personnel.

Figure 13.8   Student Abilities That Teaching Strategies Should Enhance

1. Identifying similarities and differences (comparing, classifying, and creating metaphors and analogies)

2. Summarizing and note taking (analyzing, sifting, and synthesizing information)

3. Reinforcing effort and providing recognition (teaching that effort enhances achievement and recognizing identified levels of performance)

4. Doing homework and practicing (providing opportunities to learn and to practice)

5. Representing knowledge (helping students generate nonlinguistic representations of information, such as graphic organizers, pictures and pictographs, mental pictures, concrete representations, and kinesthetic activities)

6. Participating in cooperative learning groups (creating opportunities to develop positive interdependence, face-to-face interaction, individual and group accountability, interpersonal and small group skills, and group processing)

7. Setting objectives and providing feedback (helping students set learning goals and providing timely feedback)

8. Generating and testing hypotheses (helping students generate and test hypotheses through systems analysis, problem solving, decision making, historical investigation, experimental inquiry, and invention)

9. Using cues, questions, and advance organizers (using helpful guides to the learning)

10. Activating prior knowledge (helping students retrieve specific types of knowledge, such as vocabulary and details, how to organize ideas, and using related skills and processes)

Note: A description of these research-based strategies that improve student achievement are available as a free download (see Marzano, Gaddy, & Dean, 2000; http://www.mcrel.org/PDF/Instruction/5992TG_What_Works.pdf).

An extensive book about these strategies, *Classroom Instruction That Works: Research-Based Strategies for Increasing Student Achievement* (Marzano, Pickering, & Pollock, 2001) and a coordinated handbook, *A Handbook for Classroom Instruction That Works* (Marzano, Norford, Paynter, Pickering, & Gaddy, 2005) can be purchased.

SOURCE: Adapted from Marzano (2000, 2003).

See "Suggested Reading for Further Learning" (School Effects Research, Integrating Curriculum, and Technology in Learning) at the end of Part II of this book.

ELEMENT 6: EFFECTIVE TEACHING PRACTICES ACROSS CONTENT AREAS

High-performing principals also expected teachers to refine their teaching by emphasizing the use of research-driven practices for different content areas. For a comprehensive list of these practices, see Figure 13.9.

Figure 13.9 Enhancing Student Learning Through Research-Driven Practices Across Content Areas

EFFECTIVE GENERAL PRACTICES

Parental involvement

Graded homework

Aligned time on task

Direct teaching

Advance organizers

Teaching of learning strategies

Tutoring

Mastery learning

Cooperative learning

Adaptive education

EFFECTIVE PRACTICES IN THE CONTENT AREAS

The Arts

Direct instruction

Immediate feedback

Interdisciplinary learning

Questioning techniques

Reflecting on learning and nonlearning

Individual performance

Use of creative drama and theater

Visual and aural thinking

Sequencing for understanding

Use of psychomotor principles

Correct body use

Improving memory

Instruction about the role of symbols

Nonverbal aids to reading

Focus on the arts as separate disciplines

Arts and special needs students

Understanding culture in and through the arts

Foreign Language

Beginning instruction early

Language acquisition and opportunities for interaction

Communicative language practice

Instruction in learning strategies

Instruction in listening and reading for meaning

Writing instruction

Explicit grammar instruction

Integration of culture

Appropriate assessment of student progress

Use of technology

Health Education

Developing personal competence

Developing social competence

Practice in goal setting and decision making

Development of values awareness

Practice in critical analysis of health information

Activity-oriented, interactive learning

Using the student as teacher

Encouraging and developing parental involvement

Language Arts

Extensive reading

Interactive learning

Extension of background knowledge

Instruction in strategic reading and writing

Interrelated activities

Teaching critical reading and writing skills

Discussion and analysis

Emphasis on the writing process

Balanced reading and writing

Early intervention

Exposure to different types of literature

Appropriate assessment

Oral Communication

Improving oral communication competence

Addressing voice and articulation

Reducing oral-communication anxiety

Emphasizing communication ethics

Facilitating interpersonal and small-group communication

Increasing listening effectiveness

Developing media literacy

Mathematics

Opportunity to learn

Focus on learning

Learning new concepts and skills while solving problems

Opportunities for invention and practice

Openness to student solution methods and student interaction

(Continued)

Figure 13.9 (Continued)

Small-group learning

Whole-class discussion

Number sense

Concrete materials

Student use of calculators

Physical Education

Time for practice

Appropriate, meaningful practice

Cognitive engagement

Content sequencing

Spiral curriculum

Developmental program focus

Administrative support

Science

Learning-cycle approach

Collaborative learning

Analogies

Wait time

Concept mapping

Computer simulations

Microcomputer-based laboratories

Systematic approaches in problem solving

Conceptual understanding in problem solving

Science-technology society

Real-life situations

Discrepant events

Social Studies

Thoughtful classrooms

Jurisprudential teaching

Appropriate classroom environment

Teaching critical thinking

Support for concept development

Effective questioning

Cognitive-prejudice reduction

Computer technology

Student participation in the community

Constructivist teaching

SOURCE: Adapted from Cawelti (2004).

ELEMENT 7: ORDERING AND PACING OF CONTENT AND INSTRUCTIONAL STRATEGIES

Effective curriculum design requires far more than the use of particular instructional strategies; it also requires attention to learning goals established by the teacher, the proper organization of goals, activities to help students meet goals, and effective spacing and pacing of activities (Marzano, Pickering, & Pollock, 2001). Principals in our study expected careful sequencing of instructional strategies and often referred teachers to published planning guides. One excellent guide is outlined in Figure 13.10.

See "Suggested Reading for Further Learning" (Cooperative Learning) at the end of Part II of this book.

Figure 13.10   Planning Guide for Use of Instructional Strategies

When Strategies Might be Used at the Beginning of a Unit

Setting Learning Goals

1. Identify clear learning goals.

2. Allow students to identify and record their own learning goals.

When Strategies Might Be Used During a Unit

Monitoring Learning Goals

1. Provide students feedback and help them self-assess their progress toward achieving their goals.

2. Ask students to keep track of their achievement of the learning goals and of the effort they are expending to achieve the goals.

3. Periodically celebrate legitimate progress toward learning goals.

Introducing New Knowledge

1. Guide students in identifying and articulating what they already know about the topics.

2. Provide students with ways of thinking about the topic in advance.

3. Ask students to compare the new knowledge with what is known.

4. Have students keep notes on the knowledge addressed in the unit.

5. Help students represent the knowledge in nonlinguistic ways, periodically sharing these representations with others.

6. Ask students to work sometimes individually, but other times in cooperative groups.

Practicing, Reviewing, and Applying Knowledge

1. Assign homework that requires students to practice, review, and apply what they have learned; and, be sure to give students explicit feedback as to the accuracy of all of their homework.

(Continued)

Figure 13.10 (Continued)

> 2. Engage students in long-term projects that involve generating and testing hypotheses.
>
> 3. Have students revise the linguistic and nonlinguistic representations of knowledge in their notebooks as they refine their understanding of the knowledge.
>
> **When Strategies Might Be Used at the End of a Unit**
>
> *Helping Students Determine How Well They Have Achieved Their Goals*
>
> 1. Provide students with clear assessments of their progress on each learning goal.
>
> 2. Have students assess themselves on each learning goal and compare these assessments with those of the teacher.
>
> 3. Have students articulate what they have learned about the content and about themselves as learners.

SOURCE: Marzano, Pickering, and Pollock (2001).

ELEMENT 8: ADDRESSING DIVERSE STUDENTS' NEEDS

A key premise of contemporary (or progressive) legislation (e.g., the No Child Left Behind Act) is that schools should provide a high-quality education to all students. Despite the extensive and, at times, overwhelming reporting and accountability requirements called for by this legislation, the principals we studied embraced their responsibility to educate students with diverse needs and cultural and economic backgrounds. Clearly, these principals were consumers of research, and they worked hard in their schools to implement research-based practices. To illustrate, they investigated up-to-date resources to help teachers design appropriate instruction. For example, at www.mcrel.org, one can find research reports focused on student populations such as culturally and linguistically diverse students, students who are at risk, students with special needs, students in rural communities, American students, and students who are low performing.

Principals also took an active role in the search for research-based interventions for learning-challenged students, shared their findings with teachers, and supported teachers in their implementation and monitoring of these strategies. See, for instance:

- www.interventionscentral.org. A comprehensive site on response to intervention, includes hundreds of free research-based interventions for students who are at risk, in remedial education, special education students, and students who are in a student support team process. One can download free staff training materials, access a warehouse of curriculum-based measurement tools, and print endless RTI-related forms for record keeping.
- www.whatworksclearinghouse.com. This Web site has free practice guides in various content areas, topic reports that summarize findings from topic-specific intervention reports, specific interventions within topic areas, ratings of their effectiveness, and improvement indices for relevant outcomes, as well as a what works documents library.
- www.centeroninstruction.org. This site has a plethora of information on K–12 instruction in the reading, math, science, special education, and English language learning strands, and one can follow links to topic-based materials, syntheses of recent research, and exemplars of best practice.
- www.preventionaction.org/reference/best-evidence-encyclopedia-bee. This site has a section called "Best Evidence Encyclopedia" that includes reliable and unbiased reviews of educational programs, strategies, and interventions that answer principals' and teachers' questions about what works.
- www.rti4success.org. This Web site has a library of free RTI materials and resources with numerous links to other sites that offer free online training and Webinars on various aspects of RTI, such as the link to the National Center on Progress Monitoring located at www.student progress.org.

In addition, high-performing principals supported and participated in myriad forms of peer collaboration among teachers to address such students' diverse needs. For instance, principals recognized special educators' expertise in reaching and teaching students who were struggling with academic concepts; thus, in these schools, special educators were valued as in-house resources and were regularly called upon as peer collaborators when students had conceptual difficulties.

See "Suggested Reading for Further Learning" (Addressing Every Child's Needs and Challenged and Culturally Different Students) at the end of Part II of this book.

ELEMENT 9: USE OF TECHNOLOGY IN INSTRUCTION

Technological tools are a critical part of today's effective instructional environment (Fox, 2008). In addition to the deployment of technology teams, committees, and specialists, and in addition to the use of technology for decision making about all-school management matters (such as in the data-driven instructional system discussed in Part I), the principals in our study asserted that excellent teaching includes sophisticated use of technology in the classroom, and such use requires careful integration of technology into the curriculum and alignment with learning goals. Therefore, principals provided best-practice professional learning programs and peer coaching in technology literacy and leadership (e.g., integration specialists), opportunities to visit model schools, access to online and networked learning communities for teachers, access to technology tools, and funding to maintain highly effective professional development. Specifically, principals of high-performing schools provided access to and encouraged the use of resources such as:

- Educational technology newsletters;
- Meta-analyses of the effectiveness of teaching and learning with technology on student achievement (including high-performing, high-technology schools with predominantly low-income, African American, or Latino populations);
- Reviews of model professional development programs on technology;
- Reviews of state-level policy for K–12 online learning;
- Reports of the effects of technology use on teaching, learning, and leading;
- Guides for evaluating educational software; and
- Guides for data-driven decision making about technology.

For excellent matrices on technology policy development, planning, professional development, assessment, and evaluation, see the "Technology in Education" section of the North Central Regional Educational Laboratory's Web site (http://ncrel.org.tech).

See "Suggested Reading for Further Learning" (Technology in Learning) at the end of Part II of this book.

ELEMENT 10:
MODELS OF TEACHING

High-performing principals encouraged all teachers to become skillful at using a variety of teaching models, concepts, and approaches. To illustrate, principals discussed the use of jurisprudential inquiry and group investigation in social studies classes, role-playing and social inquiry in literature classes, and the use of advance organizers and mnemonics in most classes. *Models of Teaching* (Joyce, Weil, & Calhoun, 2009), a highly-respected staple of university instruction on teaching, includes a description of the research base for each model within the four families of models (i.e., information-processing, social, personal, and behavioral-systems models), instructions for how to teach using a model, and peer-observation protocols keyed to the models (see Figure 13.11).

Figure 13.11 Families of Teaching Models

Information-Processing Models

Inductive thinking

Concept attainment

Scientific inquiry

Inquiry training

Cognitive growth

Advance organizer

Mnemonics

Synectics

Social Models

Group investigation

Social inquiry

Jurisprudential inquiry

Laboratory method

Role playing

Positive interdependence

Structured social inquiry

Personal Models

Nondirective teaching

Awareness training

Classroom meeting

Self-actualization

Conceptual systems

Behavioral-Systems Models

Social learning

Mastery learning

Programmed learning

Simulation

Direct teaching

Anxiety reduction

SOURCE: Joyce, Weil, & Calhoun (2009).

ELEMENT 11: CLASSROOM MANAGEMENT (DISCIPLINE)

High-performing principals understood that frequent misbehavior by students (i.e., poor student management in classrooms and throughout the school) would be experienced by teachers as invasive and a constant struggle that interrupts learning and requires an inordinate amount of teachers' and administrators' time and energy; many noted that they had learned this early in their careers.

> *Never a day went by that some discipline problem wasn't going on . . . and serious discipline issues can have far-ranging ramifications.*
>
> —High School Principal

Thus, beyond the challenges of encouraging excellent classroom instruction, developing skills to support the instructional growth of teachers, and helping teachers work with diverse students, high-performing principals also helped teachers support their classroom instruction with *classroom management practices that contribute to student achievement*. This often necessitated professional learning about classroom and schoolwide student management principles based on meta-analyses of relevant research. Figure 13.12 identifies effective, research-based classroom-management actions.

Figure 13.13 presents an excellent set of learning activities designed to improve student management.

Figure 13.12   Teachers' Research-Based Classroom-Management Actions

Classroom management is defined as teachers' actions related to

1. Establishing and enforcing rules and procedures:

   General classroom behavior

   Beginning the day or period

   Transitions and interruptions

   Materials and equipment

   Group work

   Seat work

2. Carrying out disciplinary actions:

   Teacher reaction

   Tangible recognition

   Direct cost

   Group contingency

   Home contingency

3. Maintaining effective teacher-student relationships:

   Establish clear learning goals

   Exhibit assertive behavior

   Flexible learning goals

   Personal interest in students

   Equitable and positive behavior

   Appropriate response to incorrect response

   Practice "being with" people

SOURCE: Marzano, Marzano, and Pickering (2003).

Figure 13.13 Activities for Developing Research-Based Schoolwide and Classroom-Management Systems

---

ACTIVITY 1

Define classroom management.

Effective classroom management should be understood as a gestalt based on several interdependent components: (1) an engaging curriculum; (2) working with anger, projection, and depression; (3) students as responsible citizens; (4) the teacher as a self-aware model; (5) classroom-management skills; (6) working with resistance, conflict, and stress; and (7) robust instruction. If any of these components is neglected, the whole process may be compromised and result in discipline problems (Hanson, 1998).

Educators should visit the "Education Topics: Classroom Management" section at the Association for Supervision and Curriculum Web site: http://www.ascd.org/. Here, practitioners discuss their views on classroom management; this can provide a basis for collaborative discussions about creating an appropriate classroom-management system in your school.

ACTIVITY 2

Consider the implications of the best research on classroom and schoolwide student management.

Research indicates that effectively managed classrooms can make a significant difference in students' achievement gains—as much as 20 percentile points of gain! However, only recently has research clarified what teachers actually *do* to create effectively managed classrooms. As a whole-school study group, refine your thinking about classroom management by either viewing the PowerPoint program or reading the informative books listed below. These resources draw from more than 100 studies of classroom management to explain the four most important general components of effective classroom management and their impact on student engagement and achievement.

- Download the free PowerPoint presentation produced from the research-based approach to classroom management, with many examples: http://www.marzanoandassociates.com/html/resources.htm#powerpoint (see classroom management).
- Read these books:

  Marzano, R. J., Marzano, J. S., & Pickering, D. J. (2003). *Classroom Management That Works: Research-Based Strategies for Every Teacher.* Alexandria, VA: Association for Supervision and Curriculum Development.

  Marzano, R. J., Gaddy, B. B., Foseid, M. C., Foseid, M. P., & Marzano, J. S. (2005). *A Handbook for Classroom Management That Works.* Alexandria, VA: Association for Supervision and Curriculum Development.

A Summary of the research on student management:

Based on the sophisticated meta-analysis of research on school-, teacher-, and student-level variables that affect student achievement (Marzano, 2000, 2003), the authors of the PowerPoint program and books referred to above describe and apply this knowledge base in the areas of student and schoolwide student management (i.e., discipline). The authors identify concrete action steps educators should take as they establish rules and procedures, use effective disciplinary interventions, build positive student-teacher relationships, and develop a sound mental set to overcome the most difficult situations. Real-life classroom stories illustrate how to

---

(Continued)

Figure 13.13 (Continued)

get every class off to a good start, involve students in classroom management, and develop effective schoolwide management policies. These books also provide practical strategies based on substantial research for establishing rules, procedures, and disciplinary interventions. Topics such as establishing an orderly environment, developing policies that articulate rules and codes of behavior, implementing thoughtful prevention of disruptions, consistent enforcement, teacher-student relationships, and management at the school level are discussed.

In brief, effective classroom management is characterized by teacher behaviors such as high dominance and cooperation, use of rubrics to clarify learning goals, assertive—not aggressive—control, with-it-ness (i.e., being attentive to all that is happening), mastering the art of displaying little discernible reaction (i.e., emotional objectivity), and active speaking and listening with students. The principal's role in promoting good classroom management includes establishment of (1) *schoolwide rules and consequences* (e.g., for repeated disruption of class, bullying, verbal harassment, disregarding the safety of others, use of drugs, gang behavior, sexual harassment, fighting, theft, and truancy) and (2) *a discipline hierarchy* (e.g., Level 1—behavioral offenses are handled by the teacher; Level 2—behavioral offenses are addressed by the administration or the safety and discipline committee, with due process provided; and Level 3—behavioral offenses warrant immediate suspension or expulsion.)

ACTIVITY 3

As a study group, apply what you have learned about student management and how it influences student achievement.

Devise a comparison chart: On the left side, list several effective and ineffective features of your classroom's and your school's student-management system. On the right side, list changes you could make (consistent with the research you have studied) to improve student management; for example, minimizing interruptions, professional development for teachers about group work, clarifying learning goals, increasing teacher with-it-ness). Next, discuss what actions you should take. Be sure to include the purpose of your management plan, how you will establish schoolwide behavior expectations, and how you will teach and sustain behavior expectations. Describe how you will correct problem behaviors, collect and utilize data, and maintain the plan over time.

Our study demonstrates that high-performing principals fashioned exemplary, far-reaching subsystems to deal with student discipline. Such subsystems were comprehensive; they typically required active involvement from all stakeholders, both individuals and teams of assistant principals, teachers, counselors, students, parents, and staff. Frequently, principals used the materials listed above or similar materials for professional learning sessions designed to align faculty members' and administrators' approach to discipline and to create student-management policies and procedures based on solid research.

Everyone is on board with discipline . . . We have eyes and ears everywhere.

—Elementary School Principal

We can't handpick the children or the parents we get, but we can handle them correctly. Bottom line, I expect the child to be responsible, I expect the teachers to have discipline plans for inside their walls (the assistant principal signs off), and I expect parent support. Students and parents get a copy of the discipline plan, they sign it, and we file it, so everybody knows the plan. All adults in our school are empowered to enforce discipline. When rules are broken, we follow the plan, with teachers and administrators facilitating it in a positive manner. We also have specific procedures, which are pretty black and white; too many principals are wishy-washy today.

—Elementary School Principal

Proactive discipline is teaching what behavior is appropriate. We have high expectations and we give out consequences, but we make sure students know what they did and what to better choose next time. Good discipline means that most kids don't keep coming back.

—Middle School Principal

Principals used collaborative-empowering approaches with individuals and teams to elicit deep levels of ownership essential to creating and maintaining effective discipline in the school.

You can't have an effective school if discipline is out of control and if the school climate is fraught with anxiety. All your stakeholders—your administrative team, teachers, and students—have to buy into having a safe school, free of anxiety. By having a collaborative decision-making approach to discipline, you get buy in, and your stakeholders support you.

—High School Principal

Discipline is one of the principal's jobs that can become overwhelming, can consume you to the point that it takes you completely away from the instructional focus of the school. So, you need to use a collaborative model of management for discipline, which is based on building capacity in the school. We don't call it discipline; we call it safety or school climate.

—High School Principal

High-performing principals promoted a positive approach to discipline:

Our discipline team set up a prosocial approach; we reward staying out of trouble and we have consequences for inappropriate behavior. The kids learn that if they don't shape up, they will lose out on the rewards.

—Middle School Principal

Discipline policies and procedures were designed to be proactive and preventative to reduce discipline problems.

> *We try to be proactive about discipline, so we spend a good deal of time in the summer planning for an environment that will eliminate some behavior. We place students so they have a ways to travel between classes, we keep teachers in close proximity, we route large groups of students through certain hallways to avoid disrupting classes, and we require passes for students to go to the bathrooms. When school starts we make sure everyone is on the same page.*
>
> —Middle School Principal

Operationally, the comprehensive approaches to discipline developed by the principals we studied included collaborative-planning sessions, efficient communication mechanisms (e.g., handbooks, newsletters, Web sites, e-mail, telephone calls), clear procedures (e.g., monitoring referrals, reward-and-punishment systems, debriefings, feedback and evaluation), and full use of technology.

> *Monitoring the data is crucial, and we use a computer program that does wonders; it tells us what time of day, time of year, and where we have [discipline] occurrences. We monitor these data all year long and share everything with our discipline team because we can't afford to let anything get out of hand before trying to do something about it.*
>
> —Middle School Principal

In part, a comprehensive approach to discipline also required educating parents, even difficult or negative parents, to become positively involved in their children's behavior.

> *There's a cycle to parents' response to discipline issues. Response number one is shock and remorse. Response number two is, "Now that I've had a chance to think about this and talk with my child, I have some serious questions." Suddenly, all the blame is shifted to me and the bus driver, for instance. We must have created the situation where the kid threw something . . . I teach assistant principals to be consistent and firm at this time, to never tolerate any disrespect from parents, and to avoid a tone of voice that tells the parent she or he is horrible and the child is horrible because all that does is enrage the parent and make the child angry and determined to continue being bad. Some parents will become your ally if they know your goal is to save the child and not to beat the child down.*
>
> —High School Principal

Sometimes, angry, aggressive parents required a more no-nonsense approach:

> *I just won't tolerate disrespect from parents; I'll tell them, "You have been given a warning and you are not allowed to come back on this campus, although you can send your spouse back. We'll reconvene later and have this meeting without you. If you do come back, you will be arrested." A lot of principals won't take that stand, but I think it's in the best interest of our school.*
>
> —High School Principal

In many high-performing schools, every person, including support personnel such as bus drivers, was trained to address discipline in a constructive manner:

> *Riding on a bus is not my favorite thing because I get carsick, but it shows the bus driver that you care; in fact, I have a meeting with a bus driver tomorrow, and I'll try to help her out.*
>
> —Middle School Principal

Principals also involved custodial and food-services staff members in student-management training and empowered them to redirect students or to handle students' transgressions; in fact, these staff members were highly valued for stimulating schoolwide positive behavior and compliance to rules as well as enhancing school climate.

Once discipline subsystems (e.g., beginning the day, establishing goals, making transitions, being assertive) were fully and effectively developed, implemented, and routinized (although all required occasional tweaking), principals' direct, day-to-day involvement was minimal. Principals reported that this freed up significant amounts of time and energy that they and the assistant principals devoted to instructional leadership and school improvement.

> *Now, I get involved in discipline issues only with the most serious offenses—drugs, weapons, serious fighting, very difficult parents.*
>
> —Middle School Principal

From the principals' perspective, effective discipline subsystems had strong positive effects on classroom teaching, student achievement, and instructional leadership.

> *In the past, we saw discipline as being disconnected from student achievement; but now, a lot of research shows a direct link.*
>
> —Middle School Principal
>
> *The effect on classrooms is high. Students have to feel safe and secure in order to function, but more than that they have to be in an environment free from disruptive people who derail the students' and the teacher's attention. The more we do to maintain a learning environment, the more conducive to student learning it is.*
>
> —Middle School Principal
>
> *Discipline can take up too much time, massive amounts of time that could be spent in classrooms, meeting with teachers, and working with parents to improve curriculum offerings. Massive amounts of time could be spent meeting with parents who are hostile and disgruntled about discipline matters, which impact instruction in a very negative way. You must be fair and consistent about discipline, and you must never, never, never, never allow a student's disruptive behavior to interfere with the education of another child.*
>
> —High School Principal

> *We went from an average of 12 discipline referrals to 1 discipline referral a day by adopting a routine discipline system. Now, our administrators have the time to do more instructionally based things as opposed to dealing with discipline all day long.*
>
> —High School Principal
>
> *Although we now have more students than ever, we have less referrals than ever, and students are more focused on instruction.*
>
> —Elementary School Principal

In sum, high-performing principals' approaches to classroom management are consistent with effective approaches described in the best research (noted in Figure 13.12 on p. 142) and with the approaches of teachers studied by Blase and Blase (2006). (See Figure 13.14.)

Figure 13.14 Lessons From Peer Consultants

Nine Guiding Principles of Classroom Management

1. Match academics to student needs
2. Take a constructive approach (stress cooperation, take a personal interest in students)
3. Insist on student responsibility and invoke natural consequences for misbehavior
4. Do not take discipline problems personally (be emotionally objective)
5. Remain calm and composed (use equitable and positive behavior)
6. Be consistent
7. Consider students' misguided goals when misbehaving
8. Be proactive (be alert to what is happening—with-it-ness)
9. Do not overdo it (be assertive, not aggressive)

Setting Up and Maintaining Classroom Routines

1. Begin the year right
2. Have plans and systems
3. Use warm-ups
4. Use signals
5. Use proximity
6. Adjust seating
7. Track misbehaviors
8. Experiment with varied techniques according to students' issues
9. Use body language
10. Vary approaches to work with challenged and culturally varied students

SOURCE: Adapted from Blase and Blase (2006).

CONSIDERING THE VALUE OF WALK-THROUGHS

All of the high-performing principals we interviewed indicated that teaching and learning were their priority. Once proper subsystems were in place and a context for dialogue about instruction was established, everyone focused on teaching and learning and continuous instructional improvement. Principals and assistant principals provided teachers with various forms of instructional support (e.g., support for professional learning opportunities such as peer coaching, critical-friends talks among groups of supportive peer teachers who observe each other, and action-research teams) consistent with the 11 elements discussed above. Moreover, principals took personal responsibility for classroom observation (i.e., informal walk-throughs). Working with teachers of diverse backgrounds and a variety of skill levels, many principals used various forms of the Downey walk-through model (Downey, Steffy, English, Frase, & Poston, 2004). Such models are grounded in a reflective-practice approach and thus use questions, such as the following, to guide observations and conversations about teaching and learning:

a. How does this teacher align his or her instruction with the curriculum?

b. How is this teacher using research-based best practices?

c. How is this teacher choosing instructional strategies that will impact student achievement?

d. How do I motivate this teacher to be reflective in practice and personally accountable for teaching decisions?

All principals we studied also trained and collaborated with assistant principals, department and grade level chairpersons, and teacher-leaders to properly and routinely conduct classroom walk-throughs.

> *You don't want faculty turning over every two or three years, so department chairpersons and teachers have been prepared to do walk-throughs, make recommendations, help correct weaknesses, and make each person a valuable member of the instructional team. It's nonthreatening.*
>
> —High School Principal
>
> *The assistant principals and I are being trained to do five-minute walk-throughs, walking and seeing what's going on under our roof, seeing if teachers are really following through with learning-focused strategies.*
>
> —Elementary School Principal

In particular, as principals and assistant principals regularly conducted classroom walk-throughs to monitor instruction and to reinforce the school's focus on school improvement, they made sure that their observations were informed by educational research on teaching and learning as defined by the 10 elements described in Figure 13.8 on p. 133.

> *The teachers aren't doing anything for me; they're doing it for the children. That's our focus, continuous improvement, constantly learning. Teachers know that when I visit classrooms all I want to see is what children are doing, and [I want us to] consider how we can do it better. I have high expectations, but I leave teachers a lot of room to be creative.*
>
> —Elementary School Principal
>
> *I have taken the research by Marzano and created a kind of mantra, and I preach: focused curriculum, school safety, student motivation, faculty morale, community. I made a personal decision that I was going to live or die—in classrooms and throughout the school—by those five things. I think a lot of principals get too many balls in the air and lose their focus. I don't neglect anything, but I do try to focus on certain things at different times.*
>
> —Middle School Principal

To increase the efficiency and effectiveness of walk-throughs, principals and assistant principals used "highlights" forms—carefully crafted by their administrative or leadership team, based on relevant research, and adopted by faculty and staff—to provide succinct, meaningful, informal observations of teaching and learning in classrooms. Completed forms were used to provide nonevaluative, constructive feedback to individual teachers and to acknowledge their compliance with the school's adopted, research-based, effective-teaching practices.

> *All of our assistant principals and department chairpersons have had a full day of training on classroom walk-throughs and what to look for in effective instruction. We use a form to note things we see, such as students being on task and active teaching, but we do not write something negative on this form, something that would call for a conversation with the teacher. It's a simple process of inspecting what you expect, focusing on what the kids are learning.*
>
> —High School Principal
>
> *We want to do something that is real, and we want to praise teachers for having child-centered classrooms, so we set a goal for each administrator to do three visits to each teacher. We use little cards with a list of about 15 things we'd like to see going on and a space for comments.*
>
> —Middle School Principal
>
> *The hardest thing to do is to get into classrooms and give teachers feedback; we felt so guilty about it that we made it a goal for the administrative team. We developed our own little form we use to do 10-minute snapshots and make quick remarks.*
>
> —Middle School Principal

> *We asked ourselves what were the things we should legitimately look for and ask about, so our walk-throughs are based on our common language about what we have talked about, and that's our vision. We never do it in an evaluative or judgmental way, though.*
>
> —Elementary School Principal

Walk-throughs provided administrators with valuable information about teaching and learning that they believed could not be obtained in other ways.

> *I have come to the conclusion that you must set aside time to be in classrooms and set aside time to do the paperwork; they're two different entities. Also, you can't do it all in an eight-hour day. As a teacher, I seldom had an administrator in my classroom ... only twice, and I see a problem with that. I can't understand what teachers are going through if I am not in the classrooms. I'm in and out enough to see their concerns, to see if they are having trouble with a strategy.*
>
> —Elementary School Principal
>
> *I carry a little notebook to help me remember who to visit, and one day I might go into 20 rooms and another day only 2 or 3. Sometimes, I expect to stay a few minutes, but I stay thirty. It gives you so much more of a feel of the pulse of the school. The teachers really appreciate it, and it's a deterrent for students [to misbehave].*
>
> —High School Principal
>
> *Some of my principal buddies are at the point they don't visit classrooms; they really and truly need to get out of education. I teach our teachers, but they also teach me so much. I've been out of the classroom for nine years; but if I went back now, I would be the best teacher because of what I have learned from the teachers here.*
>
> —Elementary School Principal

A few principals explained that they were able to collect valuable information about classrooms by simply walking the halls of the school and by visiting with students.

> *In my leadership classes, I learned that management by walking around was the best type of management, so I make a habit of doing that, being out in the school, eating with the children, talking with the children. That becomes part of my evaluation of teaching.*
>
> —Elementary School Principal
>
> *I also observe teachers by walking up and down the hall and watching what's going on in the classrooms. If I'm not even going in the classrooms, I know what's going on. I walk the halls at least three times a day.*
>
> —Elementary School Principal

Making Time for Walk-Throughs

Although high-performing principals reported that their priority was to support teaching and learning in part by creating a systematic approach to classroom walk-throughs, our data also indicate that finding time to conduct walk-throughs on a routine basis, even for veteran principals, was a challenge and required deliberately setting time aside in the face of competing administrative responsibilities; indeed, high-performing principals conscientiously scheduled regular (e.g., daily) blocks of time for walk-throughs, observations, instructional conferences with teachers, and curriculum and professional-development activities. We noted earlier that principals generally fail to overcome administrative responsibilities and fail to devote substantial amounts of time and energy to instructional leadership responsibilities (e.g., Blase & Blase, 2004; Buckley, 2004; Cusick, 2003; Glickman, 2002; Kellogg, 2005).

> *I'm in every classroom every day. I tell my secretary, "I'm going on my wonderful walk now," and then I just walk in and out of every classroom to see what's happening. I schedule it, I put everything else on the sideline, and I do it.*
>
> —Elementary School Principal

> *I formulate an agenda, and I have it in my mind. Every morning, I am like a doctor doing rounds. I can't do 50 classrooms in a day, but I can do them within five days.*
>
> —Elementary School Principal

> *We administrators really hold to the fact that instructional time is dedicated time, time to be with children. Consequently, every morning we are in and out of classrooms, talking with kids, sprinkling or pollinating ideas from classroom to classroom; we are the eyes and ears.*
>
> —Elementary School Principal

> *On occasion, I have visited as many as eight classes in a single department for 5 minutes each, gone back to my office to review and reflect on what I have seen, and then sent an e-mail commending the teachers on certain things or mentioning things I noticed (even if I saw two students off-task, the teacher knows that and will correct it). All those teachers can see that the principal was in the classes, noticed things, and they can reflect on that.*
>
> —High School Principal

For a handful of principals we studied, getting into classrooms was more difficult:

> *Though my ideal would be to go into every classroom during every period, which I can seldom do, I do try to see every class every day, to see if teachers are doing what we all embrace. It's very informal, and I don't write anything, though I have thought about using a feedback form.*
>
> —High School Principal

> *I don't get into the classrooms as much as I'd like to, and not enough. We spread responsibilities around; but to be honest, sometimes I just have to stay in my office to get things done . . . deadlines, reports, inventories.*
>
> —Elementary School Principal

Principals believed that teachers appreciated and valued classroom walk-throughs.

> *With walk-throughs, which are informal, I have a way to observe in five minutes, and the staff feel valued when I observe them.*
>
> —High School Principal

> *A lot of times teachers e-mail me with invitations to come to their classrooms to see or participate in what they are doing.*
>
> —Elementary School Principal

CONSIDERING FORMAL EVALUATIONS

For decades, traditional top-down, bureaucratic approaches to supervision of instruction (i.e., an inexorable process of observation, checklists, and judgment with or without conferences) have been challenged by educational scholars (e.g., Blase & Blase, 2004; Glanz, 1995; Pajak, 2000). Clearly, the ritualistic nature of a formal evaluation process, with its attendant fear, stress, and anxiety (for teachers and administrators) has interfered with teachers' professional development. Interestingly, principals of high-performing schools rarely discussed formal evaluation as an instructional leadership function or as an instructional improvement vehicle; instead, they typically preferred walk-throughs and other less formal and more constructive approaches to monitor and support classroom instruction and to help teachers improve.

At the same time, principals were bound by district policy to implement evaluation policies and procedures for quality assurance purposes; therefore, when engaged in required formal evaluation processes, they tended to use growth-oriented approaches similar to Danielson's (2002) approach, which includes (1) an initial track for beginning teachers—frequent observations and mentoring; (2) a second track for tenured teachers—self-assessment, goal setting, data collection, study groups, action planning, peer observation and coaching, and an active role in evaluation; and (3) a third track for tenured teachers needing assistance—remediating difficulties and recommending further action.

> *We do formal teacher evaluations pretty frequently, in August and then in mid-January, and we meet with the teacher at the mid point of the year to talk about kids, curriculum issues, and concerns that they might have.*
>
> —Elementary School Principal

I meet with each teacher after an observation, rather than just giving the written feedback. We talk about the great things they did and what might be better. Even for the written feedback, I put a lot of reflection and thought into that, so most of that I do at home.

—Elementary School Principal

Like every school system, we have a set of procedures set in place that have to be followed in evaluating teachers, and we are duty bound to follow them, though the procedures are ever evolving. We observe nontenured teachers three times during the year, and we provide written feedback and face-to-face time to discuss what we observed. The annual evaluation also has to do with the entire set of teacher duties and responsibilities. The hard part, the hurdle, is convincing teachers that it is for the good, because they can think that somebody is out to get them, that there is an X by their name if somebody observes and everything goes wrong. And it's very time consuming for principals if you have a lot of new teachers.

—High School Principal

Being in classes, observing teachers, seeing what's going on, and even teaching classes, meeting with department chairpersons for an hour or two each week—it's all about curriculum and evaluation.

—High School Principal

We all have our share of teachers to observe, and I particularly observe the two instructional lead teachers and the administrators.

—High School Principal

If necessary, I put weak teachers on professional-development plans, and most of the time their work improves. A principal has to decide how much effort to put into the negative side (that may be ultimately terminating a teacher) and how much to put into capacity building; everyone knows, whether they want to admit it or not, there is greater payoff on the capacity-building side.

—High School Principal

A teacher who will not show initiative, will not take responsibility, is a weak link. Once you recognize that you have a weak link, you start the process of strengthening that link, thinking, "I'm not in favor of firing you; I'm in favor of discussing your weakness and helping with specific ways to work on it." You invest in that teacher.

—High School Principal

SUMMARY

This chapter examined our findings about high-performing principals' use of a systems-development approach to the 11 research-based elements (achievement factors, planning, standards, instructional components, student abilities and teaching strategies, teaching for content areas, ordering and pacing, diverse students' needs, technology, models of teaching, and classroom management) as they worked with teachers. Principals' approaches to class-room walk-throughs and formal evaluations were also discussed, and related resources and activities that can be used for school improvement were presented. It is clear that effective instructional leadership (i.e., leadership for school improvement) requires a serious, ongoing commitment to studying the professional knowledge base on the part of the school administrator.

TIPS AND SUGGESTIONS

Observing Instruction and Talking with Teachers

1. Never become complacent and never allow teachers to become complacent. Celebrate the successes of the previous school year, but do not rest on these successes. Talk with teachers who have a tendency toward complacency, and let them know that complacency is not acceptable. Pay attention to teachers via walk-throughs, especially at the beginning of the year.

2. Accept no excuses from administrators, including yourself, for failing to conduct walk-throughs. Provide feedback to teachers and discuss your expectations and the research supporting these expectations.

3. As in the Brazosport model, build reteaching and extension time into your scheduling and pacing. As in the 90/90/90 schools, emphasize writing.

4. Provide teachers with standards, and ask them to self-evaluate after each instructional unit. Suggest that they review summative-assessment data to ascertain whether the data confirm what they believe about the quality of their teaching of a standard.

5. Become a connoisseur of research about teaching and learning, and encourage teachers to do the same.

6. If walk-throughs suggest that a teacher's teaching is not up to the school's standard, schedule a conference. Share your walk-through summaries and any data gathered during observations and discuss concerns (e.g., expectation shortfalls). Provide the teacher with a copy of Figure 13.7, Danielson's 2007 Framework for Teaching: Components of Professional Practice, and provide a copy of best practices for his or her content area. Provide copies of pertinent research and books at no charge to the teacher—and expect results.

7. Require and monitor integration of technology in teaching. Ask the teacher to reflect on your conversations about the use of technology, and set a time to again discuss his or her thoughts and action plan for meeting the school's standard of technology use.

8. Use Marzano's list of most effective teaching strategies (see Figure 13.8) as part of your walk-through–observation list. Expect to see these teaching strategies used consistently. React swiftly and decisively when these teaching strategies and other best practices are not observed during walk-throughs; in such cases, provide copies of pertinent research and books at no charge to the teacher, and expect an instructional return.

(Continued)

(Continued)

9. Take an active role with teachers and students in students' achievement by monitoring student learning that occurs in groups and among those with diverse needs. For example, consider observing "Kid Talk" meetings held by teachers with groups having diverse needs, and occasionally meet with individual students to discuss their learning experiences; such activities encourage and ensure accountability.

10. Require consistent use of technology in all classes and observe for compliance.

11. Ensure that teachers are familiar with and use a variety of teaching models coordinated with content and student needs. (Refer teachers to the work of Joyce, Weil, & Calhoun, 2009.) Engage teachers in dialogue about characteristics, preparation for use, and effective use of the models. (To save time, meet with all new teachers at one time to discuss these models.)

12. Use observations from walk-throughs and data from discipline reports to engage teachers in dialogue about their classroom management plans, skills, and effectiveness. Assist struggling teachers by matching them with strong classroom managers for peer observations and coaching.

13. Make walk-through time a sacrosanct part of your day. Communicate to all stakeholders the value of walk-throughs, and elicit their cooperation in support of this dedicated time. Advise secretarial and other staff that walk-through times are to be interrupted only for emergencies. Provide some type of visual cue to your staff that you are involved in walk-throughs (e.g., some high-performing principals carried a walk-through binder).

Development 14

Principals of high-performing schools provide effective, ongoing professional learning (staff development).

We found that high-performing principals systematically used a number of methods to enhance professional learning in their schools. First, principals were acutely aware of their own need for specific knowledge and skills to advance professional learning in their schools, including

1. An understanding of adult learning and development as it relates to the work of teachers;

2. The ability to help teachers deal with diverse students;

3. The ability to develop teachers' knowledge and skills in the areas of self-development, reflection, collegial sharing, and coaching;

4. The ability to assist in the instructional growth of teachers;

5. An understanding of the relationships among direct assistance to teachers, professional learning, curriculum development, group and organization development, and action research; and

6. The ability to design and implement effective staff development programs.

Consequently, to enhance their professional learning, principals were actively involved as participants in their own professional learning programs and opportunities.

> *I compare test scores of the schools in our county, and I talk with principals of those schools doing better than we are doing. I find out what they are doing and how they are doing it. In some instances, we go visit, and the visits to those schools have been very powerful. We even visit schools outside the county.*
>
> —Elementary School Principal
>
> *Just last week, I went with a group of three teachers to another middle school that has high science scores; they are doing a phenomenal job. Last year, I went with a math study team to another middle school also doing a phenomenal job; we took a whole day, and it was a great experience. Afterwards, we have debriefing sessions, and it's just incredible to hear the teachers' dialogue.*
>
> —Middle School Principal

Principals also actively encouraged teachers to be lifelong learners:

> *I encourage all teachers to be lifelong learners, because things are changing so much; strategies that worked last year might not work this year. One of my goals is to get all the teachers older than 35 to go back to school, especially because of changing performance standards. I also invite colleges to come out and help teachers with going back to school.*
>
> —Elementary School Principal
>
> *I encourage teachers to go back to school. The first principal I had said, "Don't let the teacher next door be more employable than you. Get your master's degree."*
>
> —Middle School Principal

With respect to teachers' professional learning, principals indicated that they provided teachers with opportunities at the school—on the job—to earn staff development credit and that they were flexible about activities teachers needed.

> *By having our own [in-house] staff development, we don't waste valuable time during the school day to go to something that we can do right here.*
>
> —High School Principal
>
> *You have to get it done, but the how is just as important as the what, so our staff development stays in the school. Our teachers can get professional learning units (credit toward new or renewed state credentials) "on the clock." They learn on the job.*
>
> —High School Principal
>
> *At the beginning of each year, the faculty members get a form about staff development on which they document all the different classes they take. I tell them that they can use anything that will build them up and that goes along with our school improvement plan, even if it is offered outside of the school system, and that I will pay for it.*
>
> —Middle School Principal

On-the-job staff development opportunities helped to embed professional learning in the school's culture. Principals valued and showcased faculty members' expertise, having them run faculty meetings in which they presented and modeled teaching strategies. A number of high-performing principals developed and published directories of in-house teaching talents and resources; new and weak teachers were encouraged to access such resources to shore up or enhance their skills.

A PROFESSIONAL LEARNING COMMUNITY

Our findings point out that principals of high-performing schools conceptualized staff development broadly and inclusively as creating professional learning communities (PLCs) in a manner consistent with the research literature. Viable professional learning communities include such elements as peer collaboration, teacher leadership, access to resources, guidelines for best practice, empowerment, constructivist learning, support for the risk taking inherent in transforming one's teaching practice, and instructional leadership (Blase & Blase, 2004; Danielson, 2006, 2007; DuFour, 2003; Hord & Sommers, 2007; Joyce & Showers, 2002; Martin-Kniep, 2004; Roberts & Pruitt, 2003).

> *I wanted to develop a plan for our school to build a professional learning community, which fits very nicely with what we are doing.*
>
> —Elementary School Principal
>
> *Here, everybody's learning from everybody; it's a professional learning community, which is so important.*
>
> —Middle School Principal

Thus, professional learning (i.e., staff development) in high-performing schools is based on action research and classroom experiences, focused on student learning, and designed to be collaborative. Furthermore, principals reported that teachers participating in professional learning in their schools discovered, as did Blase and Blase (2006), that peer collaboration (i.e., informal, spontaneous, timely assistance) by and for teachers not only honored their expertise and professionalism but also promoted inquiry and reflection on teaching (see Figure 14.1).

The principals we studied also described teachers' participation on district-level committees, their work with teachers based on that participation, and other forms of teacher-to-teacher learning, collaboration, and assistance:

> *I'm doing a lot to build leadership capacity in the school. For example, I have a teacher who is struggling with a strategy work with another teacher who is very good at it.*
>
> —Elementary School Principal

Figure 14.1   The Value of Teachers Teaching Teachers: Excerpts From Research

- [It is] clear that peer consultation among teachers is at the crux, indeed, is the very heart of school improvement. In peer consultation, teachers spontaneously, gently, and skillfully help each other; teachers teach teachers about teaching; and they collaboratively solve the complex problems of teaching in today's schools. This is a natural marriage of self-help and spirit among teachers whose time has come. (p. 24)
- Without a doubt, learning to teach and to solve the myriad, complex problems of teaching are challenges of the first order, and this often necessitates working effectively with other teachers. Our study demonstrates that peer consultants help colleague teachers create a bridge between knowledge and practice through practical reasoning and reflection (e.g., thinking and elaborating on thinking to connect it to practice). We also found that in teacher-to-teacher collaborative talk, the subtleties of teachers' knowledge were revealed and examined for merit and adaptation to the problems at hand. (p. 46)
- Naturally occurring collaboration expands teachers' repertoires of teaching and learning strategies, increases teachers' ability to meet diverse students' needs, enhances teachers' confidence and self-esteem, and increases teachers' commitment to continuing professional growth and development. Peer consultants build healthy relationships with [other] teachers by communicating, caring, and developing trust; exploiting the knowledge base; planning and organizing with teachers for learning; showing and demonstrating different kinds of lessons and sharing professional expertise and artifacts; and guiding teachers for classroom management. (pp. 111–112)

Conclusions About Peer Consultation

Teachers can and should learn from each other.

Teachers can and should be models for each other.

Teachers can and should share their motivation and inspiration with each other.

Teachers can and should reflect, discuss, and debate instructional matters with their colleagues.

Teachers can and should learn about cognition and learning from colleagues.

Teachers can and should use their own classrooms and artifacts from their teaching as the context for learning from peers.

Teachers can and should help each other learn how to deal with students' behavior. (pp. 112–113)

SOURCE: Blase and Blase (2006).

Our leadership team attends conferences and does presentations at other schools as well. They are out there, serving on district committees, so they know what's going on and so our teachers here get the benefit of having first-hand knowledge from them. It eliminates some of the teachers' fears, getting information from somebody directly involved in instructional initiatives; plus, they're not wasting their time learning something new incorrectly and inefficiently.

—Middle School Principal

> *Every March, we do a needs assessment, vote on the items, and then have a schoolwide retreat. We select only the top items for work at the retreat, have teachers make the presentations, and invite presenters from other regional high schools. Then, teachers follow up during the year.*
>
> —High School Principal

> *I encourage teachers who are working on advanced degrees to share research on effective practices with their colleagues.*
>
> —Elementary School Principal

> *All of our teachers observe each other and share in faculty meetings what they have observed.*
>
> —High School Principal

> *We do a two-year mentoring program with our new teachers. In that, we have monthly meetings and continuous contact.*
>
> —Middle School Principal

> *The grade-level lead teachers automatically mentor the new teachers; they just take them by the hand and guide them. They are nurtured by all the grade-level teachers, who guide them or send them to a counselor or administrator if needed.*
>
> —Elementary School Principal

THE RIGHT APPROACH

Specifically, analysis of our data indicates that high-performing principals' approaches to professional learning involved studying the teaching-learning knowledge base, contextualizing it ("personalizing it") for their particular school, and embedding it in the school culture.

> *Every school has a different culture, and staff development has to be personalized to each school. For example, it wasn't clear to us what differentiated instruction was and just how we could use it until we personalized it, owned it, saw what it meant to us, and understood why it was important to us.*
>
> —Middle School Principal

> *I have provided staff development presentations and held discussions and dialogues to learn the research on best practices using learning-focused strategies.*
>
> —Elementary School Principal

> *Our data team and curriculum team were asked by faculty to train them; it was a grass-roots thing. Then, two of our most reluctant teachers were the first to jump on the bandwagon and get trained. Now, everyone is so excited, and I will definitely help to schedule all of it.*
>
> —Elementary School Principal

Our teachers are part of the staff development decisions from the beginning, and they tell me what they want to learn that will support their efforts in the class-room. Teachers set the goals, and the goals are related to the school plan.

—Middle School Principal

You need teachers who are leaders, who can pull others along.

—Elementary School Principal

Generally, principals aligned professional development plans with a form of best practice. Highlights of an excellent toolkit for professional development based on the National Awards Program for Model Professional Development can be found in Figure 14.2 (Hassel, 1999). Professional development was also consistent with the principles of adult learning as pioneered by Malcolm Knowles (Knowles, Holton, & Swanson, 1998) (e.g., adults are self-directed, have a foundation of life experiences and knowledge, are goal oriented, are relevancy oriented, are practical, and need to be shown respect).

Figure 14.2 Action Planning for Professional Development

Step One: Designing Professional Development

1. Include professional development participants and organizers in the professional development design process.

2. Make a clear plan that describes
   a. How professional development supports the school's or district's long-term plan;
   b. A professional development needs assessment process;
   c. Professional development goals;
   d. Professional development content, process, and activities;
   e. Research that supports the chosen content or process for professional development;
   f. Resources available to support professional development; and
   g. Professional development evaluation steps.
      Share the plan.

Step Two: Implementing Professional Development

   a. Stay abreast of best practices.
   b. Ensure district policies support professional development.
   c. Identify critical implementation factors.
   d. Identify a process to ensure successful implementation and problem solving.
   e. Ensure that resources remain available.
   f. Make professional development part of everyday school experiences.

Step Three: Evaluating and Improving Professional Development

   a. Ensure implementation of the evaluation plan.
   b. Schedule time to review and improve the evaluation process.

Step Four: Sharing Professional Development Learning

   a. Keep records of professional development decisions in order to guide future decisions.
   b. Keep materials organized and accessible.

SOURCE: Adapted from Hassel (1999).

For a guide to creating a comprehensive professional development strategic plan, see *Professional Development Criteria: A Study Guide for Effective Professional Development* (Colorado Statewide Systemic Initiative for Mathematics and Science [CONNECT], 1999) at www.mcrel.org. This guide includes goals related to (1) *context* (i.e., the when, where, and why of professional development that address the organization and the nature of the system in which change will occur), (2) *process* (i.e., the how of professional development, including the way activities are planned, organized, carried out, and followed up), and (3) *content* (i.e., the what of professional development, including new knowledge, skills, and understanding that are the foundation of academic disciplines and pedagogical processes).

GOING FURTHER

Appointment by the principal (or, alternatively, designation by peer teachers) of a student-achievement coach in a school is an example of the natural outgrowth of the kind of teacher-to-teacher assistance and collaboration discussed above. This has been done successfully in a Colorado school district, where coaches often engage in activities such as (1) providing support, mentoring, and coaching for new teachers; (2) facilitating training and coaching for all teachers in adopted instructional programs; (3) coordinating with district instructional leaders or directors; (4) facilitating training and coaching in differentiation, classroom management, effective instruction, standards-based instruction, data-driven instruction, and teaching for diverse learners; (5) collaborating with the principal, individual teachers, and teams of teachers; (6) assisting with data collection regarding the impact of activities on student achievement; (7) supporting the school improvement team; (8) assisting with design and implementation of all building-level professional development; (9) coteaching and modeling instruction; (10) attending district training and support sessions; (11) assisting in developing a professional learning community; (12) facilitating protocols for looking at student work to drive instructional decisions; and (13) coordinating coaching cadres (see a sample job description for this position at the Web site of the National Staff Development Council, www.ascd.org).

A MULTITUDE OF PERSONALIZED LEARNING OPPORTUNITIES

Principals of high-performing schools indicated that they also encouraged teachers to engage in a variety of other professional learning opportunities such as taking courses focused on school improvement, visiting other schools with exemplary programs that might help them address deficiencies, enrolling in advanced degree programs that would enhance their instructional and curriculum-development skills, participating in retreats designed to address instructional improvement, and various forms of mentoring one another on both a routine and an as-needed basis (see Figure 14.3 for examples of useful professional learning activities).

Figure 14.3 Variations on Staff Development Activities and Strategies: Beyond Lecture-Style Workshops

- Learning from online education portals (education portals provide coaching and guidance to teachers in order to strengthen a standards-based curriculum, provide formative assessments, provide equitable access to resources, and support high-quality teaching. Portals may include, for example, subscriptions, data systems, content standards, lesson plans, courses of study, research-based training models, model-classroom examples, interactive media, Web resources, listservs, and online portfolios).
- Peer coaching
- Critical friends talks
- Protocols for examining student work
- Portfolio development
- Mentoring
- Observing in classrooms
- Lesson study
- Content-specific staff development programs
- Study groups
- Research-based evaluations
- Technology coaching
- Action research
- Examining standards-based multimedia resources

SOURCE: Adapted from SEDTA (2008); Web site of the National Staff Development Council, www.nsdc.org (2008).

A GOOD USE OF MONEY

When possible, principals used certified substitute teachers to fill in for regular teachers so they could attend staff development sessions. This enhanced instruction during the teacher's absence.

> *Sometimes, teachers are away from the classroom a lot for training, but we have excellent, certified substitute teachers so kids don't lose instructional time. Letting teachers go for development is a balancing act between teacher development and student learning; you have to look at the big picture.*
>
> —Middle School Principal

As mentioned earlier, another strategy that enabled principals to provide teachers with half-day releases so they could attend focused development sessions was hiring "roving" substitute teachers; for example, in one elementary school, substitute teachers were provided for teachers at one grade level in the morning and for a different grade level in the afternoon (in high schools, this could be arranged by content areas or by interests).

Principals also used grants as an important financial resource for needed staff development.

I had funds for curriculum development and teacher training because of our curriculum reform grant. It has given teachers so many more ways to deliver instruction, made their teaching more linked to specific outcomes, and definitely made them better teachers.

—Middle School Principal

THE NATIONAL STAFF DEVELOPMENT COUNCIL STANDARDS

Without exception, the principals we studied declared that professional learning should fill an identified instructional need, be readily available, include both teachers and administrators, provide debriefings and follow-up help for implementation, and focus on the improvement of teaching and student achievement. Overall, it appears that high-performing principals enacted leadership approaches consistent with the National Staff Development Council's Standards for Staff Development (2001), particularly for context, process, and content (see Figure 14.4).

Figure 14.4   Standards for Staff Development

Context Standards—Staff development that improves the learning of all students:

1. Organizes adults into learning communities whose goals are aligned with those of the school and district. (**Learning Communities**)
2. Requires skillful school and district leaders who guide continuous instructional improvement. (**Leadership**)
3. Requires resources to support adult learning and collaboration. (**Resources**)

Process Standards—Staff development that improves the learning of all students:

1. Uses disaggregated student data to determine adult learning priorities, monitor progress, and help sustain continuous improvement. (**Data driven**)
2. Uses multiple sources of information to guide improvement and demonstrate its impact. (**Evaluation**)
3. Prepares educators to apply research to decision making. (**Research-Based**)
4. Uses learning strategies appropriate to the intended goal. (**Design**)
5. Applies knowledge about human learning and change. (**Learning**)
6. Provides educators with the knowledge and skills to collaborate. (**Collaboration**)

Content Standards—Staff development that improves the learning of all students:

1. Prepares educators to understand and appreciate all students; create safe, orderly, and supportive learning environments; and hold high expectations for their academic achievement. (**Equity**)
2. Deepens educators' content knowledge, provides them with research-based instructional strategies to assist students in meeting rigorous academic standards, and prepares them to use various types of classroom assessments appropriately. (**Quality teaching**)
3. Provides educators with knowledge and skills to involve families and other stakeholders appropriately. (**Family involvement**)

SOURCE: National Staff Development Council (NSDC, 2001).

As mentioned earlier in this book, high-performing principals were committed to the development of professional learning communities, wherein empowerment, teacher leadership, peer collaboration, and the ongoing study of teaching and learning are common; in such schools, educators share power, vision, values, and personal practice. Several principals suggested the usefulness of some popular materials (DuFour, DuFour, & Eaker, 2006a, 2006b; DuFour, Eaker, & DuFour, 2008) in transforming schools into PLCs:

1. DuFour, R., Eaker, R., & DuFour, R. (2008). *Revisiting Professional Learning Communities at Work: New Insights for Improving Schools.* Bloomington, IN: Solution Tree. (This book merges research and practice.)

2. DuFour, R., DuFour, R., & Eaker, R. (2006). *Learning by Doing: A Handbook for Professional Learning Communities at Work.* Bloomington, IN: Solution Tree. (This is a handbook and CD-ROM for developing a common vocabulary, assessing current reality, and taking purposeful steps to develop as a professional learning community.)

3. DuFour, R., DuFour, R., & Eaker, R. (2006). *Professional Learning Communities at Work Plan Book.* Bloomington, IN: Solution Tree. (This is a weekly planning booklet with ideas, activities, critical issues, collective inquiry methods, and action research strategies for team consideration.)

See also the "Suggested Reading for Further Learning" (Developing Professional Learning Communities) at the end of Part II of this book.

THE SPECIAL CASE OF EMPOWERING SPECIAL EDUCATION TEACHERS

Several high-performing principals defined their role vis-à-vis special education as an important administrative function. Principals explained that oversight, general support (e.g., budget allocations) and training for special educators at the school level were primary responsibilities of the district office. Principals admitted their lack of expertise in special education matters and, as a result, carefully and systematically worked to empower and support special educators in numerous ways; building trust was critical, as was support for designated teacher-leaders of special education programs and professional development for all special education teachers and support personnel. Our data indicate that the work of fully empowered special educators led to gains in student achievement and allowed principals to devote time to other instructional-leadership responsibilities.

> *I acknowledge their [special education teachers'] knowledge of children's individual needs and educational plans, and I appreciate their attention to detail and creativity. They're prepared, and they place children with special needs in the right classes so as not to create imbalances.*
>
> —Elementary School Principal

> *Our goal as a system is to have special education students exposed to as much of the general curriculum as possible. So, we're out on a limb with some students, but we're seeing positive results on test scores and graduation rates.*
>
> —Middle School Principal

High-performing principals' use of data did not stop when students moved on to the next school level. In fact, principals continued to track their students' performance and successes at the next level. Indeed, data tracking from vertical (in-house, grade-to-grade) planning and with the next school level informed principals' school improvement planning. One principal noted:

> *We have a lot of data that say we are doing well by kids; in fact, we have a high percentage of special education kids who go on to receive high school diplomas, not certificates of attendance.*
>
> —Middle School Principal

Although assistant principals were often the school-level administrators responsible for special education, principals selected the most experienced and knowledgeable teachers to serve as heads of special education departments.

> *You have to be careful who takes that job. Teachers who head the special education program must have good knowledge of special education policy and regulations, and they must have lots of experience.*
>
> —High School Principal
>
> *Our special education department chairperson attends the special education instructional-planning meetings, and it's a good feeling to have someone as knowledgeable as she is about the regulations and policies. If she needs to, she calls on one of the assistant principals for help. Dealing with special education issues inappropriately is the quickest way to go from being in administration to being in the courtroom.*
>
> —Middle School Principal

High-performing principals provided the essential training and resources to special education teachers to help them accomplish administrative functions such as planning, scheduling, completing the voluminous amount of required paperwork, and enhancing inclusion programs (i.e., providing least-restrictive environments). In particular, principals acknowledged the daunting nature of the large number of special education requirements and tasks and often provided extra resources for special education teachers (e.g., time to work as teams, secretarial assistance).

We were limping along trying to make it all work, so we had a visiting group come out the first year to help us. Now, the special education teachers do all their own scheduling. (There's no way I could do it; I don't know what Johnny needs in the regular classroom.) Together, they put it all up on a big white board and move it all around until they get it where they can manage it. Now, our teachers are training other teachers in the county, and I am just the cheerleader.

—Elementary School Principal

The big hindrance for special education is that the paperwork teachers are required to complete such as in-depth IEPs [individual educational plans] and computer programs are not perfected. In fact, computer program glitches occur . . . and teachers get frustrated.

—Elementary School Principal

Principals encouraged special education departments to directly plan for inclusion and to target increases in student achievement. Positive effects of special education inclusion programs included fewer classroom disruptions, more learning time, higher student achievement, and increased teacher growth.

We have so much less disruption in the regular classrooms now because the children don't want to leave all the good stuff that is going on. They have more ownership. It's not all a utopia, but the teachers like what they're doing, so their attitude is one of maintaining a high standard.

—Elementary School Principal

There is no doubt in my mind: The kids know they have to work harder, they see the other children reading and writing, and they can see the bar all the time, so they try harder.

—Elementary School Principal

We have an environment in which not only the children are learning but the teachers are learning as well. Everyone's learning something new every day, which is what makes it exciting.

—Elementary School Principal

As noted earlier, high-performing principals valued special educators' expertise and encouraged other teachers to tap into that expertise; at the same time, principals were vigilant about the use (or misuse) of special educators' time in the team teaching and coteaching models, insisting that special educators are partners with regular educators and are not assistants or paraprofessionals in cotaught classrooms.

PROFESSIONAL LEARNING FOR ADMINISTRATIVE TEAMS

Our data demonstrate that high-performing principals felt singularly responsible for the professional development of their administrative team members; accordingly, they provided administrative teams with a range of professional learning opportunities as well as rotation of responsibilities to build leadership capacity throughout the school.

I am constantly building leadership capacity through the assistant principals. In my first five years as principal, three of our assistant principals have become principals; that's building capacity.

—Middle School Principal

I have found that our school district is lacking in leadership initiatives for others beyond the principal, so I am building in opportunities for my leadership team to learn more about leadership, particularly how to enable teacher leadership throughout the school.

—Elementary School Principal

This year, I am going to assign to one of our assistant principals something she has never done, because I want her to have the experience of doing that task. In this case, she has worked on special programs, but not yet on the school improvement plan.

—Elementary School Principal

I give the assistant principal the opportunity to work with the whole community— business partners, parents, teacher-leaders, students, district executive committees— on things like strategic planning; that way, they interact with teachers from every grade level and department and other people as well.

—Middle School Principal

Every assistant principal is involved in staff development for the whole staff. We administrators have all been trained in collaborative-teaching models, learning-focused schools, writing across the curriculum, differentiated instruction. Where there are new teachers, the assistant principals bring them up to speed by providing the staff development and then being a back-up resource for the year.

—Middle School Principal

I read a lot, so I am always placing articles about things we may want to implement in the assistant principals' mailboxes, and we talk about them as a group.

—Middle School Principal

SUMMARY

This chapter described high-performing principals' systems-development approach to professional development. Such principals took a broad, inclusive approach to professional development, which included peer consultation, action planning for professional development, personalized and on-the-job learning opportunities, grant writing, and the special situation of special educators as part of their professional development programs. Notably, just as they encouraged teachers to be lifelong learners, these principals were themselves learners, models of active involvement in local and off-site professional learning programs and opportunities. Principals' approaches to professional learning were consistent with the standards of the National Staff Development Council.

TIPS AND SUGGESTIONS

Providing Effective, Ongoing Professional Learning

1. Tap the gold mine of teacher talent in your school. Use in-house teachers to provide professional learning programs (aka staff development) for faculty, and pay them if professional development funds allow this. Pursue certification credit hours for in-house professional learning.

2. Use school and classroom data and needs assessments to make decisions about professional learning programs.

3. Use the school improvement plan, along with specific teacher needs, to budget for and plan professional learning programs.

4. Use needs derived from data, teaching, testing, and results of professional learning surveys to develop new professional learning opportunities.

5. Make available a variety of professional development opportunities, including a range of content, process, and evaluation components.

6. Model ongoing professional development: Read and share research, attend professional development sessions, participate in book studies, take university credit courses, and pursue an advanced degree.

Part II

Suggested Reading for Further Learning

Instructional Leadership

Leadership for Learning

Cotton, K. (2003). *Principals and student achievement: What the research says.* Alexandria, VA: Association of Supervision and Curriculum Development.

Kimmelman, P. L. (2006). *Implementing NCLB: Creating a knowledge framework to support school improvement.* Thousand Oaks, CA: Corwin.

Lambert, L. (1998). *Building leadership capacity in schools.* Alexandria, VA: Association for Supervision and Curriculum Development.

Mooney, N. J., & Mausbach, A. T. (2008). *Align the design: A blueprint for school improvement.* Alexandria, VA: Association for Supervision and Curriculum Development.

Roberts, S. M., & Pruitt, E. Z. (2003). *Schools as professional learning communities: Collaborative activities and strategies for professional development.* Thousand Oaks, CA: Corwin.

Sparks, D. (2006). *Leading for results: Transforming teaching, learning, and relationships in schools.* Thousand Oaks, CA: Corwin.

Strike, K. A. (2006). *Ethical leadership in schools: Creating community in an environment of accountability.* Thousand Oaks, CA: Corwin.

Waters, T., Marzano, R. J., & McNulty, B. A. (2004). Developing the science of educational leadership. *Spectrum, 22*(1), 4–13.

Waters, T., Marzano, R. J., & McNulty, B. A. (2004). Leadership that sparks learning. *Educational Leadership, 61*(7), 45–81.

Walk-Throughs and Observing in Classrooms

Acheson, K. A., & Gall, M. D. (1992). *Techniques in the clinical supervision of teachers: Preservice and inservice applications* (3rd ed.). White Plains, NY: Longman.

Blase, J., & Blase, J. (2004). *Handbook of instructional leadership* (2nd ed.). Thousand Oaks, CA: Corwin.

Blase, J., & Blase, J. (2006). *Teachers bringing out the best in teachers: A guide to peer consultation for administrators and teachers.* Thousand Oaks, CA: Corwin.

Danielson, C. (2007). *Enhancing professional practice: A framework for teaching* (2nd ed.). Alexandria, VA: Association for Supervision and Curriculum Development.

Downey, C. J., Steffy, B. E., English, F. W., Frase, L. E., & Poston, W. K. (2007). *The three-minute classroom walk-through: A multimedia kit for professional development.* Thousand Oaks, CA: Corwin.

Glickman, C. D. (2002). *Leadership for learning: How to help teachers succeed.* Alexandria, VA: Association for Supervision and Curriculum Development.

Sullivan, S., & Glanz, J. (2005). *Supervision that improves teaching: Strategies and techniques.* Thousand Oaks, CA: Corwin.

Planning and Organizing for Teaching

Andrade, H. G. (2000). *Using rubrics to promote thinking and learning.* Alexandria, VA: Association for Supervision and Curriculum Development.

Burke, L. M. (2002). *The teacher's ultimate planning guide.* Thousand Oaks, CA: Corwin.

Hunter, R. (2004). *Madeline Hunter's mastery teaching: Increasing instructional effectiveness in elementary and secondary schools.* Thousand Oaks, CA: Corwin.

Jacobs, H. H. (2004). *Getting results with curriculum mapping.* Alexandria, VA: Association for Supervision and Curriculum Development.

Joyce, B., & Calhoun, E. (1996). *Creating learning experiences: The role of instructional theory and research.* Alexandria, VA: Association for Supervision and Curriculum Development.

Joyce, B., Weil, M., & Calhoun, E. (2000). *Models of teaching* (6th ed.). Needham Heights, MA: Allyn and Bacon.

Marlowe, B., & Page, M. L. (Eds.). (2005). *Creating and sustaining the constructivist classroom.* Thousand Oaks, CA: Corwin.

Silver, H. F., Strong, R. W., & Perini, M. J. (2007). *The strategic teacher: Selecting the right research-based strategy for every lesson.* Alexandria, VA: Association for Supervision and Curriculum Development.

Stergar, C. (2005). *Performance tasks, checklists, and rubrics.* Thousand Oaks, CA: Corwin.

Stronge, J. H., Tucker, P. D., & Hindman, J. L. (2004). *Handbook for qualities of effective teachers.* Alexandria, VA: Association for Supervision and Curriculum Development.

Wachter, J. C., & Carhart, C. (Eds.). (2003). *Time-saving tips for teachers.* Thousand Oaks, CA: Corwin.

Walsh, J. A., & Sattes, B. D. (Eds.). (2005). *Quality questioning: Research-based practice to engage every learner.* Thousand Oaks, CA: Corwin.

Wilke, R. L. (2003). *The first days of class: A practice guide for the beginning teacher.* Thousand Oaks, CA: Corwin.

Maintaining High Expectations and Developing Critical-Thinking Skills

Caine, R. N., Caine, G., McClintic, C., & Klimek, K. (Eds.). (2005). *12 Brain/mind learning principles in action.* Alexandria, VA: Association for Supervision and Curriculum Development.

Jensen, E. (2005). *Teaching with the brain in mind.* Alexandria, VA: Association for Supervision and Curriculum Development.

Sousa, D. A. (2001). *How the special needs brain learns.* Alexandria, VA: Association for Supervision and Curriculum Development.

Sousa, D. A. (2003). *How the gifted brain learns.* Alexandria, VA: Association for Supervision and Curriculum Development.

Sylwester, R. (2005). *How to explain a brain: An educator's handbook of brain terms and cognitive processes.* Alexandria, VA: Association for Supervision and Curriculum Development.

Tomlinson, C. A., Kaplan, S. N., Renzulli, J., Purcell, J., Leppien, J., & Burns, D. (Eds.). (2002). *The parallel curriculum: A design to develop high potential and challenge high-ability learners.* Thousand Oaks, CA: Corwin.

School Effects Research

Marzano, R. J. (1998). *A theory-based meta-analysis of research on instruction.* Aurora, CO: Mid-continent Research for Education and Learning. Available from http://www.mcrel.org/instructionmetaanalysis and http://www.mcrel.org/topics/productDetail.asp?productID=83.

Marzano, R. J. (2000). *A new era of school reform: Going where the research takes us.* Aurora, CO: Mid-continent Research for Education and Learning. Available from http://www.mcrel.org/newera and http://www.mcrel.org/topics/productDetail.asp?productID=81.

Marzano, R. J., (2000). *Transforming classroom grading.* Alexandria, VA: Association for Supervision and Curriculum Development.

Marzano, R. J. (2003). *What works in schools: Translating research into action.* Alexandria, VA: Association of Supervision and Curriculum Development.

Marzano, R. J. (2007). *The art and science of teaching: A comprehensive framework for effective instruction.* Alexandria, VA: Association for Supervision and Curriculum Development.

Marzano, R. J., Gaddy, B. B., & Dean, C. (2000). *What works in classroom instruction.* Aurora, CO: Mid-continent Research for Education and Learning (McREL). Available from http://www.mcrel.org/topics/productDetail.asp?productID=110.

Marzano, R. J., Marzano, J. S., & Pickering. D. J. (2003). *Classroom management that works: Research-based strategies for every teacher.* Alexandria, VA: Association for Supervision and Curriculum Development.

Marzano, R. J., Norford, J. S., Paynter, D. E., Pickering, D. J., & Gaddy, B. B. (2001). *A handbook for classroom instruction that works.* Alexandria, VA: Association for Supervision and Curriculum Development.

Marzano, R. J., Pickering, D. J., & Pollock, J. E. (2001). *Classroom instruction that works: Research-based strategies for increasing student achievement.* Alexandria, VA: Association for Supervision and Curriculum Development.

Marzano, R. J., Waters, T., McNulty, B. A. (2005). *School leadership that works: From research to results.* Alexandria, VA: Association for Supervision and Curriculum Development.

Miller, K. (2003). *School, teacher, and leadership impacts on student achievement* (policy brief). Aurora, CO: Mid-continent Research for Education and Learning. Available from http://www.mcrel.org/topics/productDetail.asp?productID=149.

Integrating Curriculum

Drake, S. (1998). *Creating integrated curriculum: Proven ways to increase student learning.* Alexandria, VA: Association for Supervision and Curriculum Development.

Drake, S. M., & Burns, R. C. (2004). *Meeting standards through integrated curriculum.* Alexandria, VA: Association for Supervision and Curriculum Development.

Exline, J. (2005). *Integrating inquiry across the curriculum.* Alexandria, VA: Association for Supervision and Curriculum Development.

Jacobs, H. H. (1997). *Mapping the big picture: Integrating curriculum & assessment K–12.* Alexandria, VA: Association for Supervision and Curriculum Development.

Cooperative Learning

Jacobs, G. M., Power, M. A., & Inn, L. W., (Eds.). (2002). *The teacher's sourcebook for cooperative learning: Practical techniques, basic principles, and frequently asked questions.* Thousand Oaks, CA: Corwin.

Johnson, D. W., Johnson, R. T., & Holubec, E. J. (1994). *Cooperative learning in the classroom.* Alexandria, VA: Association for Supervision and Curriculum Development.

Addressing Every Child's Needs

Capper, C. A., & Frattura, E. M. (2008). *Meeting the needs of students of ALL abilities: How leaders go beyond inclusion* (2nd ed.). Thousand Oaks, CA: Corwin.

Chapman, C., & King, R. (2003). *Differentiated instructional strategies for reading in the content areas.* Thousand Oaks, CA: Corwin.

Chapman, C., & King, R. (2005). *Differentiated assessment strategies.* Thousand Oaks, CA: Corwin.

Ferguson, D., Droege, C., Guojóbsdóttir, H., Lester, J., Meyer, G., Ralph, G., Sampson, N., et al. (2001). *Designing personalized learning for every student.* Alexandria, VA: Association for Supervision and Curriculum Development.

Frattura, E., & Capper, C. A. (2007). *Leading for social justice: Transforming schools for all learners.* Thousand Oaks, CA: Corwin.

Gore, M. C. (2004). *Successful inclusion strategies for secondary and middle school teachers: Keys to help struggling learners access the curriculum.* Thousand Oaks, CA: Corwin.

Gregory, G. H. (2005). *Differentiating instruction with style.* Thousand Oaks, CA: Corwin.

Gregory, G. H., & Kuzmich, L., (Eds.). (2004). *Data driven differentiation in the standards-based classroom.* Thousand Oaks, CA: Corwin.

Karten, T. (2005). *Inclusion strategies that work! Research-based methods for the classroom.* Thousand Oaks, CA: Corwin.

Stone, R. (2004). *Best teaching practices for reaching all learners.* Thousand Oaks, CA: Corwin.

Tomlinson, C. A. (2001). *How to differentiate instruction in mixed-ability classrooms* (2nd ed.). Alexandria, VA: Association for Supervision and Curriculum Development.

Tomlinson, C. A., (2003). *Fulfilling the promise of the differentiated classroom: Strategies and tools for responsive teaching.* Alexandria, VA: Association for Supervision and Curriculum Development.

Challenged and Culturally Different Students

Baldwin, A. Y. (Ed.). (2004). *Culturally diverse and underserved populations of gifted students.* Thousand Oaks, CA: Corwin.

Bender, W. N. (2002). *Differentiating instruction for students with learning disabilities: Best teaching practices for general and special educators.* Thousand Oaks, CA: Corwin.

Bender, W. N. (2005). *Differentiating instruction for students with learning disabilities: A multimedia kit for professional development.* Thousand Oaks, CA: Corwin.

Bender, W. N., & Larkin, M. J. (2003). *Reading strategies for elementary students with learning difficulties.* Thousand Oaks, CA: Corwin.

Calderón, M. E., & Minaya-Rowe, L. (2003). *Designing and implementing two-way bilingual programs.* Thousand Oaks, CA: Corwin.

Haver, J. J. (2003). *Structured English immersion: A step-by-step guide for K–6 teachers and administrators.* Thousand Oaks, CA: Corwin.

Kottler, E., & Kottler, J. A. (2002). *Children with limited English: Teaching strategies for the regular classroom.* Thousand Oaks, CA: Corwin.

Lachat, M. A. (2004). *Standards-based instruction and assessment for English language learners.* Thousand Oaks, CA: Corwin.

Lauer, P. A., Akiba, M., Wilkerson, S. B., Apthorp, H. S., Snow, D., & Martin-Glenn, M. (2004). *The effectiveness of out-of-school-time strategies in assisting low-achieving students in reading and mathematics: A research synthesis* (updated ed.). Aurora, CO: Mid-continent Research for Education and Learning.

McLeskey, J., & Waldron, N. L. (2000). *Inclusive schools in action: Making difference ordinary.* Alexandria, VA: Association for Supervision and Curriculum Development.

McNary, S. J., Glasgow, N. A., & Hicks, C. D. (2005). *What successful teachers do in inclusive classrooms: 60 research-based teaching strategies that help special learners succeed.* Thousand Oaks, CA: Corwin.

Robins, K. N., Lindsey, R. B., Lindsey, D. B., & Terrell, R. D. (2002). *Culturally proficient instruction: A guide for people who teach.* Thousand Oaks, CA: Corwin.

Rong, X. L., & Preissle, J. (2008). *Educating immigrant students in the 21st century: What educators need to know* (2nd ed.). Thousand Oaks, CA: Corwin.

Snow, D. R. (2005). *Classroom strategies for helping at-risk students.* Alexandria, VA: Association for Supervision and Curriculum Development.

Sousa, D. A. (2001). *How the special needs brain learns.* Thousand Oaks, CA: Corwin.

Villa, R. A., & Thousand, J. S. (2005). *Creating an inclusive school.* Alexandria, VA: Association for Supervision and Curriculum Development.

Technology in Learning

Bray, M., Brown, A., & Green, T. (Eds.). (2004). *Technology and the diverse learner.* Thousand Oaks, CA: Corwin.

Jukes, I., Dosaj, A., & Macdonald, B. (Eds.). (2000). *NetSavvy.* Thousand Oaks, CA: Corwin.

Ormiston, M. J. (2004). *Conquering InfoClutter: Timesaving technology solutions for teachers.* Thousand Oaks, CA: Corwin.

Pflaum, W. D. (2004). *The technology fix: The promise and reality of computers in our schools.* Alexandria VA: Association for Supervision and Curriculum Development.

Staudt, C. (2005). *Changing how we teach and learn with handheld computers.* Thousand Oaks, CA: Corwin.

Discipline and Classroom Management

Beaudoin, M., & Taylor, M. (2004). *Breaking the culture of bullying and disrespect, grades K–8: Best practices and successful strategies.* Thousand Oaks, CA: Corwin.

Colvin, G. (2007). *7 Steps for developing a proactive schoolwide discipline plan.* Thousand Oaks, CA: Corwin.

Cummings, C. (2000). *Winning strategies for classroom management.* Alexandria, VA: Association for Supervision and Curriculum Development.

Gordon, S. P., & Maxey, S. (2000). *How to help beginning teachers succeed.* Alexandria, VA: Association for Supervision and Curriculum Development.

Hanson, J. R. (1998). *Developing a classroom management repertoire. In Classroom management: An ASCD professional inquiry kit* (Folder 3). Alexandria, VA: Association for Supervision and Curriculum Development.

Kohn, A. (2006). *Beyond discipline: From compliance to community* (10th anniversary edition). Alexandria, VA: Association for Supervision and Curriculum Development.

Kounin, J. S. (1970). *Discipline and group management in classrooms.* New York: Holt, Rinehart & Winston.

Lee, C. (2004). *Preventing bullying in schools: A guide for teachers and other professionals.* Thousand Oaks, CA: Corwin.

Marzano, R. J., Gaddy, B. B., Foseid, M. C., Foseid, M. P., & Marzano, J. S. (2005). *A Handbook for classroom management that works.* Alexandria, VA: Association for Supervision and Curriculum Development.

Marzano, R. J., Marzano, J. S., & Pickering, D. J. (2003). *Classroom management that works: Research-based strategies for every teacher.* Alexandria, VA: Association for Supervision and Curriculum Development.

McLeod, J., Fisher, J., & Hoover, G. (2003). *The key elements of classroom management: Managing time and space, student behavior, and instructional strategies.* Alexandria, VA: Association for Supervision and Curriculum Development.

Shores, C., & Chester, K. (2008). *Using RTI for school improvement.* Thousand Oaks, CA: Corwin.

Smith, R. (2004). *Conscious classroom management: Unlocking the secrets of great teaching.* Thousand Oaks, CA: Corwin.

Stone, R. (2005). *Best classroom management practices for reaching all learners: What award-winning classroom teachers do.* Thousand Oaks, CA: Corwin.

Sullivan, K., Cleary, M., Sullivan, G. (2004). *Bullying in secondary schools: What it looks like and how to manage it.* Thousand Oaks, CA: Corwin.

Wessler, S. L., & Preble, W. (2003). *The respectful school: How educators and students can conquer hate and harassment.* Alexandria, VA: Association for Supervision and Curriculum Development.

Developing Professional Learning Communities

Blase, J., & Blase, J. (2006). *Teachers bringing out the best in teachers: A guide to peer consultation for administrators and teachers.* Thousand Oaks, CA: Corwin.

Blase, J., & Kirby, P. C. (2008). *Bringing out the best in teachers: What effective principals do* (3rd ed.). Thousand Oaks, CA: Corwin.

Crow, G. M., & Pounder, D. G. (2000). *Interdisciplinary teacher teams.* Alexandria, VA: Association for Supervision and Curriculum Development.

DuFour, R. (2003). *Building a professional learning community.* Arlington, VA: American Association of School Administrators.

DuFour, R., DuFour, R., & Eaker, R. (2006). *Learning by doing: A handbook for professional learning communities at work.* Bloomington, IN: Solution Tree.

DuFour, R., DuFour, R., & Eaker, R. (2006). *Professional learning communities at work plan book.* Bloomington, IN: Solution Tree.

DuFour, R., Eaker, R., & DuFour, R. (2008). *Revisiting professional learning communities at work: New insights for improving schools.* Bloomington, IN: Solution Tree.

Hord, S. M., & Sommers, W. A. (2007). *Leading professional learning communities: Voices from research and practice.* Thousand Oaks, CA: Corwin.

Joyce, B., & Showers, B. (2002). *Student achievement through staff development* (3rd ed.). White Plains, NY: Longman.

Killion, J., & Harrison, C. (2006). *Taking the lead: New roles for teachers and school-based coaches.* Oxford, OH: National Staff Development Council.

Martin-Kniep, G. (2004). *Developing learning communities through teacher expertise.* Thousand Oaks, CA: Corwin.

Murphy, C. (1999). *Use time for faculty study.* Alexandria, VA: Association for Supervision and Curriculum Development.

Novick, B., Kress, J. S., & Elias, M. J. (2002). *Building learning communities with character: How to integrate academic, social, and emotional learning.* Alexandria, VA: Association for Supervision and Curriculum Development.

Osterman, K. F., & Kottkamp, R. B. (2004). *Reflective practice for educators: Professional development to improve student learning.* Thousand Oaks, CA: Corwin.

Roberts, S. M., & Pruitt, E. Z. (2003). *Schools as professional learning communities: Collaborative activities and strategies for professional development.* Thousand Oaks, CA: Corwin.

Senge, P. M. (2006). *The fifth discipline: The art and practice of the learning organization.* New York: Doubleday.

Sklare, G. B. (2005). *Brief counseling that works: A solution-focused approach for school counselors and administrators.* Thousand Oaks, CA: Corwin.

Tichenor, M., & Heins, E. (2000). *Study groups: An inquiry-based approach to improving schools.* Alexandria, VA: Association for Supervision and Curriculum Development.

Part III

Conclusion

*Systems Thinking and
the Systems-Development
Approach in Educational Leadership*

INTRODUCTION TO PART III
OF THE *HANDBOOK*

Parts I and II of the *Handbook* have focused on the action foci of administrative leadership and the goals of instructional leadership, respectively, as demonstrated in the practice of high-performing principals; clearly, these two strands of the double helix model of leadership for school improvement operate in concert. Part III of the *Handbook* emphasizes the importance of the strategic underpinning of both strands of leadership for school improvement: systems thinking and the systems-development approach. Implications of systems thinking and the systems-development approach for preparation programs in educational leadership are also discussed.

15 The Importance of Systems Thinking and the Systems-Development Approach for School Improvement

Systems thinking is a discipline for seeing wholes. It is a framework for seeing interrelationships rather than things, for seeing patterns of change rather than static "snapshots." It is a set of general principles—distilled over the course of the twentieth century, spanning fields as diverse as the physical and social sciences, engineering, and management. . . . During the last thirty years, these tools have been applied to understand a wide range of corporate, urban, regional, economic, political, ecological, and even psychological systems. And systems thinking is a sensibility—for the subtle interconnectedness that gives living systems their unique character.

—Peter Senge, *The Fifth Discipline* (1990, pp. 68–69)

A study by the Council of Chief State School Officers (CCSSO; 2002) found that school-level leadership is crucial for success and that effective principals improve schools by setting high expectations, sharing leadership, staying engaged, encouraging collaboration, using assessment data, keeping the focus on students, addressing barriers to learning, reinforcing classroom instruction at home, addressing special education needs, and employing systems to identify interventions. Indeed, as we pointed out earlier, high-performing principals reported that "putting a school together," administratively and instructionally, requires systems thinking; based on our study data, these high-performing principals used, in fact, a systems-development approach to leadership. That is, each high-performing principal we studied used a bottom-up approach to create an integrated system comprising a host of subsystems at the school level to address both administrative leadership and instructional leadership tasks. The subsystems comprising the whole school system were arranged in coordinated, dynamic, constructive, and progressive ways to emphasize school improvement; principals achieved this regardless of the nature of the school district within which their schools were located. Principals also used their discretion at the school level, in collaboration with others (administrators, faculty members, staff members, and parents) to create and sustain high-performing school *cultures* based on deeply-embedded values, beliefs, ways of thinking, and behavior that worked together for whole-school improvement.

Formal *systems theory* is a broad framework for understanding and changing organizations. Systems thinkers assume that organizational phenomena (e.g., goals, behavior, events, and problems) can best be understood in the *context* of the whole system. Because school districts and schools are open systems, context also includes the relevant external environment. Systems thinkers are able to see how the components of a system or the major components within a subsystem (an individual school) are related or hang together. Systems thinkers also assume that successful change may require that all *related* components be changed; changing one component without also changing other related components is often an exercise in futility. In short, systems thinkers see things holistically, "as they are," and they approach change holistically to create systems "as they should be" (Fullan, 2005; Hoy & Miskel, 2005; Owens & Valesky, 2007; Senge, 1990; Wagner et al., 2006).

Unfortunately, although the importance of formal systems theory has been discussed in the organizational literature (e.g., Fullan, 2005; Hoy & Miskel, 2005; Owens & Valesky, 2007; Senge, 1990; Wagner et al., 2006) and, undoubtedly, systems theory has been a part of most university preparation programs in educational leadership for decades, little progress has been made in applying this perspective to school reform or improvement efforts (Fullan, 2005; Wagner et al., 2006). This suggests, for instance, that even if principals have competencies to deal with separate administrative and instructional-leadership challenges, too few have the ability to put it all together as a viable whole, to *create* both the essential subsystems and constructive relationships among such subsystems within a school, as well as the essential cultural components to focus on school improvement.

We strongly recommend that prospective and practicing school administrators develop their abilities to apply systems thinking and, in particular, a bottom-up systems-development approach to administration and leading in schools. To develop further insight into systems thinking, we suggest reading the work of scholars such as Fullan (2005), Senge (1990), and Wagner and colleagues (2006). Specifically, Wagner and colleagues' powerful, practical, and straightforward systems framework is well suited to understanding the *interrelated elements and challenges* of school improvement within a whole-school context. This framework consists of four arenas of change, referred to as the 4 Cs:

1. *Competencies* refers to skills and knowledge that affect student learning. Wagner and colleagues (2006) contend that professional development activities are most efficacious when they are collaborative, continuous, and embedded in the workday world of the school, a conclusion consistent with our study of high-performing principals. These researchers also suggest that implementation of this form of professional development requires collaboration among many of the school's different subsystems.

2. *Conditions* includes the environment that surrounds teaching and learning, or the "tangible arrangements of time, space, and resources" (Wagner et al., 2006, p. 101).

3. *Culture* consists of shared values, beliefs, behaviors, symbols, ways of thinking, and meanings related to teaching and learning within and outside the school.

4. *Context* identifies the socio-historical-political-economic environment in which school improvement efforts occur; in particular, this is the community in which a school is located and the people in that community. Knowledge of context should be used to inform efforts to transform school-based competencies, conditions, and culture.

To demonstrate how the 4 Cs framework can be used as both a *diagnostic* and *transformative* tool for school improvement, we shall consider the case of Washington Middle School and its *use of data*.

USING THE 4 Cs MODEL AS A DIAGNOSTIC AND PRESCRIPTIVE TOOL

Although we cannot fully explicate Wagner and colleagues' 4 Cs model here, this realistic though imaginary example is helpful. Let us assume that the administrators and faculty members of Washington Middle School realize that they have difficulty *using data to inform decisions about teaching, learning, and school improvement*. The 4 Cs model (competencies, conditions, culture, and context) can be used to (1) diagnose potential aspects of the problem, and then to (2) develop appropriate strategies to remedy the situation.

Within the *competencies* realm of the model, several questions could be considered by the administrators and faculty:

- What skills and knowledge are required for effective data collection, analysis, interpretation, and application?
- In particular, which skills do administrators and faculty need to improve?

- What relevant knowledge and skills are available among the school's personnel, the professional literature, Web sites, or the community?

Next, faculty and administrators should consider the *conditions* realm of the model. Answers to the following questions (as well as others) should be sought:

- Are there sufficient time, space, and resources for data analysis?
- If additional training is required, how can it be acquired?
- Subsequent to any necessary training, how much time, space, and other resources will be needed for the ongoing, collaborative work of data-study teams? For example, can administrators and faculty create schedules that allow common meeting time for study teams? Do personnel have the technology needed to support ongoing data analysis throughout the school? Should time be made available for the entire administration and faculty to meet and share their experiences with data for teaching, learning, and school improvement?

The *culture* of the school should also be considered. The following questions might be asked.

- Which values, beliefs, symbols, shared understandings, and patterns of behavior are essential to effective use of data by individuals and groups in the school?
- What can school leaders (administrators and teachers) do to facilitate the development of core factors such as collaboration, trust, ownership, and openness, all of which are essential to productive working relationships? What activities can be encouraged that may enhance trust and ownership?
- Are expectations for collaboration among professionals clearly communicated, regularly reinforced, and acknowledged?
- What level of trust exists among teachers and between teachers and administrators?

Then, all of the above should be considered in terms of the *context* of the school. For instance,

- What are the community and parent expectations about the use of data for school improvement? Its dissemination?
- What data sources exist within the community that could be helpful in making decisions about teaching and learning? What methods should administrators and teachers use to collect and analyze such data?
- How can all personnel use data to help parents understand this school's approach to the use of data for teaching, learning, and school improvement?

Having used systems thinking to gain a broad, deep, and clear understanding of the school's competencies, conditions, culture, and context with respect to data use, the next step would be *to create and implement strategies that address each of the four arenas of change* in order to improve the school's use of data. The goal would be to produce a comprehensive *data-use subsystem* that would work in concert with other established subsystems in the school to support school improvement efforts. *Keep in mind the fact that changes in one area of a school-level system (e.g., data use) typically require changes in other areas of the system (e.g., professional development); in short, components of a school-level subsystem are interrelated and interactive, and they must be designed to work together to effect school improvement.* (See Figure 15.1 Wagner and colleagues' 4 Cs model, a useful systems thinking tool for principals interested in applying systems thinking to school improvement efforts.)

Figure 15.1 The 4 Cs Model for School Improvement: Diagnosing and Overcoming Educational Problems

Competencies

How could we better

- Think strategically?
- Identify student-learning needs?
- Gather and interpret data?
- Collaborate?
- Give and receive critiques?
- Productively disagree?
- Reflect and make midcourse corrections?

Conditions

How could we better create and maintain

- Time for problem solving, for learning, for talking about challenges?
- Relevant and user-friendly student data?
- Agreed-upon performance standards?
- Clear priorities and focus for each person's work?
- District- and building-level support?

Culture

How would we describe

- Our level of expectations for all students' learning? (Consistently high? Medium? Low? Or a mix of these depending on which students?)
- Our school's agenda? (Multiple and unrelated? Frequent changes? Steady, consistent focus? Related initiatives that build on each other?)
- The communications between district and school leadership to teachers? (Directive? Compliance oriented? Engaged in building cosponsorship and ownership?)
- Adult relationships with each other? (Lacking trust? Trusting?)
- Adult view of responsibility for all students' learning? (Blames others? Sees various contributors, including oneself?)

Context

How could we better

- Understand and work with students' families?
- See clearly the core competencies students will need for work, citizenship, and continuous learning?

SOURCE: Wagner et al. (2006).

SUMMARY

Chapter 15 has reiterated a theme discussed throughout the *Handbook:* High-performing principals employ systems thinking and, in particular, a systems-development approach to school improvement; this is a bottom-up, systematic, comprehensive, approach to reorganizing and reculturing all major administrative/management and instructional leadership responsibilities and functions to emphasize school improvement.

16 Afterword

A Summary and a Note About Preparation for Educational Leadership

Findings drawn from our study and reviews of relevant professional studies clearly demonstrate that school principals, like managers generally, are increasingly confronted with a daunting number of diverse, complex, and even incompatible managerial and leadership responsibilities (Bass, 1990; Buckley, 2004; Cusick, 2003; Dunklee, 2000; Kotter, 1990, 1998; Kowalski, 2003; McPeake, 2007; Yukl, 2006). This means that a simplistic approach to school leadership, to understanding and implementing administrative/managerial and instructional leadership processes in schools, would be grossly inadequate (Bass, 1990; Gardner, 1989). Kotter (1990) writes, "Indeed, any combination other than strong management and strong leadership has the potential for producing highly unsatisfactory results" (p. 7). Moreover, consistent with our findings, other scholars have argued that managerial and leadership processes in organizations are, in reality, highly intertwined. *In fact, Yukl (2006) has concluded that the question of how to successfully integrate the two processes is now considered a crucial leadership issue.*

The *Handbook* provides a compelling research-based answer to the long-standing question, How do principals create high-performing schools? It consists of findings from a groundbreaking study of principals who created high-performing schools and recommendations of the best available resources for school improvement. It should be reiterated that our study of high-performing principals' administrative and instructional leadership practices solidly confirms the findings of other research with regard to effective leadership for school improvement. In addition—and consistent with the above—the *Handbook* demonstrates that a balanced, empowering approach to school leadership based on systems thinking and a systems-development approach is essential to effectively and efficiently addressing a school's administrative and instructional leadership functions, responsibilities, and activities for sustained school improvement. In short, for high-performing principals, student achievement is, in part, driven by a systems-development approach. The following summary and acrostic (derived from the double helix model of leadership we presented in the preface of this book) may be helpful in considering our findings.

HIGH-PERFORMING PRINCIPALS

What are their goals? They:

- Focus on teaching and learning (see Chapter 10 of this *Handbook*);
- Develop a culture that supports instruction (Chapter 11);
- Establish a context for dialogue about instruction (Chapter 12);
- Reference research-based instructional elements (Chapter 13); and
- Provide ongoing, effective professional development (Chapter 14).

What do they do to achieve their goals, and how do they do it? High-performing principals:

- Use a systems-development approach (Chapter 6); and
- Focus on practices associated with increased student achievement (Chapter 3).

Here are some additional reminders, keyed to action foci:

Reminders for Prospective and Practicing Principals	High-Performing Principals' Action Foci (Handbook Chapter)
Set the example.	Be a model of learning. (Chapter 1)
Yield not to barriers to instruction.	Lead for maximum impact on achievement. (Chapter 4)
Set the standard.	Be an exemplar of leadership standards. (Chapter 2)
Take data to the limit.	Use data to inform instructional development. (Chapter 9)
Employ the best.	Hire strong people. (Chapter 8)
Mind the mission.	Work with teachers on the mission: ongoing, collaborative study of schoolwide instructional improvement. (Chapter 5)
Share the power.	Take an empowering approach to create a learning community. (Chapter 7)

Despite the incredible challenges of creating a school focused on sustained school improvement and the concomitant knowledge and skills required (Gronn, 2002), the fluid and developing nature of administration (Willower & Uline, 2001), and the pressures of external accountability (e.g., NCLB, 2001), studies—though few in number—have demonstrated the impact of leadership on measurable school outcomes (Spillane, 2003). Therefore, we strongly recommend that university and district-based preparatory and professional development programs provide sufficient opportunities for prospective and practicing administrators to develop the requisite skills—particularly those of systems thinking—for all administrative and instructional leadership responsibilities. We have shown that a principal must understand that school improvement is contingent on instructional approaches that have been validated through solid and rigorous empirical research (Slavin, 2008) rather than approaches defined by invalid beliefs, popular practices, limited objectivity, anecdotal knowledge, and the recycling of ineffective programs (Ginsberg, 1996; Hall & Hord, 2006; Kowalski, 2009). We have also shown that a principal must have the ability to view a school in its entirety (i.e., as a complex set of relationships and interactions among various subsystems, components, or arenas). Further, we have shown that a principal must realize that changes in one subsystem will frequently result in or require changes in another; to be sure, this implies systems thinking and a systems-development approach on the part of the principal. Preparation programs must therefore develop in prospective and practicing principals the ability to create subsystems and to put all the subsystems together into a whole-school organization with collaborative, empowering cultures characterized by significant leadership density (i.e., distributed or shared leadership) in which administrators and teachers define problems and make decisions about them (Hall & Hord, 2006). Preparation programs should also help students develop firmly held beliefs, shared understandings, and a deep sense of ownership and responsibility that works toward school change and improvement. In such a school, teachers and administrators frequently ask questions such as, What do we expect of students? What is good instructional practice? Who is responsible for student learning? and, How do students and teachers account for their work and learning? (Elmore & Fuhrman, 2001). This is the essence of culture building through democratic leadership described many years ago by Burns (1978), and it is "only with certain kinds of cultures . . . one find[s] leadership emerging throughout the organization," (Kotter, 1990, p. 138), and such administrative and teacher leadership is the linchpin of school improvement.

Research Method and Procedures

The study which serves as the basis for this book examined how high-performing principals overcome managerial responsibilities and create instructionally effective high-performing schools. Here, we describe the research method and procedures used to conduct this study.

Data collection and analysis of data were consistent with symbolic interaction theory. This theory recognizes the importance of structural factors that influence human behavior, but it emphasizes the meanings people attribute to such behavior; in essence, human reflexivity is given more importance than structural factors. That is, individuals are influenced by others but maintain efficient distance to construct unique action (Blumer, 1969; Mead, 1934). Thus, symbolic interaction theory focuses on individual action, perception, and experience.

Consistent with symbolic interaction theory, a priori concepts from the literature were not employed to determine data collection techniques. Moreover, we did not review the relevant literature on school-level management and leadership until after we analyzed all data; rather, we used only sensitizing concepts (e.g., management, instructional leadership, instructional effectiveness) to determine what to investigate and to reduce the probability that principals would be influenced by the researchers' preconceived ideas about the research topic. The meanings discussed by the principals we studied constitute the core findings presented throughout this book (Bogdan & Biklen, 1982; Glaser, 1978, 1992, 1998; Glaser & Strauss, 1967; Taylor & Bogdan, 1998).

The high-performing principals selected for participation in our study worked in schools in which students achieved greater-than-expected test results on the state standardized achievement tests for the elementary and middle schools and the state graduation test for high schools as identified by the School Improvement Office of the state department of education. Furthermore, all elementary and secondary schools had met state AYP (annual yearly progress) standards for three consecutive years (2004–2007) and achieved "Distinguished AYP" status. Of the six high schools represented in the study, four had achieved "Distinguished AYP" status for three consecutive years. Of the two remaining high schools, which were both Title I schools, one achieved "Distinguished AYP" status for the 2004–2005 and 2007–2008 school years and then received a state award as a "Title I Distinguished School." All six of the high schools outperformed the state average and their respective district averages on the state composite academic scorecard in all or a majority of categories. In addition, all principals participating in the study were designated "exemplary" instructional leaders by the School Improvement Office of the state department of education and/or by the local district administration.

We also selected principals for this study on the basis of achieving the broadest possible representation for gender, race, and setting (elementary, middle, and high school). The final study sample included 20 principals: female (n = 13) and male (n = 7); Caucasian (n = 17) and African American (n = 3); elementary (n = 9), middle (n = 5), and high schools (n = 6); urban (n = 3), suburban (n = 7), and rural (n = 4) schools. The sample included married (n = 16) and single (n = 4) principals, with an average age of 50 years. Degrees earned by these principals included masters' (n = 1), specialist (n = 11), EdD (n = 7), and PhD (n = 1) degrees. The mean number of years of experience as a principal was 9.3 years, and the mean number of years working at the current school six years. The mean number of assistant principals at these schools was 2.4, and the mean number of faculty members at these schools was 95.8. Eight of the twenty schools had 40% to 97% of students on free or reduced lunch. Seven schools had 40%–97% African American and Hispanic students. The range of per capita student expenditure was $7260–$11,215. Data collection for this study occurred during 2006 through 2008.

One researcher contacted individuals, explained the nature of our study, and answered all questions; this researcher also shared our general research questions and asked principals to think about them before the first interview.

The study described throughout this book examined the broad question: How have you overcome managerial responsibilities to create an instructionally effective school? Among other things, principals were asked to describe how they addressed major administrative functions, instructional leadership, and instructional improvement. In a word, we attempted to learn how this elite group of principals put together a well-managed and well-led, instructionally effective school. (As noted in Part I, to our knowledge, no published research exists that directly explores this research question, although it is widely acknowledged in the professional literature that an overwhelming percentage of principals fail to sufficiently overcome ever-expanding managerial responsibilities and create high-performing schools.)

Data were collected between 2006 and 2008. Two tape-recorded telephone and/or face-to-face semistructured interviews were conducted with each research participant. In addition to the research questions described above, we asked principals to provide general background information about themselves and their schools. All audiotapes were reviewed for quality and subsequently transcribed, generating over 1200 pages of usable data.

Given the limitations of using computer software for grounded theory research, especially for conceptual and theoretical work (Charmaz, 2000; Glaser, 1998; Taylor & Bogdan, 1998), we analyzed all of our data line by line and by hand; this is consistent with a Blumerian emphasis on meaning in symbolic interaction studies (Charmaz, 2000). This procedure, although very time consuming, allowed us to keep principals' perspectives at the center of our research and to generate robust descriptions of each participant's experience (Fontana & Frey, 2000). A subsequent interview with each of our participants was used to fill out emergent categories, clarify areas of ambiguity, and explore relationships between and among emergent categories (Bogdan & Biklen, 1982; Glaser, 1978, 1992, 1998; Strauss & Corbin, 1998; Taylor & Bogdan, 1998).

Accordingly, our study complied with guidelines for inductive-exploratory research that focuses on generating meanings as well as descriptive and conceptual results. Specifically, we used constant comparative analysis to analyze our data; this approach requires a comparison of each new incident in the data base to emergent categories and subcategories coded previously (Bogdan & Biklen, 1982; Charmaz, 2000; Glaser, 1978, 1992, 1998; Glaser & Strauss, 1967; Lofland, 1971; Strauss & Corbin, 1998; Taylor & Bogdan, 1998).

Two researchers analyzed the entire data set independently, and another examined the results of these analyses. All three researchers met to resolve issues of interpretation that arose. Subsequent to completion of a series of cycles of analysis, comparisons were made with the existing relevant academic literature; we made no changes in our analysis based on this last procedure. Careful data collection and constant comparative analysis of our data reduced the probability of inappropriate use of concepts from the literature (Charmaz, 2000).

Although interview-based protocols are essential to qualitative studies that focus on meanings (Bogdan & Biklen, 1982; Glaser, 1978, 1992, 1998; Glaser & Strauss, 1967; Strauss & Corbin, 1998; Taylor & Bogdan, 1998), interviewees may present idealized versions of themselves and their situations. To address this and other issues related to trustworthiness and reliability of our findings, we used an inductive-generative approach to data collection and analysis; we used no a priori concepts to control data collection, developed rapport and trust with our participants, conducted multiple interviews with each participant, audiotape recorded and transcribed all interviews, probed for detailed responses, examined data for inconsistencies and contradictions within and between interviews for each participant as well as across participants, searched for negative and disconfirming evidence, generated low-inference descriptors, and checked for researcher effects. Finally, as a supplemental validation of our findings, we made comparisons with the existing literature (Bogdan & Biklen, 1982; Glaser, 1978, 1992, 1998; Glaser & Strauss, 1967; Strauss & Corbin, 1998; Taylor & Bogdan, 1998).

In sum, all the findings discussed in this book were derived directly from our study database. Relevant empirical findings and theoretical ideas from the extant literature were presented throughout this book for interpretive and comparative purposes and for supplemental validation of emergent findings (Bogdan & Biklen, 1982; Charmaz, 2000; Glaser, 1978, 1992, 1998; Taylor & Bogdan, 1998). Due to space limitations, only brief excerpts from our data are presented to illustrate select ideas.

References

Achilles, C. M., Keedy, J. L., & High, R. M. (1999). The workday world of the principal: How principals get things done. In L. W. Hughes (Ed.), *The principal as leader* (2nd ed., pp. 25–58). Upper Saddle River, NJ: Merrill.

Apthorp, H., Dean, C., Florian, J., Lauer, P., Reichardt, R., Sanders, N., et al. (2001). *Standards in classroom practice research synthesis.* Aurora, CO: Mid-continent Research for Education and Learning.

Bass, B. M. (1990). *Bass & Stogdill's handbook of leadership: Theory, research, and managerial applications* (3rd ed.). New York: The Free Press.

Bennis, W. (1989). *Why leaders can't lead: The unconscious conspiracy continues.* San Francisco: Jossey-Bass.

Blase, J., & Blase, J. (2004). *Handbook of instructional leadership: How successful principals promote teaching and learning.* Thousand Oaks, CA: Corwin.

Blase, J., & Blase, J. (2006). *Teachers bringing out the best in teachers: A guide to peer consultation for administrators and teachers.* Thousand Oaks, CA: Corwin.

Blumer, H. (1969). *Symbolic interactionism: Perspective and method.* Englewood Cliffs, NJ: Prentice Hall.

Bogdan, R. C., & Biklen, S. K. (1982). *Qualitative research for education: An introduction to theory and methods* (2nd ed.). Boston: Allyn & Bacon.

Boris-Schacter, S., & Langer, S. (2006). *Balanced leadership: How effective principals manage their work.* New York: Teachers College Press.

Brown, J. J., & Duguid, P. (1991). Organizational learning and communities of practice: Toward a unified view of working, learning, and organization. *Organization Science, 2*(1), 40–50.

Bryk, A., & Schneider, B. (2002). *Trust in schools: A core resource for improvement.* New York: Russell.

Buckley, M. F. (2004). *Questionnaire study of Connecticut high school principals.* Cheshire, CT: Connecticut Association of Schools.

Burns, J. M. (1978). *Leadership.* New York: Harper & Row.

Cawelti, G. (2004). *Handbook of research on improving student achievement.* Arlington, VA: Educational Research Service.

Chan, T. C., & Pool, H. (2002, April). *Principals' priorities versus their realities: Reducing the gap.* Paper presented at the annual meeting of the American Educational Research Association, New Orleans, LA.

Charmaz, K. (2000). Grounded theory: Objectivist and constructivist methods. In N. Denzin & Y. Lincoln (Eds.), *Handbook of qualitative research* (2nd ed., pp. 509–535). Thousand Oaks, CA: Sage.

Colorado Statewide Systemic Initiative for Mathematics and Science (CONNECT). (1999). *Professional development criteria: A study guide for effective professional development.* Aurora, CO: Mid-continent Research for Education and Learning.

Cotton, K. (2003). *Principals and student achievement: What the research says.* Alexandria, VA: Association for Supervision and Curriculum Development.

Council of Chief State School Officers (CCSSO). (2002). *Expecting success: A study of five high-performing, high poverty schools.* Washington, DC: Author.

Council of Chief State School Officers (CCSSO). (2008). *Educational leadership policy standards: 2008.* Washington, DC: Author.

Cunningham, W. G., & Cordiero, P. A. (2006). *Educational leadership: A problem-based approach* (3rd ed.). Boston: Pearson.

Cusick, P. A. (2003). *A study of Michigan's school principal shortage (Policy Report No. 12).* East Lansing: The Education Policy Center, Michigan State University.

Daft, R. L., & Weick, K. E. (1984). Toward a model of organizations as interpretation systems. *Academy of Management Journal, 9*(2), 287–295.

Danielson, C. (2002). *Enhancing student achievement: A framework for school improvement.* Alexandria, VA: Association for Supervision and Curriculum Development.

Danielson, C. (2006). *Teacher leadership that strengthens professional practice.* Alexandria, VA: Association for Supervision and Curriculum Development.

Danielson, C. (2007). *Enhancing professional practice: A framework for teaching* (2nd ed.). Alexandria, VA: Association for Supervision and Curriculum Development.

Danielson, C. (2008). *The handbook for enhancing professional practice: Using the framework for teaching in your school.* Alexandria, VA: Association for Supervision and Curriculum Development.

Danielson, C. (2009). *Talk about teaching: Leading professional conversations.* Thousand Oaks, CA: Corwin.

Danielson, C., & Abrutyn, L. (1997). *An introduction to using portfolios in the classroom.* Alexandria, VA: Association for Supervision and Curriculum Development.

Davenport, P., & Anderson, G. (2002). *Closing the achievement gap: No excuses.* Houston, TX: American Productivity and Quality Center.

Dean, C.B., & Bailey, J.A. (2003). A report documenting the process for developing an integrated standards-based instructional unit. Retrieved January 1, 2010, from http://www.mcrel.org/PDF/Standards/5031TG_DevelopingaStandards-basedUnit.pdf

Deming, W. E. (2000). *Out of the crisis.* Cambridge: MIT Press.

Dewey, J. (1933). *How we think.* Lexington, MA: D.C. Heath.

DiPaola, M., & Tschannen-Moran, M. (2003). The principalship at a crossroads: A study of the conditions and concerns of principals. *National Association of Secondary School Principals Bulletin, 81*(634), 43–65.

Downey, C. J., Steffy, B. E., English, F. W., Frase, L. E., & Poston, W. K. (2004). *The three-minute classroom walk-through: Changing school supervisory practice one teacher at a time.* Thousand Oaks, CA: Corwin.

Doyle, M. E., & Rice, D. M. (2002). Model for instructional leadership. *Principal Leadership, 3*(3), 49–52.

Drake, T. L., & Roe, W. H. (2003). *The principalship* (6th ed.). Upper Saddle River, NJ: Pearson Education.

DuFour, R. (2003). *Building a professional learning community.* Arlington, VA: American Association of School Administrators.

DuFour, R., DuFour, R., & Eaker, R. (2006a). *Learning by doing: A handbook for professional learning communities at work.* Bloomington, IN: Solution Tree.

DuFour, R., DuFour, R., & Eaker, R. (2006b). *Professional learning communities at work plan book.* Bloomington, IN: Solution Tree.

DuFour, R., Eaker, R., & DuFour, R. (2008). *Revisiting professional learning communities at work: New insights for improving schools.* Bloomington, IN: Solution Tree.

Dunklee, D. R. (2000). *If you want to lead, not just manage: A primer for principals.* Thousand Oaks, CA: Corwin.

Elmore, R. (2003). *Knowing the right thing to do: School improvement and performance-based accountability.* Washington, DC: National Governors Association (NGA) for Best Practices. Retrieved October 13, 2009, from http://www.nga.org/cda/files/0803knowing.pdf.

Elmore, R. F. (2000). *Building a new structure for school leadership.* Washington DC: Albert Shanker Institute.

Elmore, R. F. (2002). Building capacity to enhance learning: A conversation. *Principal Leadership 2*(5), 39–43.

Elmore, R. F., & Fuhrman, S. H. (2001). Research finds the false assumption of accountability. *Education Digest, 67*(4), 9–14.

Farrace, B. (2002, January). Building capacity to enhance learning: A conversation with Richard Elmore. *Principal Leadership (High School Ed.), 2*(5), 39–43.

Fontana, A., & Frey, J. H. (2000). The interview: From structured questions to negotiated text. In N. Denzin & Y. Lincoln (Eds.), *Handbook of qualitative research* (2nd ed., pp. 645–672). Thousand Oaks, CA: Sage.

Fox, C. (2008). *Empowering teachers: A professional and collaborative approach.* Arlington, VA: State Educational Technology Directors Association.

Fullan, M. (2003). *The moral imperative of school leadership.* Thousand Oaks, CA: Corwin.

Fullan, M. (2005). *Leadership and sustainability: Systems thinkers in action.* Thousand Oaks, CA: Corwin.

Fullan, M. (2007). *The new meaning of educational change* (4th ed.). New York: Teachers College Press.

Fullan, M. G. (2001). *Leading in a culture of change.* San Francisco: Jossey-Bass.

Gardner, J. W. (1989). *On leadership.* New York: The Free Press.

Ginsberg, R. (1996). The new institutionalism, the new science, persistence and change: The power of faith in schools. In R. L. Crowson, W. L. Boyd, & H. B. Mawhinney (Eds.), *The politics of education and the new institutionalism: Reinventing the American school* (pp. 153–166). London: Falmer.

Glanz, J. (1995). Exploring supervision history: An invitation and agenda. *Journal of Curriculum and Supervision, 10*(2), 95–113.

Glaser, B. G. (1978). *Theoretical sensitivity: Advances in the methodology of grounded theory.* Mill Valley, CA: Sociology Press.

Glaser, B. G. (1992). *Emergence vs. forcing: Basics of grounded theory.* Mill Valley, CA: Sociology Press.

Glaser, B. G. (1998). *Doing grounded theory: Issues and discussions.* Mill Valley, CA: Sociology Press.

Glaser, B. G., & Strauss, A. L. (1967). *The discovery of grounded theory: Strategies for qualitative research.* Chicago: Aldine.

Glickman, C. D. (2002). *Leadership for learning: How to help teachers succeed.* Alexandria, VA: Association for Supervision and Curriculum Development.

Gould, S. M. (1998). *The perceptions of elementary school principals regarding their role in helping teachers increase student learning.* Unpublished doctoral dissertation, University of Massachusetts, Amherst.

Groff, F. (2001, October/November). Who will lead? The principal shortage. *State Legislatures, 27*(9), 16.

Gronn, P. (2002). Leader formation. In K. Leithwood & P. Hallinger (Eds.), *Second international handbook of educational leadership and administration* (pp. 1031–1070). Dordrecht: Kluwer Academic.

Hall, G. E., & Hord, S. M. (2006). *Implementing change: Patterns, principles, and potholes* (2nd ed.). Boston: Allyn & Bacon.

Halverson, R., Grigg, J., Prichett, R., & Thomas, C. (2007). The new instructional leadership: Creating data-driven instructional systems in schools. *Journal of School Leadership, 17*(2), 159–194.

Halverson, R., Prichett, R. B., & Watson, J. G. (2007). *Formative feedback systems and the new instructional leadership* (WCER Working Paper No. 2007–3). Madison: University of Wisconsin–Madison, Wisconsin Center for Education Research.

Hansen, J. B., Schalock, M. D., McConney, A., & Rudd, A. (2001, April). *Self-evaluation and peer observation of early career teachers in a standards-based context: Preliminary results.* Paper presented at the annual meeting of the American Educational Research Association, Seattle, WA.

Hanson, R. (1998). *Classroom management professional inquiry kit.* Alexandria, VA: Association for Supervision and Curriculum Development.

Hassel, E. (1999). *Professional development: Learning from the best.* Oak Brook, IL. North Central Regional Educational Laboratory.

Hord, S. M., & Sommers, W. A. (2007). *Leading professional learning communities: Voices from research and practice.* Thousand Oaks, CA: Corwin.

Hoy, W. K., & Miskel, C. G. (2005). *Educational administration: Theory, research, and action.* Boston: McGraw Hill.

Joyce, B., & Showers, B. (2002). *Student achievement through staff development* (3rd ed.). White Plains, NY: Longman.

Joyce, B., Weil, M., & Calhoun, E. (2009). *Models of teaching* (8th ed.). Needham Heights, MA: Allyn and Bacon.

Kellogg, S. (2005). *Principals' organizational activities: An analysis of the differences between actual and ideal time expenditures as a function of career stage.* Unpublished doctoral dissertation, Ashland University, Ashland, OH.

Kendall, J. S., & Marzano, R. J. (2004). *Content knowledge: A compendium of standards and benchmarks for K–12 education.* Aurora, CO: Mid-continent Research for Education and Learning. Available from http://www.mcrel.org/standards-benchmarks/.

Knowles, M. S., Holton, E. F., & Swanson, R. A. (1998). *The adult learner: The definitive classic in adult education and human resource development* (6th ed.). Boston: Elsevier Science.

Kotter, J. P. (1990). *A force for change: How leadership differs from management.* New York: The Free Press.

Kotter, J. P. (1998). *On what leaders really do.* Boston: HBS Press.

Kowalski, T. (2009). Need to address evidence-based practice in educational administration. *Educational Administration Quarterly, 45*(3), 351–374.

Kowalski, T. J. (2003). *Contemporary school administration: An introduction.* Boston: Pearson Education.

Lashway, L. (2002, Spring). *Research roundup: Rethinking the principalship.* ERIC Clearinghouse on Educational Management, 18(3). Retrieved October 15, 2009, from http://hdl.handle.net/1794/3484.

Lave, J., & Wenger, E. (1991). *Situated learning: Legitimate peripheral participation.* Cambridge, MA: Cambridge University Press.

League of Professional Schools (1991). *Focus of governance: Educational impact.* Athens, GA: The University of Georgia College of Education PSI League of Professional Schools.

Leithwood, K., Seashore-Louis, K. S., Anderson, S., & Wahlstrom, K. (2004). *How leadership influences student learning.* Minneapolis, MN: The Center for Applied Research and Educational Improvement; Toronto, ON: Ontario Institute for Studies in Education; and New York, NY: The Wallace Foundation.

Levin, B., & Wiens, J. (2003). There is another way: A different approach to education reform. *Phi Delta Kappan, 84*(9), 658–664.

Lieberman, M. (2007). The educational morass: Overcoming the stalemate in American education. Lanham, MD: Rowman & Littlefield.

Lofland, J. (1971). *Analyzing social settings.* Belmont, CA: Wadsworth.

Martin-Kniep, G. (2004). *Developing learning communities through teacher expertise.* Thousand Oaks, CA: Corwin.

Marzano, R. J. (1998). Models of standards implementation. Aurora, CO: Mid-continent Research for Education and Learning. Retrieved October 15, 2009, from http://www.mcrel.org.topics/products/92.

Marzano, R. J. (2000). *A new era of school reform: Going where the research takes us.* Retrieved October 13, 2002, from http://www.mcrel.org/PDF/SchoolImprovement Reform/5002RR_NewEraSchoolReform.pdf.

Marzano, R. J. (2003). *What works in schools: Translating research into action.* Alexandria, VA: Association for Supervision and Curriculum Development.

Marzano, R. J., Gaddy, B. B., & Dean, C. (2000). *What works in classroom instruction.* Aurora, CO: Mid-continent Research for Education and Learning. Available from http://www.mcrel.org/PDF/Instruction/5992TG_What_Works.pdf.

Marzano, R. J., Gaddy, B. B., Foseid, M. C., Foseid, M. P., & Marzano, J. S. (2005). *A handbook for classroom management that works.* Alexandria, VA: Association for Supervision and Curriculum Development.

Marzano, R. J., Marzano, J. S., & Pickering, D. J. (2003). *Classroom management that works: Research-based strategies for every teacher.* Alexandria, VA: Association for Supervision and Curriculum Development.

Marzano, R. J., Norford, J. S., Paynter, D. E., Pickering, D. J., & Gaddy, B. B. (2005). *A handbook for classroom instruction that works.* Alexandria, VA: Association for Supervision and Curriculum Development.

Marzano, R. J., Pickering, D. J., Arredondo, D. E., Paynter, D. E., Blackburn, G. J., Brandt, R. J., et al. (1997). *Dimensions of learning teacher's manual* (2nd ed.). Aurora, CO: Mid-Continent Research for Education and Learning.

Marzano, R. J., Pickering, D. J., & Pollock, J. E. (2001). *Classroom instruction that works: Research-based strategies for increasing student achievement.* Alexandria, VA: Association for Supervision and Curriculum Development.

Marzano, R. J., Waters, T., & McNulty, B. A. (2005). *School leadership that works: From research to results.* Alexandria, VA: Association for Supervision and Curriculum Development.

McBrien, J. L., & Brandt, R. S. (1997). *The language of learning: A guide to education terms.* Alexandria, VA: Association for Supervision and Curriculum Development.

McCarthy, M. M. (1998). The evolution of educational leadership programs. In J. Murphy & K. Lewis (Eds.), *Handbook of research on educational administration* (2nd ed., pp. 119–139). San Francisco: Jossey Bass.

McPeake, J. A. (2007). *The principalship: A study of the principal's time on task from 1960 to the twenty-first century.* Unpublished doctoral dissertation, Marshall University, Huntington, WV.

Mead, G. H. (1934). *Mind, self, and society.* Chicago: University of Chicago Press.

Murphy, C. W., & Lick, D. W. (2005). *Whole-faculty study groups creating professional learning communities that target student learning* (3rd ed.). Thousand Oaks, CA: Corwin.

Murphy, J. (1994). Transformational change and the evolving role of the principal: Early empirical evidence. In J. Murphy & K. S. Louis (Eds.), *Reshaping the principalship: Insights from transformational reform efforts* (pp. 20–53). Thousand Oaks, CA: Corwin.

Murphy, J. (2003, September). *Reculturing educational leadership: The ISLLC standards ten years out.* Paper prepared for the National Policy Board of Educational Administration, Austin, TX.

National Staff Development Council. (2001). *Standards for staff development.* Oxford, OH: Author.

No Child Left Behind Act of 2001 (NCLB). (2002). Pub. L. No. 107–110, 115 Stat. 1425.

Nonaka, I. (1994). A dynamic theory of organizational knowledge creation. *Organization Science, 5*(1), 14–37.

Owens, R. G., & Valesky, T. C. (2007). *Organizational behavior in education: Adaptive leadership and school reform.* Boston: Pearson.

Pajak, E. (2000). *Approaches to clinical supervision: Alternatives for improving instruction* (2nd ed.). Norwood, MA: Christopher-Gordon.

Pounder, D., & Merrill, R. (2001). Job desirability of the high school principalship: A job choice theory perspective. *Educational Administration Quarterly, 37*(1), 27–57.

Quinn, T. (2002). *Succession planning: Start today.* Retrieved February 6, 2009, from http://www.principals.org/s_nassp/bin.asp?TrackID=&SID=1&DID=46936&CID=482&VID=2&DOC=FILE.PDF.

Reeves, D. B. (2000). *Accountability in action: A blueprint for learning organizations.* Denver, CO: Advanced Learning Press.

Roberts, S. M., & Pruitt, E. Z. (2003). *Schools as professional learning communities: Collaborative activities and strategies for professional development.* Thousand Oaks, CA: Corwin.

Robinson, V. M. J., Lloyd, C. A., & Rowe, K. J. (2008). The impact of leadership on student outcomes: An analysis of the differential effects of leadership types. *Educational Administration Quarterly, 44*(5), 635–674.

Schein, E. H. (2004). *Organizational culture and leadership.* San Francisco: Jossey-Bass.

Schon, D. A. (1987). *Educating the reflective practitioner: Toward a new design for teaching and learning in the professions.* San Francisco: Jossey-Bass.

Senge, P. M. (1990). *The fifth discipline: The art and practice of learning organizations.* New York: Doubleday.

Sharp, W. L., & Walter, J. K. (2003). *The principal as school manager* (2nd ed.). Lanham, MD: Scarecrow Press.

Shellard, E. (2003). *Using professional learning communities to support teaching and learning.* Arlington, VA: Educational Research Service.

Slavin, R. E. (2008). Evidence-based reform in education: Which evidence counts? *Educational Researcher, 37*(1), 47–50.

Spillane, J. (2003). Educational leadership. *Educational Evaluation and Policy Analysis, 25*, 343–346.

Spillane, J. P., Halverson, R., & Diamond, J. B. (2004). Towards a theory of leadership practice: A distributed perspective. *Journal of Curriculum Studies, 36*(1), 3–34.

Strauss, A. L., & Corbin, J. (1998). *Basics of qualitative research: Techniques and procedures for developing grounded theory* (2nd ed.). Thousand Oaks, CA: Sage.

Stronge, J. H. (2007). *Qualities of effective teachers* (2nd ed.). Alexandria, VA: Association for Supervision and Curriculum Development.

Stronge, J. H., & Hindman, J. L. (2006). *The teacher quality index: A protocol for teacher selection.* Alexandria, VA: Association for Supervision and Curriculum Development.

Taylor, S. J., & Bogdan, R. (1998). *Introduction to qualitative research methods: A guidebook and resource* (3rd ed.). New York: Wiley.

Thompson, M., & Thompson, J. (2000). *Learning focused strategies notebook.* Boone, NC: Learning Concepts.

Thompson, S. D. (1998). Causing change: The National Policy Board for Educational Administration. In J. Murphy & P. B. Forsyth (Eds.), *Educational administration: A decade of reform* (pp. 93–114). Thousand Oaks, CA: Corwin.

Thornton, B., & Perrault, G. (2002). Becoming a data-based leader: An introduction. *NASSP Bulletin, 86*(630), 86–96.

Wagner, T., Kegan, R., Lahey, L., Lemons, R. W., Garnier, J., Helsing, D., et al. (2006). *Change leadership: A practical guide to transforming our schools.* San Francisco: Jossey-Bass.

Waters, J. T., Marzano, R. J., & McNulty, B. A. (2003). *Balanced leadership: What 30 years of research tells us about the effect of leadership on student achievement.* Aurora, CO: Mid-continent Research for Education and Learning.

Willower, D. J., & Uline, C. L. (2001). The alleged demise of science: A critical inquest. *Journal of Educational Administration, 39*(5), 455–471.

Yukl, G. (2006). *Leadership in organizations* (6th ed.). Upper Saddle River, NJ: Pearson/Prentice Hall.

Index

Abrutyn, L., 121
Accessibility, 18–19
Accountability, 13
Achievement gap, 125–126
Achievement recognition, 16–18
Achilles, C. M., xxiv
Across-content area teaching, 133–136
Action research resources, 93–94, 101
Activities
   classroom management, 143–144
   effective school leadership, 36
   Hexagon Exercise, 62–63
   instructional improvement strategies,
      41, 120–121
   leadership performance standards, 25–27
   student achievement focus, 30
   time management, 48–50
Administrative leadership
   action foci, xxiv, xxvi, 1–5
   administrative/managerial activities, 42–64
   balance strategies, 9
   budget management, 51–56
   effective leadership characteristics, 4–5
   leadership teams, 69–73
   physical plant management, 56–61
   planning strategies, 50–51
   problem-solving strategies, 59, 61
   reading suggestions, 98–102
   systems-development approach,
      xxvii, 43–64
Administrative teams, 65–73, 169
Allen, D., 121
Anderson, G., 126, 128
Anderson, S., 32
Approachability, 18–19
Apthorp, H., 131
Arredondo, D. E.
   see Marzano, R. J.
Assessment strategies, 87–88, 96
Assistant principals, 72–73, 99, 167
At-risk students, 138–139, 174–175

Bailey, J. A., 130
Balance strategies
   administrative-instructional leadership
      balance, 9
   effective school leadership, 33, 35
   work–home balance, 8

Bambino, D., 120
Bass, B. M., 184
Beginning teachers, 100, 153
   see also Newly hired teachers
Behavioral-systems teaching models, 141
Belief systems
   high-performing principals, 13
   reculturing approaches, xxvi, 43–45
Bennis, W. G., xxii, xxix
Biklen, S. K., 187, 189
Blackburn, G. J.
   see Marzano, R. J.
Blase, Jo, 4, 115, 116, 118, 119, 120, 148,
      152, 153, 159, 160
Blase, Joseph, 4, 115, 116, 118, 119, 120,
      148, 152, 153, 159, 160
Blumer, H., 187
Blythe, T., 121
Bogdan, R. C., 187, 188, 189
Bookkeepers, 51–52
Book studies, 41
Boris-Schacter, S., xxiv
Bower, B., 121
Brain research, 172–173
Brandt, R. S., 128
Brazosport schools (Texas), 126, 128
Brown, J. J., 119
Bryk, A., 119
Buckley, M. F., xxiii, 45, 152, 184
Budget management, 51–56
Burns, J. M., 186

Calhoun, E., 39, 140–141, 156
Capacity-building strategies, 65–69
Caring capacity, 10–12, 102
Cawelti, G., 136
Certificates of achievement, 17
Certified substitute teachers, 164
Challenged students, 138–139, 174–175
Chan, T. C., xxiii
Charmaz, K., 188, 189
Classroom management strategies,
      141–148, 175–176
Collaborative teams, 65–70, 95–96,
      118–121, 145–146, 159–160
Colorado Statewide Systemic Initiative
      for Mathematics and Science
      (CONNECT), 163

Common planning time, 121–122
Communication skills
    high-performing principals, 10–12
    reading suggestions, 102
    standards-based instructional units, 130
Community relations, 19–20
Compendium of Standards (Kendall &
    Marzano), 129–130
Competencies
    see 4 Cs Model (competencies, conditions,
        culture, and context)
Conditions
    see 4 Cs Model (competencies, conditions,
        culture, and context)
Constructive relationships, 10–12
Content standards, 128
Context
    see 4 Cs Model (competencies, conditions,
        culture, and context)
Context-building strategies, 115–123
Contribution recognition, 16–18
Cooperative learning, 173–174
Corbin, J., 189
Cordiero, P. A., xxiii
Cotton, K., 2, 3
Council of Chief State School Officers
    (CCSSO), 23, 25, 178
Critical-thinking skills, 172–173
Culturally different students, 138–139,
    174–175
Culture
    see 4 Cs Model (competencies, conditions,
        culture, and context)
Cunningham, W. G., xxiii
Curriculum integration, 173
Cusick, P. A., xxii–xxiii, 45, 152, 184
Custodial staff, 56–61, 147

Daft, R. L., 119
Daggett, W. R., 39
Danielson, C., 77, 120, 121, 131–132,
    153, 155, 159
Data collection and use
    reading suggestions, 101
    research methods and procedures, 187–189
    research resources, 93–96
    tips and suggestions, 97
    usage improvement strategies, 92–93
    usage strategies, 87–92
Data-driven instructional improvement
    system (DDIS), 88
Davenport, P., 126, 128
Dean, C., 130, 131, 133
Decision-making strategies, 13
Delegation, 14–15, 21
Deming, W. E., 87
Dewey, J., 115
Dialogue-building strategies, 115–123
Diamond, J. B., 4
Differentiated instruction, 174

DiPaola, M., 47
Disciplined reflection, 6–7
Discipline strategies, 141–148, 175–176
Distributed leadership, 4, 13–14
Diverse students' needs, 138–139, 174–175
Diversity resources, 95
Double Helix Model of Leadership, xxv, xxvi
    see also Systems-development approach
Downey, C. J., 149
Downey walk-through model, 149
Doyle, M. E., 45
Drake, T. L., xxii
DuFour, Rebecca, 70, 166
DuFour, Richard, 70, 159, 166
Duguid, P., 119
Dunklee, D. R., 184

Eaker, R., 70, 166
Educational leadership policy standards,
    24–25
Effective change resources, 99
Effective leadership, 32–35
Effective teachers, 77, 172
Elmore, R. F., xxiv, 3, 5, 28, 30, 87, 186
Empowerment
    capacity-building strategies, 65–69
    classroom management, 145–147
    high-performing principals, 13–16, 74
    hiring strategies, 78–83
    reading suggestions, 102
    special education teachers, 166–168
English, F. W., 149
Evaluation strategies, 153–154
Exemplars of leadership standards, 23–27
Expectations
    see High expectations; Student achievement

Faculty meetings, 49–50, 67–68, 117
Farrace, B., xxiv
Feedback, 87–88
Financial grants, 164–165
Florian, J., 131
Focus
    see Teaching and learning focus
Fontana, A., 189
Food-services staff, 147
Formal evaluations, 153–154
Formative assessment, 87–88
Foseid, M. C., 143
Foseid, M. P., 143
4 Cs Model (competencies, conditions,
    culture, and context), 180–182
Fox, C., 139
Frase, L. E., 149
Frey, J. H., 189
Fuhrman, S. H., 186
Fullan, M., xxii, xxiii, 5, 119, 179, 180

Gaddy, B. B., 133, 143
Gardner, J. W., 184

Garnier, J.
   see Wagner, T.
Ginsberg, R., 186
Glanz, J., 153
Glaser, B. G., 187, 188, 189
Glickman, C. D., 39, 118, 152
Gould, S. M., xxiii
Grants, 164–165
Greenfield, W., 63
Grigg, J., 4, 87, 88
Groff, F., 47
Gronn, P., xxii, 185
Group development, 10–12, 102

Hale, S. H., 38
Hall, G. E., 186
Halverson, R., 4, 87, 88
Hansen, J. B., 129
Hanson, R., 143
Hassel, E., 162
Helsing, D.
   see Wagner, T.
Hexagon Exercise, 62–63
High expectations, 172–173
High-performing principals
   across-content area teaching, 133–136
   action foci, xxiv, xxvi, 1–5, 124
   administrative/managerial activities,
      42–64
   belief and value systems, 13
   budget management, 51–56
   characteristics, xxviii–xxix, 3–4, 185–186
   classroom management, 141–148,
      175–176
   data collection and use, 87–97
   dialogue-building strategies, 115–123
   diverse students' needs, 138–139,
      174–175
   empowerment, 13–16, 65–69, 74, 78–83
   as exemplars of leadership standards,
      23–27
   formal evaluations, 153–154
   goals, xxv, xxvi
   hiring strategies, 75–86
   instructional improvement strategies,
      37–41, 105–123
   instruction planning strategies, 127–128,
      137–138
   leadership teams, 69–73
   as models of learning, 6–22
   physical plant management, 56–61
   planning strategies, 50–51
   problem-solving strategies, 59, 61
   research-based instruction, 124–156
   school culture development, 111–114,
      161–162
   school leadership effects, 32–36
   special education teachers, 166–168
   standards-based instructional units,
      128–131
   student ability enhancement, 132–133
   student achievement focus, 28–30, 108,
      124–126
   systems-development approach, xxvi,
      43–64, 177–183, 184
   teaching and learning focus, 105–110
   teaching components framework, 131–132
   teaching models, 140–141
   technology integration strategies,
      139–140, 175
   time management, 107
   walk-throughs/walk-abouts, 17, 22, 68,
      148–153, 171–172
   see also Professional development
High-performing schools
   action foci, xxiv, xxvi
   characteristics, 2–3
   planning strategies, 50–51
High, R. M., xxiv
Hindman, J. L., 77
Hiring strategies
   faculty involvement, 78–83
   importance, 75–76
   interviews, 82
   problematic teachers, 83–85
   reading suggestions, 99
   recruitment protocols, 80–83
   strong people, 8–9
   teacher characteristics, 76–78
   tips and suggestions, 86
Holcomb, E. L., 96
Holton, E. F., 162
Hopkins, D., 39
Hord, S. M., 159, 186
Hoy, W. K., 179

Information-processing teaching models, 141
Instructional improvement strategies,
   37–41, 105–123
Instructional leadership
   across-content area teaching, 133–136
   balance strategies, 9
   classroom management, 141–148,
      175–176
   data collection and use, 87–97
   dialogue-building strategies, 115–123
   diverse students' needs, 138–139,
      174–175
   formal evaluations, 153–154
   goals, xxv, xxvi, 103–104, 137–138
   instructional improvement strategies,
      37–41, 105–123
   leadership teams, 69–73
   planning strategies, 127–128, 137–138,
      172–173
   reading suggestions, 102, 171–176
   research-based instruction, 124–156
   school culture development, 111–114
   standards-based instructional units,
      128–131

student ability enhancement, 132–133
student achievement focus, 28–30, 108,
    124–126
systems-development approach,
    xxvii, 43–51
teaching components framework,
    131–132
teaching models, 140–141
technology integration strategies,
    139–140, 175
time management, 107
tips and suggestions, 155–156
walk-throughs/walk-abouts, 17, 22, 68,
    148–153, 171–172
Instructional strategies, 2–3, 127–128,
    137–138, 172–173
Integrated Standards-Based Instructional Unit
    (Dean & Bailey), 130
Interstate School Leaders Licensure
    Consortium (ISLLC) standards, 23, 24–27

Jones, R., 39
Joyce, B., 5, 39, 140–141, 156, 159

Keedy, J. L., xxiv
Kegan, R.
    see Wagner, T.
Kellogg, S., xxiii, 45, 152
Kendall, J. S., 129–130
Knowles, M. S., 162
Kotter, J. P., 184, 186
Kowalski, T. J., xxii, xxiii, xxiv, 184, 186

Lahey, L.
    see Wagner, T.
Langer, S., xxiv
Lashway, L., 45
Lauer, P., 131
Lave, J., 119
Leadership for learning, 171
Leadership teams, 69–73
League of Professional Schools, 49
Learning-challenged students, 138–139,
    174–175
Learning goals, 137–138
Learning models, 6–22, 127–128
Learning subsystems
    action foci, xxiv, xxvi
    bottom-up processes, xxvi, 43–45
    classroom management, 144–147
    high-performing principals, 5, 43–47
Leithwood, K., 32
Lemons, R. W.
    see Wagner, T.
Levin, B., 29
Lick, D. W., 96
Lieberman, M., 129
Lifelong learning, 9–10, 131, 158
Linguistically different students, 138–139,
    174–175

Lloyd, C. A., 35
Lofland, J., 189
Looper, S., 121

Maintenance personnel, 56–61
Managerial activities, 42–64
Martin-Kniep, G., 159
Martin-Kniep, G. O., 159
Marzano, J. S., 142, 143
Marzano, R. J., 3, 29–30, 32, 33–35, 36, 39,
    77, 125, 127, 129–133, 137–138,
    142, 143, 155
McBrien, J. L., 128
McCarthy, M. M., xxii
McConney, A., 129
McNulty, B. A., 3, 32, 33–35, 36
McPeake, J. A., xxiii, 45, 184
Mead, G. H., 187
Meetings, 49–50, 67–68, 117
Mentoring approaches, 15–16, 100
Merrill, R., xxiv
Miskel, C. G., 179
Mission
    see School mission
Models of learning, 6–22
Models of Standards Implementation
    (Marzano), 130–131
Models of teaching, 140–141
Motivation, 12–13
Murphy, C. W., 96
Murphy, J., xxiii, 105

National Association of Secondary School
    Principals (NASSP), xxiii
National Staff Development Council,
    164, 165–166
Negative role models, 6–7
Newly hired teachers, 83–85, 153
    see also Beginning teachers
90/90/90 schools (Milwaukee), 126
No Child Left Behind Act (2001), xxiii, 47,
    87, 185
Nonaka, I., 119
Norford, J. S., 133

Observation resources, 100
Open-door policies, 18–19
Opportunity to learn standards, 128
Owens, R. G., xxiv, 179
Ownership, 13

Pajak, E., 153
Parental involvement
    discipline strategies, 146
    high-performing principals, 11–12
    newly hired teachers, 85
    reading suggestions, 102
Paynter, D. E., 133
Peer coaching, 100
Peer collaboration, 118–121, 159–160

Performance standards, 128

Perrault, G., 47

Personalized learning opportunities, 163–164

Personal teaching models, 141

Physical plant management, 56–61

Pickering, D. J., 29–30, 77, 125, 127, 132–133, 137–138, 142, 143

Planning strategies, 50–51, 121–122, 127–128, 137–138, 172–173

Pollock, J. E., 29–30, 77, 125, 127, 132–133, 137–138

Pool, H., xxiii

Positive role models, 6–7

Poston, W. K., 149

Pounder, D., xxiv

Powell, B. S., 121

Prichett, R., 4, 87, 88

Principals, xxii–xxvii

  see also High-performing principals

Problematic teachers, 83–85

Problem-solving strategies, 59, 61

Professional development

  administrative teams, 169

  financial grants, 164–165

  high-performing principals, 14, 157–159

  instructional improvement strategies, 116

  lifelong learning, 9–10, 158

  personalized learning opportunities, 163–164

  planning guidelines, 161–163

  professional learning communities, 35, 37, 159–161, 176

  reading suggestions, 176

  school culture development, 161–162

  standards, 165–166

  systems-development approach, 157–170

  teacher-to-teacher collaboration, 159–160, 163

  tips and suggestions, 170

Promptness, 11

Pruitt, E. Z., 159

Public relations, 19–20

Published research analyses, 117

Quinn, T., xxiii

Reading suggestions, 98–102, 171–176

Recognition strategies, 16–18, 22

Reculturing approaches, xxvi, 43–45

Reeves, D. B., 126

Reflective practices

  high-performing principals, 6–7

  instructional improvement strategies, 115, 116

  leadership performance standards, 25–27

Reichardt, R., 131

Relationship management, 10–12

Reorganization approaches, xxvi, 43–45

Research-based instruction

  across-content area teaching, 133–136

  classroom management, 141–148, 175–176

  diverse students' needs, 138–139, 174–175

  instruction planning strategies, 127–128, 137–138, 172–173

  learning models, 127–128

  reading suggestions, 171–176

  standards-based instructional units, 128–131

  student ability enhancement, 132–133

  student achievement, 124–126

  teaching components framework, 131–132

  teaching models, 140–141

  technology integration strategies, 139–140, 175

  tips and suggestions, 155–156

  walk-throughs/walk-abouts, 148–153, 171–172

Research-based leadership responsibilities, 34–35

Research methods and procedures, 187–189

Respect, 10–12

Response to Intervention (RTI), 139

Responsiveness, 11

Rice, D. M., 45

Risk-taking strategies, 117

Roberts, S. M., 159

Robinson, V. M. J., 35

Roe, W. H., xxii

Role models, 6–7

Rolheiser, C., 121

Rowe, K. J., 35

Rudd, A., 129

Sanders, N., 131

Schalock, M. D., 129

Scheduling strategies, 121–122

Schein, E. H., 111, 113

Schneider, B., 119

Schon, D. A., 115

School climate, 22

School culture, 111–114, 161–162

School effects research, 173

School improvement resources, 98–99

School leadership, 32–36

School-level achievement-related practices, 125

School mission, 5, 38, 41, 76

Seashore-Louis, K. S., 32

Secondary problems, 61

Self-assessment strategies, 117

Senge, P., 179, 180

Senge, P. M., 178

Shared leadership, 13–14, 69–73

Sharp, W. L., xxiv

Shellard, E., 119

Showers, B., 5, 159
Slavin, R. E., 186
Snow-Renner, R., 131
Social teaching models, 141
Sommers, W. A., 159
Special education teachers, 166–168
Special needs students, 138–139
Spillane, J. P., 4, 185
Staff development, 157–159
    see also Professional development
Stakeholder involvement
    discipline strategies, 146–148
    newly hired teachers, 85
    reading suggestions, 102
Standards
    educational leadership, 23–27
    standards-based instructional units,
        128–131
    Standards for Staff Development,
        165–166
Steffy, B. E., 149
Stevahn, L., 121
Strauss, A. L., 187, 189
Strength assessments, 14–15
Stronge, J. H., 77
Strong people, 8–9
Student achievement
    across-content area teaching, 133–136
    classroom management, 141–148,
        175–176
    data-driven measurement approaches,
        87–89
    influencing factors, 124–126
    instructional focus, 28–30, 108, 124–126
    instructional improvement strategies,
        37–41, 105–110
    research resources, 93–94
    school leadership effects, 32–36
    student ability enhancement, 132–133
Study group resources, 38–40
Substitute teachers, 164
Subsystems
    see Learning subsystems; Systems-
        development approach
Suggested readings, 98–102, 171–176
Summative assessments, 87–88
Swanson, R. A., 162
Systems-development approach
    bottom-up processes, xxvi, 43–45, 179
    budget management, 51–56
    data collection and use, 87–97
    double helix model of leadership, xxv, xxvi
    empowerment, 65–69, 74
    formal evaluations, 153–154
    high-performing principals, xxvii, 43–64,
        177–183, 184
    hiring strategies, 75–86
    importance, 177
    leadership teams, 69–73
    physical plant management, 56–61

    planning strategies, 50–51
    problem-solving strategies, 59, 61
    professional development, 157–170
    research-based instruction, 124–156
    systems thinking, 177, 178–183, 184
    time management, 45–50
    tips and suggestions, 63–64
    see also Administrative leadership;
        Instructional leadership

Taylor, S. J., 187, 188, 189
Teacher dialogue and collaboration,
    118–121
Teacher leadership, 78, 99
Teacher-level achievement-related
    practices, 125
Teacher negativity, 12–13
Teacher-to-teacher collaboration,
    119, 159–160, 163
Teaching and learning focus
    instructional improvement strategies,
        105–110
    student achievement, 28–30, 108,
        124–126
Teaching components framework,
    131–132
Teaching models, 140–141
Teamwork, 65–73, 77–78
Technology integration strategies,
    101, 139–140, 175
Thinking and reasoning skills, 130
Thomas, C., 4, 87, 88
Thompson, J., 127
Thompson, M., 127
Thompson, S. D., xxii
Thornton, B., 47
Time management
    classroom management, 146–148
    instructional improvement strategies, 107
    systems-development approach, 45–50
    walk-throughs/walk-abouts, 152–153
Tips and suggestions
    data collection and use, 97
    delegation, 21
    dialogue-building strategies, 123
    effective school leadership, 36
    empowerment, 74
    hiring strategies, 86
    instructional improvement strategies, 41
    leadership performance standards, 27
    professional development, 170
    recognition, 22
    research-based instruction, 155–156
    school climate, 22
    school culture development, 113–114
    student achievement focus, 31
    systems-development approach, 63–64
    teacher empowerment and motivation, 21
    teaching and learning focus, 109–110
    walk-throughs/walk-abouts, 22

Trial and error experiences, 7
Trust, 10–13, 16, 102
Tschannen-Moran, M., 47

Uline, C. L., 185

Valesky, T. C., xxiv, 179
Value systems
   high-performing principals, 13
   reculturing approaches, xxvi, 43–45
Visibility, 18–19, 22

Wagner, T., xxv, 179, 180, 182
Wahlstrom, K., 32
Walk-abouts, 22

Walk-throughs, 17, 22, 68, 148–153, 171–172
Walter, J. K., xxiv
Waters, T., 3, 32, 33–35, 36
Watson, J. G., 88
Web sites, 139
Weick, K. E., 119
Weil, M., 140–141, 156
Wenger, E., 119
Wiens, J., 29
Willower, D. J., 185
Work–home balance, 8
World-class standards, 128
Wyatt, R. L., 121

Yukl, G., 184

CORWIN
A SAGE Company

The Corwin logo—a raven striding across an open book—represents the union of courage and learning. Corwin is committed to improving education for all learners by publishing books and other professional development resources for those serving the field of PreK–12 education. By providing practical, hands-on materials, Corwin continues to carry out the promise of its motto: **"Helping Educators Do Their Work Better."**